COMMON SENSE 101

DALE AHLQUIST

COMMON SENSE 101

Lessons from G. K. Chesterton

IGNATIUS PRESS   SAN FRANCISCO

Cover photograph: G. K. Chesterton and Frances Chesterton

Cover design by Roxanne Mei Lum

ISBN 978-1-58617-139-1
ISBN 1-58617-139-9
Library of Congress Control Number 2005933368
Printed in the United States of America ∞

To John Peterson

Wise mentor and faithful friend

CONTENTS

PREFACE

How did the world forget such an unforgettable character? Most people know almost nothing about G. K. Chesterton. And most of what they do know is wrong.

Even those of us who have gotten to know him do not see the complete picture. We see only glimpses. We know that he was a writer from the early twentieth century who wrote a hundred books and thousands of essays for the London newspapers, that he wrote and argued about everything, that he penned epic poetry but also delighted in detective fiction, that he made everyone laugh, that everyone who knew him loved him, that he was happily married but unhappily had no children, that he took on all the leading thinkers of his time and challenged them not only with his clear ideas but with the example of his own life, especially with the astounding decision he made to become a Catholic.

But looking at Chesterton is not as important as looking at the whole world through his eyes. This is not a book about Chesterton. It is a book about everything else from a Chestertonian perspective. It is an attempt to get inside of him and inhabit him like a large house so that we can see the world through the windows he provides. I have very little hope of succeeding, but I am trying to do it this way for two reasons. First, it is precisely the way Chesterton approached other writers, by getting inside of them. Second, I can't think of a more wonderful way to see the world than through Chesterton's eyes.

I have one great advantage: I don't have to make anything up. Chesterton wrote about everything. An ocean of words poured out of his pen. I have simply immersed myself in that ocean. It is deep, it is dangerous, it is delightful, it is refreshing, it is full of surprises, it is full of life.

These chapters first saw life in the form of television programs for the Eternal Word Television Network. I wish to thank Steve Beaumont and all the good folks at EWTN for inviting me into their studios and for helping me introduce Chesterton to so many people around the world. My further appreciation goes to Chuck Chalberg for trying to make himself look as though he weighs three hundred pounds. My undying thanks to Peter Floriani, whose hard work made my easy work possible. And my inexpressible gratitude to my toughest critic, without whom not one page of this book could have or would have been written: my lovely wife, Laura.

I

Another Introduction to G. K. Chesterton

When he walks in through the door, the first thing we notice is that he fills up the room. Of course, he weighs three hundred pounds, but his height is even more extraordinary than his weight. He is six foot four, but he seems even taller. He is a giant. But he is no Goliath. He is actually an overgrown elf. He casts a spell, and the spell is called joy. It is something we have certainly felt on some occasion, but this is something that sweeps into our souls. His huge body shakes with laughter. Laughter blows through his moustache.

"I suppose I enjoy myself more than most other people, because there's such a lot of me having a good time." [1]

He takes off his crumpled hat and his heavy cape. He leans his swordstick against the wall. He squints and adjusts the crooked lenses on the end of his nose, but they remain crooked still. There is geniality in his every gesture.

But what about that swordstick, is it real? Is there really a sword concealed inside the walking stick? There certainly is. Why does he carry a swordstick, of all things?

[1] Dorothy Collins, "Recollections", in John Sullivan, ed., *G. K. Chesterton: A Centenary Appraisal* (London: Harper and Row, 1974), 157.

He says it is because he likes things that come to a point.[2]
He has a romantic attachment to the sword, seen in his
endless doodles and drawings. But this sword will never draw
blood. It is the poetry without the prose. The only thing
he ever stabs with it is the pillow on the couch in his study.

But the sword is not the only weapon he carries. He also
carries ... a gun! But why?

"I bought it the day of my wedding", he explains ...
and then adds, "to defend my bride."[3] He says it has also
proved to be quite useful on other occasions. For instance,
whenever he hears a man say that life is not worth living,
he takes out the gun and offers to shoot him. "Always with
the most satisfactory results", he laughs.[4]

But wait, there's more in his arsenal. He also carries with
him a big Texas knife. (Where does he keep all these things?)
It is seven inches long when folded, fourteen inches long
when open. "The knife is only a short sword; and the
pocket-knife is a secret sword." It has, he explains, that "terrible tongue we call a blade".[5]

He sleeps with the knife under his pillow—and usually
forgets it there. His wife has to retrieve it from all the hotels
they stay at. He uses it mostly as a letter opener, and once
during a debate, he absent-mindedly took it out and started
sharpening his pencil with it, to the great amusement of
the audience and the great distress of his opponent.

[2] G.K. Chesterton (hereafter, unless otherwise noted, the author is Chesterton), *Orthodoxy*, in *The Collected Works of G. K. Chesterton* (San Francisco:
Ignatius Press, 1986–7), 1:266. (Hereafter *CW*, followed by volume number
and page number.)

[3] *Autobiography*, *CW* 16:43–44.

[4] *Illustrated London News* (hereafter *ILN*), March 17, 1906.

[5] "What I Found in My Pocket", in *Tremendous Trifles* (New York: Sheed
and Ward, 1955), 15.

Yes, the many legends of his absent-mindedness are not exaggerations. He does miss a lot of trains. And the ones he does catch are not always the right ones. He will hail a cab to take him to the editorial offices of *G.K.'s Weekly*, his own newspaper, but he will not know the address. So he will have the cab take him first to a newsstand to buy a copy of the paper so he can get the address, and since many of the newsstands are sold out of the paper, it may take several stops. He walks away from bookstalls reading a book he has picked up, and the shopkeeper, recognizing him, simply sends a bill to his wife. His pockets overflow with books and newspapers, and he reads as he walks, oblivious of traffic, which screeches to a halt as he crosses the street.

There is more in his pockets. In addition to the reading material and the weapons, he says he can find whole worlds in his pockets, that on the Day of Judgment when the sea gives up its dead, so will his pockets give up the extraordinary things buried there.[6] But what he cannot find in any of his pockets is his train ticket. Or money. The train ticket he has no doubt left on the counter where he bought it. The money he has given to beggars.

He seems so frivolous and so careless, but he gives money to beggars, not frivolously or carelessly, but because he believes in giving money to beggars, and giving it to them "where they stand". He says he knows perfectly well all the arguments against giving money to beggars. But he finds those to be precisely the arguments *for* giving money to them. If beggars are lazy or deceptive or wanting a drink, he knows only too well his own lack of motivation, his own dishonesty, his own thirst. He doesn't believe in

[6] Ibid.

"scientific charity" because that is too easy, as easy as writing a check. He believes in "promiscuous charity" because that is really difficult. "It means the most dark and terrible of all human actions—talking to a man. In fact, I know of nothing more difficult than really talking to the poor men we meet."[7] He says that if we really believed in democracy, we would not be debating about what we should do with the poor; the poor would be debating about what to do with us.[8]

And suddenly he does not seem so absent-minded and out of touch. His absent-mindedness, it turns out, is only about details that really don't matter, though they are the kinds of things that fill up the lives of most of us while we neglect the things that *do* matter. He is always focused on the larger picture and on eternal truths. But he also has a passion for justice and a genuine love for everyone. He may be lost and helpless on the street, but he is always at home in the world.

He can expound, it seems, on any subject. The history of glass-making. Gargoyles. Milton. Huxley. Cheese. The Manichees. Shakespeare. Shaw. Shirts. Tennyson. Turnpikes. Taffy. He can quote whole passages of books from memory, books that he has read years and years before. Challenge him to offer evidence for one of his historical pronouncements, he will repeat verbatim the terms of the Magna Carta, *in the original Old English!*[9] Ask him to autograph a book for you, and he will inscribe it with an original poem inside the front cover:

---

[7] *Daily News*, October 10, 1908.

[8] See *Heretics*, *CW* 1:190.

[9] There is an account of this in an unpublished letter from Thomas Derrick in the Chesterton Papers in the British Library.

> In this book the pretty pictures
> May incur your righteous strictures,
> Only do not read the verse
> Because you'll find it even worse.[10]

Or else he'll toss off a perfect epigram or refer to the book as "Bosh!"

He doesn't sign his name. He draws it. His penmanship is picturesque, as clear and clean as his prose, as full and fitting as his poetry.

And then he gives you the book as a gift. "Alas, my trade is words",[11] he says. He is embarrassed that words are the only thing he makes and the only gift that he can give. The humility is utterly sincere. It is the most striking thing about him, that such a big man should feel so small. But his very size may have something to do with his humility: "It may be that the thin monks were holy, but I am sure it was the fat monks who were humble. To be fat is to be laughed at, and that is a more wholesome experience for the soul of man."[12]

And, indeed, he laughs harder than anyone at the jokes made at his own expense, and his caricatures of himself are more hilarious than any others. He can honestly enjoy his own foolishness and mock his own accomplishments. In debates, he disarms his opponents by agreeing with them when they attack him personally. It is when they attack his ideas that he reluctantly rises and utterly demolishes their arguments. But as his secretary would say, long afterward, "It gave him no pleasure to excel over other people."[13] He

---

[10] *Collected Poetry*, *CW* 10, Part 1:286.

[11] Ibid., 333.

[12] *ILN*, May 8, 1909.

[13] Collins, "Recollections", 157.

truly understands the great virtue of humility and the great sin of pride. He says he is no preacher, but if he had only one sermon to preach, it would be a sermon against pride: "All evil began with some attempt at superiority." [14]

He reminds us that he is only a scribbler. Then he suddenly reminds himself of a deadline. He has to produce an article for one of the many newspapers he writes for. He tries to find something, anything, to write on. "The quicker goes the journalist the slower go his thoughts. The result is the newspaper of our time, which every day can be delivered earlier and earlier, and which every day is less worth delivering at all." [15] But of course, if he writes it, it is worth reading, and still worth reading almost a century after he has written it. He can deliver a provocative essay on any subject, even when there doesn't appear—at first—to be a subject. But before he plunges into thought, he takes out still another weapon. At least, some would call it a weapon. A cigar.

He makes the sign of the cross with the match before lighting the cigar. "My muse", he says, taking a puff. "Some men write with a pencil, others with a typewriter. I write with my cigar." [16] As if sensing our disapproval, he laughs and he answers our objections before we can even list them. "It is true that tobacco, though not an intoxicant, is in some sense a drug: but so is tea. It is true that tobacco, taken out of season and reason, spoils your appetite: but so do sweets.... It is true that it is a luxury, a mere keen and passing titillation or pungency: but so are pepper and salt and mustard and a hundred other blameless gifts.... It is

---

[14] *The Common Man* (New York: Sheed and Ward, 1950), 246.

[15] *Eugenics and Other Evils*, *CW* 4:343.

[16] From an article in *Chicago Daily Tribune*, reprinted in *CW* 21, appendix: 650.

true that it ends in smoke: but so do all worldly powers and pleasures. It is true that it falls into ashes: but so do we." [17] He explains that there is nothing immoral about smoking a cigar. To regard smoking as immoral shows not merely a lack of clear thinking but a lack of clear standards. Lumping the wrong things together as evils blurs the lines between right and wrong and leads to chaos. It also leads to legal and practical confusion. "The lack of clear standards among those who vaguely think of [smoking] as a vice may yet be the beginning of much peril and oppression." [18]

He defends smoking and drinking not as habits ("All habits are bad habits.") [19] but as simple, traditional pleasures that have been enjoyed by normal people for centuries. He points out that what society calls "progress" usually serves to punish all the things the common man enjoys. "There is no normal thing that cannot now be taken from the normal man. Modern 'emancipation' has really been a new persecution of the Common Man and common sense." [20] If he is proud of anything, he is proud of defending the common man and common sense. "I represent the jolly mass of mankind. I am the happy and reckless Christian." [21] The puritanical assault on smoking is an example of "the exaltation of very small and secondary matters of conduct at the expense of very great and primary ones. If there is one thing worse than the modern weakening of major morals it is the modern strengthening of minor morals. Thus it is considered more withering to accuse a man of bad taste

[17] *ILN*, June 29, 1912.

[18] *ILN*, February 5, 1927.

[19] *Manalive*, *CW* 7:294.

[20] *Common Man*, 1.

[21] Interview with Gilbert and Frances Chesterton in the *Daily News*, December 13, 1907.

than of bad ethics. Cleanliness is not next to godliness now-adays, for cleanliness is made an essential and godliness is regarded as an offence." [22] These matters of health and hygiene have been invoked to attack the simple pleasures that should be matters of personal liberty and convenience. "It is the great peril of our society that all its mechanisms may grow more fixed while its spirit grows more fickle. A man's minor actions and arrangements ought to be free, flexible, creative; the things that should be unchangeable are his principles, his ideals. But with us the reverse is true; our views change constantly; but our lunch does not change. . . ." [23]

The question occurs to us: Does he always talk this way? Does he talk the same way he writes? Does he write the same way he talks? The answer is yes. His beloved wife, Frances, assures us that when he talks his tone and his outlook never vary—whoever may be with him. Early in the morning or late at night—in company with others or alone with his wife—he has the same way of approaching life—"the same flow of a sudden idea". [24]

He also talks to himself. "If a man does not talk to himself," he says, "it is because he is not worth talking to." [25]

Better yet, he laughs at his own jokes. "If a man may not laugh at his own jokes, at whose jokes may he laugh? May not an architect pray in his own cathedral?" [26] Everything shakes with his laughter. He leans closer to us. "Nothing has been worse than the modern notion that a clever man

[22] *On Lying in Bed and Other Essays* (Calgary: Bayeux Arts, 2000), 36.
[23] Ibid.
[24] Chesterton, interview.
[25] "Chesterton on 'Magic'", in John Sullivan, ed., *Chesterton Continued: A Bibliographical Supplement* (London: University of London Press, 1968), 91.
[26] *ILN*, January 13, 1906.

can make a joke without taking part in it. . . . It is unpardonable conceit not to laugh at your own jokes. Joking is undignified; that is why it is so good for one's soul." [27]

We could sit and bask in the glow of his words and laughter all night long, but his wife suddenly reminds him that he has to give a lecture this evening, and if he doesn't hurry he will be late. Well, he will be late even if he hurries. A riot of activity follows, as Frances attempts to make her husband appear presentable, and he attempts to find out what he is supposed to be lecturing about. He scribbles a few notes on whatever scraps of paper are in reach and then is hurriedly loaded into a cab. Upon arriving at the lecture hall, the great man of great girth has trouble getting his huge frame out of the vehicle. Perhaps, someone suggests, if he tried to get out sideways. He groans: "I have no sideways." [28]

The lecture hall is completely full of people. His lectures are always sold out. He is given a long and laudatory introduction and a thundering ovation as he rises to speak and begins by saying quietly, almost to himself: "After the whirlwind, the still small voice."

He reaches into a pocket for his notes but of course does not find them. He tries another pocket and eventually realizes that he does not have them. He begins his talk, even as he continues searching through his pockets. He gives an extemporaneous lecture, touching on and tying together a dazzling array of different subjects: [29]

---

[27] *Alarms and Discursions* (New York: Dodd, Mead, 1911), 233.

[28] Maisie Ward, *Gilbert Keith Chesterton* (New York: Sheed and Ward, 1943), 585.

[29] This is not an actual lecture of Chesterton's, but is a pastiche gleaned from the following sources: *New York Times*, January 11, 1921; *ILN*, January 21, 1906; May 29, 1926; *Daily News*, January 28, 1902; January 1, 1902; *Alarms and Discursions*, 154; *Daily News*, July 29, 1905; September 28, 1907.

I have been invited tonight to give a lecture, but of course I cannot call myself a lecturer, because I fear there are some here who have actually heard one of my lectures. . . .

I am a journalist and so am vastly ignorant of many things, but because I am a journalist I write and talk about them all. . . .

I could certainly talk about the adventure of getting here this evening. An adventure is only an inconvenience rightly considered. An inconvenience is only an adventure wrongly considered. . . .

Part of the adventure of my arrival here was the journey across a modern urban landscape. It seems the modern world could easily be defined as a crowd of very rapid racing cars all brought to a standstill and stuck in a block of traffic. . . .

I think it may be cheerfully admitted that one of the strangest, largest, and most fundamental problems of modern life is . . . its ugliness. The world has grown richer and more complex, and more industrious and more orderly; upon the whole, it has grown more emancipated and more humane; but when all is said and done, upon the whole it has grown more ugly. . . . What can be the reason of this? . . . I believe that the great source of the hideousness of modern life is the lack of enthusiasm for modern life. If we really loved modern life we should make it beautiful. For all men seek to make beautiful the thing which they already think beautiful. The mother always seeks to deck out her child in what finery she possesses. The owner of a fine house adorns his house; the believer beautifies his church; the lover lavishes his lady; the patriot reforms his country. All these men improve a thing because they believe it is beautiful. . . . We do not make modern life beautiful precisely because we do not believe in modern life. . . . If we regarded the engineering of our age as the great Gothic architects regarded the engineering of their age we should make of the ordinary steam engine something as beautiful as the Christian cathedral. . . .

There was a time when art was merely a tool which served religion, but we have tried to make art replace religion. We have tried to make art the only common bond. And we have tried to avoid the religious questions altogether. But the first and most important thing about any man is his vision, his conception, of existence. Upon this depends whether he will paint a gorgeous picture or a sad one. Upon this also depends whether he will paint a sad picture or merely jump over London Bridge. . . .

The modern mind is a door with no house to it; a gigantic gate to nowhere. . . . The modern mind wishes to do away with such quaint ideas as right and wrong. The modern mind thinks that freedom somehow means breaking the rules. But here is where tradition is, as it generally is, on the side of truth. Tradition tells us that the rules are right. We cannot really prove them to be right, except perhaps when we see the consequences of trying to do away with them. The Ten Commandments, for instance. Throughout history, men have certainly failed to live up to them. But in modern times, men have more disastrously failed in trying to live without them. But it is only in establishing and obeying certain rules that freedom is possible. If we break the big laws we do not get freedom. We do not even get anarchy. We get the small laws. . . .

There are some who would argue that we should have no absolutes, that evolution tends to rub out absolute lines. I say, we must have definite lines; but it is not because definite lines are the things which restrain humanity. It is because definite lines are the things which distinguish humanity. Our black lines are not the bars of the tiger's cage. They are the stripes of the tiger's skin: they are what makes him a tiger. If you think I want rules merely to restrain some inferior mob, you are quite wrong. It is true that bridles and blinders keep a great part of the human race out of the ditch, but this is not what I am urging. I am not urging anything so profoundly undemocratic. I do not mean that there are some people stupid enough to require general rules. I mean that there are no people wise enough to do without them. Our need for rules does not arise from the smallness of our intellects, but from the greatness of our task. Discipline is not necessary for things that are slow and safe; but discipline is necessary for things that are swift and dangerous. We do not need a map for a stroll; but we do need a map for a raid. And that is what Western Democracy is now engaged in: a raid. A raid on the New Jerusalem. It is a crusade of justice. We are trying to do right; one of the wildest perils. We are trying to bring political equity on the earth; to materialise an almost incredible justice. We cannot be vague about what we believe in, what we are willing to fight for, and to die for. There are twenty ways of criticizing a battle, but only one way of winning it. The ordinary man does not obey special rules because he is too stupid to see the alternative; he obeys them because he feels, though he cannot express the fact, that they are the only way of having a rapid and reasonable human activity. Dogmatic democracy as much as dogmatic ethics are our own special creation. There are some who will be annoyed by my calling it a creation of Christianity or a creation of Europe, but certainly it is one or the other. And as the wolf dies fighting, we shall die doctrinal, and Democracy as well as Christianity will die with us. For Democracy is always difficult, and we alone have the fixed principles which face difficulties. If our raid fails no other raid will succeed, and no men, perhaps, will ever come again so near to bringing justice on the earth!

There is outburst of cheering and applause at the conclusion of his speech, which he humbly acknowledges but grows uncomfortable as it lasts too long. Then, he urges the audience to calm down and invites people to ask questions. His spontaneous answers usually upstage anything he might have said during the lecture.

"Would you prefer to be thin?"
"No. My weight gives us a subject with which to start these questions and answer sessions." [30]

"What are your thoughts on Hell?"
"I regard it as a thing to be avoided." [31]

"What do you think of the German language?"
"I regard it with a profound agnosticism." [32]

"If you were stranded on a desert island with only one book, what book would you want it to be?"
"*Thomas' Guide to Practical Shipbuilding.*" [33]

"Could you speak louder please?"
"Good sister, don't worry. You aren't missing a thing!" [34]

"What do you think will happen in the next great revolution: the revolt of Nature against Man?"
"I hope Man will not hesitate to shoot." [35]

[30] *Cleveland Press*, March 3, 1921.

[31] "The Future of Religion: Mr. G. K. Chesterton's Reply to Mr. Bernard Shaw", reprinted for The Heretics (a University of Cambridge organization that sponsored a speech by Chesterton in 1911), 7.

[32] *Capitol Times* (Madison, Wis.), March 3, 1921.

[33] Ward, *Gilbert Keith Chesterton*, 204.

[34] Cyril Clemens, *Chesterton as Seen by His Contemporaries* (New York: Haskell House, 1969), 71.

[35] *Platitudes Undone* (San Francisco: Ignatius Press, 1997), 69.

"Isn't Truth merely one's own conception of things?"

"That is the Big Blunder. All thought is an attempt to dis-
    cover if one's own conception is true or not." [36]

"Do you believe in the comradeship between the sexes?"

"Madam, if I were to treat you for two minutes like a com-
    rade, you would turn me out of the house." [37]

"You seem to know everything."

"I know nothing, Madam. I am a journalist." [38]

"In the event of your having to change your original posi-
    tion, what tactic do you adopt?"

"On such occasions, I invariably commit suicide." [39]

He steps down from the stage. We step back and see
that it is just a larger version of his favorite boyhood game,
the Toy Theatre, where the figures are fantastic and heroic,
the colors bright. He has battled the dragons once again.
The applause fades, the lights dim, the picture begins to
blur into rapidly passing images. There is the skeletal figure of Shaw, urging him to write plays and make some
money. There is the charging bull, Belloc, urging him
to attack political and corporate corruption. There is the
patient and supportive wife, Frances, urging him not to
spend so much time with journalism, to use his considerable talents to create a great and lasting work of literature rather than the fleeting work of Fleet Street. There is
H. G. Wells, with his brilliant mind and empty philosophy,

[36] Ibid., 13.

[37] *What's Wrong with the World*, *CW* 4:123.

[38] Michael Ffinch, *G. K. Chesterton: A Biography* (San Francisco: Harper
and Row, 1986), 175.

[39] Maisie Ward, *Return to Chesterton* (New York: Sheed and Ward, 1952),
147.

representing on a grand scale everything that is wrong with the world. And there are the lesser critics, urging him to stop writing about his newly found Catholic faith, even though that is what he has been writing about all along.

There are still more dragons to fight. The battle seems endless. Once again, we can hear him sigh, "Alas my trade is words." He does not feel worthy of his calling to be a bearer of beauty and justice and truth. He suddenly seems weary and overwhelmed at the awesomeness of his task. He says, "I now realize that we are trying to fight the whole world, to turn the tide of the whole time we live in, to resist everything that seems irresistible." [40] And for an instant all seems lost.

But then he lifts up his head. "The one perfectly divine thing," he says, "the one glimpse of God's paradise on earth, is to fight a losing battle—and not lose it." [41]

He still has one more weapon, more potent and more practical than all the others. He picks it up. It is his pen. His trade may be mere words, but as he himself says, "Words are deeds." [42] The unlikely costume of a journalist that he wears is really a soldier's uniform. He is ready for battle again, attacking what is bad because he must defend what is good. The bad is not so bad that we should fear it. The good is much better than we can even imagine. He exhorts us. His pen is a weapon, but it is also a tool, a trowel. Like Nehemiah, he says, a man must have a sword in one hand and a trowel in the other.[43] The sword is reason and is used for defense; the trowel is imagination and is used to build,

---

[40] *G. K.'s Weekly*, March 9, 1929.
[41] *Time's Abstract and Brief Chronicle*, CW 11:63.
[42] *ILN*, February 2, 1907.
[43] See *Varied Types* (New York: Dodd, Mead, 1909), 113.

to create something beautiful. The work is hard and good. It is daily, like a journal.

And he writes and writes and fights and fights to the very end of his life. His dying thoughts are as lucid as his living thoughts: "The issue is clear. It is between light and darkness and everyone must choose his side." [44]

We must choose our side. Then we must join the fight. We can arm ourselves with that valuable weapon of his that he has left for us. His words are still here, the words created by his pen, that help us battle the ancient enemy in all its new forms, and to defend the ancient truth that does not change. We still have that sword that is also a trowel; it is a weapon that we can use for fighting, but it is also a tool that we can use for building. It serves us still: the pen of G. K. Chesterton.

[44] Ward, *Gilbert Keith Chesterton*, 650.

2

Wonder

There is no excuse for being bored. The world is overflow-
ing with more than enough beauties and fascinations and mysteries to fill several lifetimes. There are always more books to
be read, and, amazingly enough, still more books to be written. There are more problems to be solved, and more solutions to be celebrated. And there are endless games to be
played. And yet the modern world is bored. Modern art reflects
the boredom. So do the people who patronize it. No great
literature is being produced. And, if it is, certainly no one is
reading it. On the social front, most of the genuine injustices
are being fought by only a few lonely voices, while the rest
of us languidly turn our heads. And games are something we
hire professionals to play for us, while we merely watch. Our
entertainment grows louder, flashier, and more bizarre in ever
more desperate attempts just to keep our attention.

As G. K. Chesterton proclaims: "The world will never
starve for want of wonders; but only for want of wonder." [1] There are no dreary sights, he declares, only dreary
sightseers. [2] He claims that there were two things he never

---

[1] *Tremendous Trifles* (New York: Sheed and Ward, 1955), 7.

[2] See *Alarms and Discursions* (New York: Dodd, Mead, 1911), 295.

encountered in his whole life: an uninteresting subject or an uninteresting person.[3] But he did find many *uninterested* persons. The Bored. The Cagey. The people who think the excitement is elsewhere, never here. These were the people he was trying to convince of a very important lesson in life: that the richest discoveries are the things close by, the things overlooked. "We may scale the heavens and find new stars innumerable, but there is still the new star we have not found—that one on which we were born." [4]

For Chesterton, everything is a source of fascination. As a young man, he realized that no one else seemed to take such "a fierce pleasure in things being themselves" as he did: he says he was startled and excited by "the wetness of water, the fieriness of fire, the steeliness of steel, the unutterable muddiness of mud".[5] This led him to understand that when we call a man "manly" or a woman "womanly", we touch the deepest philosophy.[6] It also led him to understand his own vocation as a writer and a literary artist. He was not selfish with his gift of being able to see the world in all its fullness. He tried to give us his eyes to see the world as he saw it, to reawaken in us a sense of wonder.

> The whole object of real art, of real romance—and, above all, of real religion—is to prevent people from losing the humility and gratitude which are thankful for daylight and daily bread; to prevent them from regarding daily life as dull or domestic life as narrow; to teach them to feel in the sunlight the song of Apollo and in the bread the epic of the plough. What is now needed most is intensive imagination.

[3] See *ILN*, January 11, 1913.

[4] *The Defendant* (London: J. M. Dent, 1907), 113.

[5] Maisie Ward, *Gilbert Keith Chesterton* (New York: Sheed and Ward, 1943), 108–19.

[6] Ibid.

I mean the power to turn our imaginations inwards, on the things we already have, and to make those things live. It is not merely seeking new experiences, which rapidly become old experiences. It is really learning how to experience our experiences. It is learning how to enjoy our enjoyments.[7]

Our first act each day should be an act of thanksgiving. We should begin by being grateful to have been created. We should regard life as an ecstasy, a mercy, an unbelievable privilege. And yet, it is the hardest of all earthly tasks to turn back and wonder at the simplicities we have come to ignore. For some strange reason the most unpopular of all doctrines is the doctrine that declares the common life divine. Though we praise democracy, it turns out that there is nothing that so terrifies men as the decree that they are all kings. And Christianity, oddly enough, is the hardest of gospels; for there is nothing that so strikes men with fear as the saying that they are all the sons of God.[8] But this *is* the Good News, and this good news flows endlessly from the pen of Gilbert Keith Chesterton.

Everywhere Chesterton looks he sees a sacramental sign or a symbol. Everything means something. "It is impossible for anything to signify nothing."[9] Where there is nothing there is Satan.[10] As an example of Chesterton's ability to see the significance in anything, one night while traveling in a train, he looked out the window and saw a brief glimpse of a scene inside a house along the tracks: a room lit with a blue light against a red curtain, and the shadow of a man stretching his arms, probably just yawning and getting ready

---

[7] *ILN*, October 20, 1924.
[8] See "Savonarola", in *Twelve Types* (Norfolk, Va.: IHS Press, 2003), 73–74.
[9] *A Handful of Authors* (New York: Sheed and Ward, 1953), 40.
[10] See *Utopia of Usurers*, *CW* 5:457.

to go to bed. But in that blue light, Chesterton saw the blue skies of eternity and the blue that clings to the Blessed Virgin in all the old pictures, and in the red he saw the blood of martyrdom, and in the figure with the out-stretched arms he saw the Crucifixion.[11]

An unsettling image? That, says Chesterton, is the whole purpose of the imagination: "The function of imagination is not to make strange things settled, so much as to make settled things strange; not so much to make wonders facts as to make facts wonders."[12]

The wonder begins with existence itself. Existence, he says, "has a value wholly inexpressible".[13] But the artist tries to express it. That is duty of the artist: to express the inexpressible.

Chesterton tries to get us to feel what he calls "the intox-ication of existence"[14] and the invaluable, incomparable gift of life. In a prophetic poem he wrote over a hundred years ago, a poem entitled "By the Babe Unborn", he portrays a baby, lying in the dark womb, trying to imagine a world of blue skies and green grassy hills, which to him in the dark-ness is just a dream. But if he could actually attain it, and see such a world and live in it, his gratitude would be unending.

> They should not hear a word from me
> Of selfishness or scorn,
> If only I could find the door,
> If only I were born.[15]

---

[11] See "The Artistic Side", in *The Coloured Lands* (New York: Sheed and Ward, 1938), 109–110.

[12] *The Defendant*, 60.

[13] *Robert Browning* (New York: Macmillan, 1903), 50.

[14] Ward, *Chesterton*, 108.

[15] *Collected Poetry*, *CW* 10, Part 1:197–98.

Consequently, babies remind us to be in awe of the world. We should never stop being in awe of babies. As Chesterton says, each time a baby is born, it is as if a whole new world has been created, because the world is being seen for the first time by a new soul as if it were the first day of creation; inside that little head, there is a new system of stars, new grass, new cities, a new sea.[16]

> A literary man who cannot see that a baby is marvelous could not see that anything was marvelous. He has certainly no earthly logical reason for regarding a movie vamp as marvelous. The movie vamp is only what happens to the baby when it goes wrong.[17]

We don't recognize that babies are marvelous because we refuse to see basic, obvious things. Chesterton says that it is only the obvious things that are never seen, the things that we have been seeing all along without seeing them. And one of those obvious things is the strangely elusive thing called happiness. All the true things about happiness have been said and are always being said, and yet we have managed to ignore them.

It is another example of us not knowing how to enjoy enjoyment. We put so much emphasis on the *pursuit* of happiness rather than on the happiness itself. All the things that we need to make us reasonably happy lie within our grasp. If we pause in our frantic pursuit of happiness, if we stop and try to picture happiness, it is something different from the fuss and frustration that fills our pursuit. Happiness is something simple and basic. And everyone knows this, if they would only stop and consider it. It is common sense.

[16] See *The Defendant*, 113.
[17] *ILN*, March 17, 1931.

> Men rush towards complexity, but they yearn towards sim-
> plicity. They try to be kings; but they dream of being
> shepherds.[18]

If we will neglect the basic pleasures, the reasonable happiness that is already available to us, we will chase after an
unreasonable sort of happiness: the impossible or the forbidden, or what we never *can* have or never *should* have.
"That sort of divine discontent is not the pursuit of happiness, but rather the pursuit of unhappiness."[19]

> The point of the story of Satan is not that he revolted against
> being in hell, but that he revolted against being in heaven.
> The point about Adam is not that he was discontented with
> the conditions of the earth, but that he was discontented
> with the conditions of the earthly paradise.[20]

This discontent leads to the loss of wonder. The world
becomes stale, and all other problems follow.

> The effect of this staleness is the same everywhere; it is
> seen in all drug-taking and dram-drinking and every form
> of the tendency to increase the dose. Men seek stranger
> sins or more startling obscenities as stimulants to their jaded
> sense. They seek after mad oriental religions for the same
> reason. They try to stab their nerves to life.... They are
> walking in their sleep and try to wake themselves up with
> nightmares.[21]

There is a clarity in contentment. And it is something that
we can control, something we can choose. It is a happiness

---

[18] *Robert Louis Stevenson, CW* 18:135–36.
[19] *ILN*, September 20, 1924.
[20] *New York American*, December 15, 1932.
[21] *Everlasting Man, CW* 2:291.

that we can choose. The misery of discontent is passive. It is muddled and it muddles. It is cynical and suspicious and short. It is hopeless. But wonder is active. It shimmers. It is full of faith and hope. And it is eternal.

The key to happiness and the key to wonder is humility. Chesterton understands this better than any modern writer. More than that, he also embodies it. Humility means being small enough to see the greatness of something and to feel unworthy of it, and privileged to be able to enjoy it. And ultimately there is only One Thing to enjoy and only One Thing that can ever make us happy. Ironically, both the skeptic and the believer think the Gospel is too good to be true. But the skeptic scorns it, and the believer falls on his knees. He sees that even goodness is too good to be true, along with the truth that is too good to be true. The only thing that prevents us from seeing this is the sinfulness of pride.

Chesterton maintains that pride is the ultimate evil, and he claims that mankind has instinct against pride, which "can be proved from the most prosaic details":

> We do not resent a schoolboy being in love with a different girl every week, nor even his being in love with all of them in the course of the same week. Our dim yet divine desire to kick him only comes when he says that they are all in love with him.... Pride is the poison in every other vice.... Gluttony is a great fault; but we do not necessarily dislike a glutton. We only dislike the glutton when he becomes the *gourmet*—that is, we only dislike him when he not only wants the best for himself, but knows what is best for other people.... Pride does not go before a fall. Pride is a fall.[22]

[22] *ILN*, August 22, 1914.

Pride, says Chesterton, dries up laughter, it dries up won-der, it dries up chivalry and energy.[23] But humility is the thing that is forever renewing the earth and the stars.[24] The sense of wonder silences us. It is the silence that comes from being in the presence of God. It is the silence that lets us listen. The fear of the Lord is the beginning of wis-dom.[25] The first thing the fear of the Lord does, as it did to Job, is compel us to put our hands over our mouths.[26]

Religion is about wonder. Wonder "has the positive ele-ment of praise".[27] The wonder of creation, and of the Cre-ator. The wonder of what we have been given, and—if we think about it—the hint of a wonder of something we have lost. We know that there is something perfect, only because we have an imperfect version of it. Paradise, says Chester-ton, is a hope, but also—in some strange way—also a mem-ory. We recognize paradise because we recognize we have been deprived of it.

Chesterton realized this, oddly enough, when he sprained his foot. Remember, everything means something—even a sprained foot. For Chesterton, the name of the lesson was: "The Advantages of Having One Leg":

> I feel grateful for the slight sprain which has introduced this mysterious and fascinating relationship between one of my feet and the other. The way to love anything is to real-ise that it might be lost. In one of my feet I can feel how strong and splendid a foot is; in the other I can realise how very much otherwise it might have been. The moral of the thing is wholly exhilarating. This world and all our powers

[23] See *Heretics*, *CW* 1:107.

[24] Ibid., 128.

[25] See Proverbs 9:10.

[26] See Job 40:4.

[27] *Orthodoxy*, *CW* 1:257.

in it are far more awful and beautiful than even we know until some accident reminds us. If you wish to perceive that limitless felicity, limit yourself if only for a moment. If you wish to realise how fearfully and wonderfully God's image is made, stand on one leg. If you want to realise the splendid vision of all visible things—wink the other eye.[28]

"The way to love anything is to realize that it might be lost." It makes us look on everything with a new appreciation. What if we did not have it? Chesterton reminds us that we could just as easily *not* have had it, or any of the good things we do have.

Thanks are the highest form of thought. Gratitude is happiness doubled by wonder.[29]

The reason why thanks are the highest form of thought is because they put us in the frame of mind where we realize that everything we have is a gift. The nature of a gift is that it is undeserved. There is a theological term for this: grace.

And what is the best kind of gift? The one that we don't expect: the surprise. Certainly it is a pleasure on Christmas morning to find our stockings filled with gifts. But Chesterton says the best gift we can ever find in our stockings is our own two legs. He wants us to experience that pleasure of the surprise gift with everything, to see everything as if seeing it for the first time, to enhance the whole world in a new light of appreciation: "The test of all happiness is gratitude." [30] For Chesterton there was one famous piece of literature that illustrates better than anything else the art

[28] *Tremendous Trifles*, 39.
[29] *A Short History of England, CW* 20:463.
[30] *Orthodoxy, CW* 1:258.

of gratitude and the appreciation of the so-called commonplace: it is the original castaway story, *Robinson Crusoe*:

> Robinson Crusoe is a man on a small rock with a few com-
> forts just snatched from the sea: the best thing in the book
> is simply the list of things saved from the wreck. The great-
> est of poems is an inventory. Every kitchen tool becomes
> ideal because Crusoe might have dropped it in the sea. It is
> a good exercise, in empty or ugly hours of the day, to look
> at anything, the coal-scuttle or the bookcase, and think how
> happy one could be to have brought it out of the sinking
> ship on to the solitary island. But it is a better exercise still
> to remember how all things have had this hair-breadth escape:
> everything has been saved from a wreck. Every man has
> had one horrible adventure [of almost not being saved]. . . .
> Men spoke much in my boyhood of restricted or ruined
> men of genius: and it was common to say that many a man
> was a Great Might-Have-Been. To me it is a more solid
> and startling fact that any man in the street is a Great
> Might-Not-Have-Been.[31]

Robinson Crusoe is an example of "the poetry of limits",
and "the wild romance of prudence". It is the best use of
the imagination. We might suppose that imagination involves
an expansion, a longing for larger and larger horizons. We
might suppose that the imagination works toward the infinite. But, if we think about it, the infinite is the opposite
of the imagination. For as Chesterton says, "The imagination deals with an image. And an image is in its nature a
thing that has an outline and, therefore, a limit."[32] The
person with the best imagination, and who quite uncon-
sciously sees this connection between imagination and

[31] Ibid., 267.
[32] *ILN*, February 8, 1930.

limitation, is the little child. "The child is positively in love with limits. He uses his imagination to invent imaginary limits." For instance, he has never been told that it is his moral duty to step on alternate paving-stones. And yet that's what he does. "He deliberately deprives this world of half its paving-stones, in order to exult in a challenge that he has offered to himself." [33] This game of self-limitation is the principle behind every game. It means drawing a line and staying within it. It is one of the secret treasures of life. It begins with a child stepping on alternate paving-stones. It means sometimes standing on one leg. It means appreciating something more because you have given something else up. There is a theological term for this, too: sacrifice.

Only Chesterton could derive such profound, eternal truths from such a simple thing as a game of hopscotch.

> If anybody chooses to say that I have founded all my social philosophy on the antics of a baby, I am quite satisfied to bow and smile. [34]

Wonder is an elementary thing. The child's sense of wonder at a fairy tale is something basic. But what is interesting is that the younger the child is, the less fantastic the fairy tale has to be. The sense of wonder is so intense that mere life is interesting enough.

> A child of seven is excited by being told that Tommy opened a door and saw a dragon. But a child of three is excited by being told that Tommy opened a door. [35]

[33] Ibid.
[34] Ibid.
[35] *Orthodoxy, CW* 1:257.

The point is that we were made to be astonished. And that is what we expect art to do for us. But the greatest work of art is the astonishing creation that God gave us.

> Astonishment at the universe is not mysticism but a transcendental common sense.[36]

When Chesterton recalled his own childhood, he said that what was wonderful about it was that anything in it was a wonder. "It was not merely a world full of miracles, it was a miraculous world."[37] Make no mistake: he grew up and came to understand sin and evil; he was not naïve about the darkness that clouds the human soul. But G. K. Chesterton maintained a supreme innocence that fills his writing. He never lost his childlike sense of wonder.

And this is important. Jesus teaches us, "I tell you truly, anyone who will not receive the Kingdom of God like a little child, will never enter it."[38] There is a challenge with Chesterton. The challenge is this: we have to adjust our whole way of thinking when we read him. We are not used to thinking in the language he uses. But if we can learn to think his thoughts with him, he can reawaken in us that sense of wonder that will enable us to become like little children. And we can step closer to the Kingdom of God.

There is indeed something that children seem to grasp about eternal life that the rest of us have lost. They have abounding vitality; they are in spirit, fierce and free, and yet, as Chesterton says, they want things repeated and unchanged. "They always say, 'Do it again'; and the

---

[36] The Defendant, 112.
[37] Autobiography, CW 16:45.
[38] Mark 10:15.

grown-up person does it until he is nearly dead. For grown-up people are not strong enough to exult in monotony. But perhaps God is strong enough to exult in monotony. It is possible that God says every morning, 'Do it again' to the sun; and every evening, 'Do it again' to the moon." [39]

World without end. Amen.

[39] *Orthodoxy, CW* 1:263–64.

3

The Riddles of God

The hand of God may be evident in the wonder of his creation, but the most evident thing about God ... is that he is hidden.

> We all feel the riddle of the earth without anyone to point it out. The mystery of life is the plainest part of it. The clouds and curtains of darkness, the confounding vapors, these are the daily weather of this world. Whatever else we have grown accustomed to, we have grown accustomed to the unaccountable. Every stone or flower is a hieroglyphic of which we have lost the key; with every step of our lives we enter into the middle of some story which we are certain to misunderstand.[1]

It may seem startling to call G. K. Chesterton a mystic. That is because we have a hard time associating the word "mystic" with a three hundred-pound, cigar-smoking London journalist. And that is because in general we have the wrong idea about what a mystic is. As Chesterton says, a verbal accident has confused the mystical with the mysterious.[2] Mysticism is thought to be something vague and cloudy

---

[1] *William Blake* (London: House of Stratus, 2000), 38.
[2] Ibid.

and impenetrable. Something mysterious. But the mystic does not bring doubts and riddles. The doubts and riddles exist already. The mystic is the man who tries to address the doubts and solve the riddles. The mystic is not the man who makes mysteries but the man who destroys them.

And that is why it is safe to say that Chesterton is a mystic. He is always diving deeply into the ocean of mystery and returning to the surface with great truths for those of us who are here along the shore, barely getting our feet wet. Chesterton not only points to the strange symbols we have missed; he reveals their surprising meanings. His greatest gift is his ability to turn things around for us when we have them exactly backwards.

For instance, we often say things like, "The marriage vow might be very convenient for commonplace public purposes, but has no place in the world of art and imagination." Chesterton says, the truth is exactly the other way. The truth is that if marriage had not existed, it would have been necessary for artists to invent it. Even if the pledge of commitment between a man and a woman had never been a social requirement, it would still have been a poetical requirement. Monogamy is romantic; it just happens to be merely practical, but "if ever monogamy is abandoned in practice, it will linger in legend and in literature." [3]

Another example of our backwardness: we often talk of "the restraints of fact and the freedom of fiction". But the truth is exactly the other way. "Nature is as free as air: art is forced to look probable. There may be a million things that do happen, and yet only one thing that convinces us as likely to happen." [4]

[3] *ILN*, July 15, 1922.
[4] *Charles Dickens, CW* 15:108.

So what does all this have to do with God? We some-times say that the concept of God is merely a symbol of some greater abstract cosmic idea of goodness. But the truth is exactly the other way. Chesterton says, "God is not sym-bol of goodness; goodness is a symbol of God." [5]

And as any true mystic draws closer to the Truth, closer to God, God does not become something vague and form-less and impersonal. God becomes more solid and definite and personal. God becomes a man.

Yet even Jesus is a mystery. He does not come as a con-quering king; he comes as a suffering servant. Not what we would have expected. Even when God reveals himself, he remains hidden. The mystic always has more work cut out for him.

There is a question that has always haunted mankind. It is a question that has perplexed everyone who has ever thought about it. The question is this: "Why does God allow suffering?" Or as we sometimes more pointedly put it: "Why does God allow bad things to happen to good people?"

There is one place that this question is dealt with more profoundly than anywhere else: the Old Testament Book of Job, which just happens to be G. K. Chesterton's favor-ite book of the Bible. He describes how Job faces the universal question of suffering. Though Job's endurance is beyond anything most of us can imagine, in spite of his great patience, he finally reaches the point that we all reach, the point where he demands an explanation. He wants some answers from God. And, finally, God himself steps onto the stage. But the amazing thing about the book is that when God enters the story, it is not to answer Job's questions; it is to ask his own questions, questions such as,

[5] *William Blake*, 40.

"Where were you when I laid the foundation of the earth?" And what is even more amazing than the fact that God doesn't really answer Job's questions is this: Job is suddenly satisfied.

> [Job] was comfortless before the speech of Jehovah and is comforted after it. He has been told nothing, but he feels the terrible and tingling atmosphere of something which is too good to be told. The refusal of God to explain His design is itself a burning hint of His design. The riddles of God are more satisfying than the solutions of man.[6]

This is a marvelous turnaround. Job and his friends had insisted that everything in the world can be explained. God himself comes and insists that everything cannot be explained, at least as far as men are concerned. In fact, as God describes the wonders of creation, he insists that it is a much stranger world than Job ever thought it was. And again Job is somehow comforted by this.

But the big question dealt with in the Book of Job is the question of whether God always punishes vice with earthly calamity and always rewards virtue with earthly prosperity. In other words, do we suffer right now because of our sins, and are we rewarded right now because of our virtues? The answer in the Book of Job is pretty obvious. The answer is no. And if it were a different answer, *that* would be a calamity. Because it would tempt us to think that all successful people are virtuous and that all unfortunate people are merely getting what they deserve. But as Chesterton says, the Book of Job is chiefly remarkable for the fact that it does not end in a way that is conventionally satisfactory.

[6] "Introduction to the Book of Job", *Chesterton Review*, vol. 11, no. 1, February, 1985.

Job is not told that his misfortunes were due to his sins or
a part of any plan for his improvement.... We see Job tor-
mented not because he was the worst of men, but because
he was the best. It is the lesson of the whole work that
man is most comforted by paradoxes; and it is by all human
testimony the most reassuring. I need not suggest what a
high and strange history awaited this paradox of the best
man in the worst fortune. I need not say [whose wounds
are] pre-figured in the wounds of Job.[7]

Paradoxical, isn't it, that man is most comforted by paradoxes. It is this tool of comfort, the paradox, that Chesterton makes the greatest use of in all his writing. He is the
prince of paradox.

What exactly is this thing, paradox? Well, first of all, it isn't
one thing; it's two things. It has two definitions. And both
definitions are equally important. The first meaning, the literal meaning, from the Greek, is *para*, which is "contrary to"
or "against", and *dox*, which is "accepted opinion or expectation". In other words something strange, something remarkable, even wonderful, unexpected or uncommon. Something
other than, even the opposite of what we would expect.

The second meaning is the notion of the proposition that
seems to contradict itself: two statements that are both true,
but absolutely contradict one another.

The Bible of course is full of paradox. "Many that are first
will be last, and the last first."[8] "Whoever would save his life
will lose it, and whoever loses his life will find it."[9] "Whoever would be great among you must be your servant."[10]

[7] Ibid.
[8] Matthew 19:30.
[9] Matthew 16:25.
[10] Matthew 20:26.

"A Virgin shall give birth."[11] "The dead shall rise."[12] "Blessed are the poor."[13] "Blessed are those who are persecuted."[14] "Count it all joy ... when you meet various trials."[15]

If you want more good examples of paradox turn to any page of G. K. Chesterton:

All men are tragic.... All men are comic.... Every man is important if he loses his life; and every man is funny if he loses his hat.[16]

All the jokes about men sitting down on their hats are really theological jokes; they are concerned with the Dual Nature of Man. They refer to the primary paradox that man is superior to all the things around him and yet is at their mercy.[17]

Men can always be blind to a thing so long as it is big enough. It is so difficult to see the world in which we live.[18]

The self is more distant than any star.[19]

The mere pursuit of health always leads to something unhealthy.[20]

Nature worship inevitably produces things that are against nature.[21]

[11] Isaiah 7:14.
[12] Isaiah 26:19.
[13] Luke 6:20.
[14] Matthew 5:11.
[15] James 1:2.
[16] *Charles Dickens, CW* 15:178–79.
[17] *ILN*, March 21, 1908.
[18] *The Superstition of Divorce, CW* 4:270.
[19] *Orthodoxy, CW* 1:257.
[20] Ibid., 280.
[21] *St. Francis of Assisi, CW* 2:39.

Charity to the deserving is not charity.[22]

It is of the new things that men tire—of fashions and proposals and improvements and change. It is the old things that startle and intoxicate. It is the old things that are young.[23]

It is easy to be solemn; it is so hard to be frivolous.[24]

Fairy tales are the only true accounts that man has ever given of his destiny. "Jack the Giant-Killer" is the embodiment of the . . . the paradox of Courage; the paradox which says, "You must defy the thing that is terrifying; unless you are frightened, you are not brave." "Cinderella" is the embodiment of the paradox of Humility which says "Look for the best in the thing, ignorant of its merit; he that abases himself shall be exalted." And "Beauty and the Beast" is the embodiment of the . . . paradox of Faith—the absolutely necessary and wildly unreasonable maxim which says to every mother with a child or to every patriot with a country, "You must love the thing first and make it lovable afterwards." [25]

Chesterton uses the concept of courage as a prime example of paradox. He says it means a strong desire to live, taking the form of a readiness to die. A man in peril can only save his life by risking it.

He can only get away from death by continually stepping within an inch of it. A soldier surrounded by enemies, if he is to cut his way out, needs to combine a strong desire for living with a strange carelessness about dying.[26]

[22] Heretics, CW 1:125.

[23] The Napoleon of Notting Hill, CW 6:153.

[24] "The Case for the Ephemeral", in All Things Considered (New York: Sheed and Ward, 1956), 3.

[25] The World, September 7, 1904.

[26] Orthodoxy, CW 1:297.

There is no way out of danger except the dangerous way.[27]

Now, before we get carried away with examples of paradox, we have to note examples of what *isn't* paradox. Paradox is not a compromise of two opposing ideas, each giving
in to a middle ground that is neither one nor the other, as
pink is neither red nor white. It is not dualism (as in the
philosophy of Hegel), where you have a thesis and an antith-
esis and put them together to produce a synthesis. It is not
the Oriental yin-yang, where reality is composed of a meta-
physical balance of opposite forces. And it is not an oxymoron, or contradiction in terms, which is simply nonsense
like "round square" or "tiny giant" or "jumbo shrimp" or
"tight slacks" or "government intelligence" (or my all-time
favorite oxymoron: "Microsoft Works"). While these are not
paradox, they point to the paradox, because each of these
others attempts to deal with contradiction, and contradiction is the essence of the paradox.

Chesterton says, "By paradox we mean the truth inher-
ent in a contradiction.... [In the paradox] the two opposite cords of truth become entangled in an inextricable knot
... [but it is] this knot which ties safely together the whole
bundle of human life." [28]

An element of paradox runs through the whole of existence itself. It begins in the two facts that we cannot imagine a space that is infinite, and that we cannot imagine a
space that is finite. It runs through the inmost complica-
tions of divinity, in that we cannot conceive that Christ in
the wilderness was truly pure, unless we also conceive that
he desired to sin. It runs, in the same manner, through all
the minor matters of morals, so that we cannot imagine

courage existing except in conjunction with fear, or mag-
nanimity existing except in conjunction with some temptation to meanness.[29]

"Thinking", says Chesterton, "means connecting things." [30]
But when we do try to connect things, one of two things
usually happens: either they don't connect, or they collide.
In other words, we encounter a contradiction. The contradiction is either a lack of continuity, a separation, or, more
likely, it is a collision, a discord, an opposition. And somehow we have to deal with it. We have to do something
about it. Our natural tendency is to do away with the contradiction. Eliminate it.

But Chesterton says,

It is only ... the man who accepts the contradictions who
can laugh and walk easily through the world. . . . He has
always cared more for truth than for consistency. If he saw
two truths that seemed to contradict each other, he would
take the two truths and the contradiction along with them.
His spiritual sight is stereoscopic, like his physical sight: he
sees two different pictures at once and yet sees all the
better for that. Thus he has always believed that there was
such a thing as fate, but such a thing as free will also.
Thus he believed that children were indeed of the kingdom of heaven, but nevertheless ought to be obedient to
the kingdom of earth. He admired youth because it was
young and age because it was not. It is exactly this balance of apparent contradictions that has been the whole
buoyancy of the healthy man. The whole secret of mysticism is this: that man can understand everything by the
help of what he does not understand. The morbid logi-

[29] *Twelve Types* (Norfolk, Va.: IHS Press, 2003), 28.
[30] *Orthodoxy*, *CW* 1:238.

cian seeks to make everything lucid, and succeeds only in
making everything mysterious. The mystic allows one thing
to be mysterious and everything else becomes lucid.[31]

Chesterton uses paradox for a purpose—not to be cute, not
to be clever, not to be confusing, and not to be merely
contradictory. He uses paradox to point to the truth. Truth
is paradoxical in both senses of the word. It is a surprise,
and it is set around a contradiction. At no point does Chesterton explain the contradiction away; he never unties that
inextricable knot. He, like the mystic to whom he refers,
"allows one thing to be mysterious" so that everything else
can be lucid. But this is important: he is not trying to encourage muddled thinking. On the contrary, he really is trying
to make everything lucid, all the while acknowledging the
insoluble mystery that lies at the heart of existence.

Now, to say that there is such a thing as an insoluble
mystery is not to attack reason. It is to say that reason, by
itself, is insufficient. Reason has its place, but first it has its
starting place, which is never reasonable. He says, "You can
never prove your first statement or it would not be your
first statement." [32] In other words, there is no such thing as
a reasonable assumption. (That would be an oxymoron.)
Chesterton points out that logic is a process that can be
performed with any assumption. He says that you can only
find truth with logic if you have already found truth without it.[33] Truth and logic have very little to do with each
other. Chesterton is not against reason; what he is against is
skepticism in all its forms, especially in the proud agnostic
who claims he is relying only on reason, when really he

[31] Ibid., 230–31.
[32] Daily News, June 22, 1907.
[33] See Daily News, February 25, 1905.

only equates reason with doubt. The skeptic begins by doubting. There is nothing reasonable about that. His only use of reason is to reinforce his doubt, and thus, says Chesterton, he "sinks through floor after floor of a bottomless universe".[34]

Reason has to have a starting point from which to build its case. But that starting point has to simply be a given, a given that has to be accepted, an assumption, which is nothing more than an act of faith. But, then, reason can only go so far. It also ends with faith.

> The ultimate paradox ... [is] that the very things we cannot comprehend are the things we have to take for granted.[35]

> Whatever may be the meaning of faith, it must always mean a certainty about something we cannot prove.[36]

> A man must take what is called a leap in the dark, as he does when he is married or when he dies, or when he is born, or when he does almost anything else that is important.[37]

Truth is paradoxical. It is strange. It is improbable. It is the opposite of what we expect. Chesterton explains why truth is stranger than fiction: because we have made fiction to suit ourselves.[38] We have not made the truth. He says, however wild he makes his fictitious examples, "Truth is always wilder." [39] Truth comes as a surprise. It is the opposite of what we expect. Why? Because we have things backwards. Why? Because of another paradox. Chesterton says, "The

[34] *Lunacy and Letters* (New York: Sheed and Ward, 1958), 123

[35] *George Bernard Shaw, CW* 11:385.

[36] *Heretics, CW* 1:127.

[37] *A Handful of Authors* (New York: Sheed and Ward, 1953), 27.

[38] See *Heretics, CW* 1:67.

[39] *ILN*, September 22, 1906.

primary paradox of Christianity is that the ordinary condition of man is not his sane or sensible condition; that the normal itself is an abnormality." [40] We are fallen. We are sinful. We are confused. And we have everything mixed up.

> Men are always speaking gravely and earnestly and with the utmost possible care about things that are not important, but always talking frivolously about the things that are. Men talk for hours with the faces of a college of cardinals about things like golf, or tobacco . . . or party politics. But all the most grave and dreadful things in the world are the oldest jokes in the world—being married; being hanged. [41]

And then there is the paradox at the heart of all truth. The ultimate paradox. The absolute paradox. Jesus Christ. That God should come to earth as a humble servant is quite contrary to expectation. That he should suffer and die is not how we would have written the script. That he should rise from the dead is beyond wonderful. Jesus is one surprise after another. He goes against our expectations. But Jesus is also the Contradiction: the collision of the eternal with the temporal, the infinite with the finite, the Creator with the creature, the invisible with the visible, the spirit with the flesh, life with death. Here we encounter the God-man, the King who is a servant, the Spirit who is a Rock, the Lion who is a Lamb: Jesus Christ.

In order to fulfill our deepest desire, to meet all our needs, to answer all our questions, in other words, to embody truth, Christ has to be a paradox. We would accept nothing less. And nothing less would be able to accept us. It must be God and man combined in one person. Not a blend or a

[40] *Orthodoxy, CW* 1:363.
[41] *Heretics, CW* 1:157–58.

compromise, but, as Chesterton says, "both things at the top of their energy; love and wrath both burning ... not a being apart from God and man, like an elf, not a being half human and half not, like a centaur, but both things at once and both things thoroughly, very man and very God." [42]

The Cross has always been called the sign of contradiction. It is the horizontal contradicted by the vertical. It is time contradicted by eternity. It is sin contradicted by forgiveness. It is death contradicted by life.

What is left for us to do? Bow down and worship. That is the final paradox. Chesterton says, "The worshipper never feels taller than when he bows." [43]

---

[42] *Orthodoxy, CW* 1:296.
[43] *The Everlasting Man, CW* 2:244.

4

The Signature of Man

It is one of the great ironies that the twentieth century's greatest writer—G. K. Chesterton, for those of you who haven't been paying attention—never went to college. He went to art school. And his definition of art school is itself a work of art: "An art school is a place where about three people work with feverish energy and everybody else idles to a degree that I should have conceived unattainable by human nature." [1]

Chesterton considered himself one of the idlers, but he at least thought that he was in art school because he was training to become an artist. But he accidentally became a writer instead. In 1900, he was asked to review some art books for a magazine, and with that he said he had discovered "the easiest of all professions", which he pursued the rest of his life.

But his training in art obviously served him well. Art is about being articulate. And G. K. Chesterton, the artist turned writer, writes visually. He illustrates everything he says with verbal images that spring to life. His words "become flesh".

[1] *Autobiography, CW* 16:94.

Although he went on to write about everything and everything else, art is a theme he returns to again and again. His writings include commentary on just about any major artist you could name: Leonardo da Vinci, Michelangelo, Raphael, Giotto, Botticelli, Turner, Reynolds, Constable, Monet, Gauguin, Picasso. What sets him apart as an art critic is the stunning way in which he puts artists into their larger contexts, that is, he puts them in their place. But he also puts art into its place.

Because we are created in the image of God, we also are creators. Man is the only one of God's creatures who is an artist.[2] Art sets man apart. "Art", says Chesterton, "is the signature of man."[3] But I suppose we could add that it is a signature that is not always legible. When someone asks, "What is art?" it is almost as bad as Pontius Pilate asking, "What is Truth?" when Truth is standing right in front of his face. (As Chesterton says, the Roman governor "showed his taste for epigram at a somewhat unlucky moment".[4]) Yet if we ask Chesterton the question "What is art?" the answer he gives is almost as challenging as the question. For he does not give just one answer. He says that the definition of art is exaggeration, but he also says that art is diminution, reducing the world to a smaller scale. He says art should be sensational, but he also says art should be subtle. He contends that art should be beautiful, overwhelmingly beautiful, yet he defends gargoyles and the grotesque and the homely peasants painted by Rembrandt. He attacks vulgarity, and he also defends it. He attacks originality, and he also vigorously defends

[2] See *ILN*, November 23, 1929.
[3] *The Everlasting Man*, *CW* 2:166.
[4] *ILN*, March 16, 1922.

it. He attacks high art, and he also defends it. He attacks popular art, and he also defends it. Is there a contradiction here?

Yes and no.

Chesterton is a complete and consistent thinker, but he has to correct errors that lie at opposite extremes and defend a truth that is being attacked from all different angles, and that is why his arguments may seem at times to contradict each other.

> All very great classics of art are a rebuke to extravagance not in one direction but in all directions. The figure of a Greek Venus is a rebuke to the fat women of Rubens and also a rebuke to the thin women of Aubrey Beardsley.... This is perhaps the test of a very great work of classic creation, that it can be attacked on inconsistent grounds, and that it attacks its enemies on inconsistent grounds. Here is a broad and simple test. If you hear a thing being accused of being too tall and too short, too red and too green, too bad in one way and too bad also in the opposite way, then you may be sure that it is very good.[5]

There is another reason for the apparent contradictions in Chesterton's explanation of art. That is because there is a contradiction at the heart of all truth. Truth is paradoxical. And so art is also paradoxical. What makes a work of art great? What makes it survive through the ages? Chesterton says, "The thing that survives is that which has *a certain combination of normality with distinction. It has simplicity with a slight touch of strangeness. . . .* It is a tale just sufficiently unusual

---

[5] "The Macbeths", in *The Spice of Life*, compiled by Dorothy Collins (Beaconsfield, Eng.: Darwen Finlayson, 1964), 43.

to be worth telling, and yet immediately intelligible when told." [6]

This is common sense. We want art to strike us and amaze us, but we also want it to comfort us and to embrace us, to be both strange and familiar at the same time. If it is only strange, or only familiar, it fails as art. It succeeds when we can look at it and say, "I have seen that a thousand times and I never saw it before." Chesterton says that the masterpieces are defined by the fact that even when we have already seen them there is something unexpected about them. [7]

Anyone who has suffered through a gallery of modern art will appreciate Chesterton's art criticism. He explains exactly why most modern art fails. Though in one sense he really doesn't have to. Most anyone can see why it fails. However, modern art critics elaborately try to explain to us why modern art succeeds. But the explanations have taken over and have become more important than the art itself. And the poor patrons of the arts have to pretend to enjoy it. Chesterton says it takes moral courage to say of the academy what the child alone had the courage to say about the emperor's new clothes. There is nothing there.

It is one thing to swallow the new art and another thing merely to swallow the new art criticism. [8]

Many critics have passed from the proposition that a masterpiece may be unpopular to the other proposition that unless it is unpopular it cannot be a masterpiece. [9]

[6] *ILN*, November 20, 1920. (Emphasis mine.)
[7] See *The Thing*, *CW* 3:173.
[8] *ILN*, February 11, 1922.
[9] *ILN*, August 19, 1922.

Suppose a man says: "Why am I not free to produce a sublime architectural effect with thirty-seven butter-tubs, three gas-pipes, and a packing case? Why should I not make beauty out of these?" There seems to be no answer except to say, "Why not, indeed?" If he will produce sublime architecture out of them, I shall not complain of the sublimity. If he will make beauty from them, I shall not condemn them for contriving to be beautiful.... My attitude toward the experiment may be described as one of patient expectancy—of hope not unmingled with doubt. I am waiting for the moment when the pagoda of tubs shall strike my soul like a thunderbolt out of the sky; when I shall stagger with admiration at some perfect poise and balance of pipes and packing-cases which I had never foreseen even in my dreams. I say nothing of that inspiring moment of my life, except that it has not yet come.[10]

The problem is this. We worship the new instead of the eternal. And when we worship the new, we are always changing our allegiances, because there will always be something newer. Look at the schools of art in the last hundred years: Impressionism, Post-Impressionism, Futurism, Modernism, Post-Modernism, Post-Post-Modernism. The very titles given to the new schools refer only to the sequence of time and what Chesterton calls "a monomania of rivalry". He says it is "just as if one controversialist were called a Thursdayite, and the other completely eclipsed him by being a Fridayite.... The notion that every generation proves the last generation worthless, and is in its turn proved worthless by the next generation, is an everlasting vision of worthlessness."[11]

[10] *ILN*, February 11, 1922.
[11] "Are the Artists Going Mad?" *Century Magazine*, December 1922.

> *The tragedy of humanity has been the separation of art from the people.* Indeed, it is a queer fact that the same progressives who insist that government shall be democratic often insist that art must be [elitist], and "the public", which is a god when they are talking about votes, becomes a brute when they are talking about books and pictures.[12]

According to Chesterton there was a time in history when art was more connected to the people, when the abyss between the sense of beauty and the sentiment of humanity was nearly bridged. And that was in the Middle Ages. Medieval artists knew that the normal person took great pleasure in seeing a cloud of scarlet and gold, and so they made sure there was plenty of scarlet and gold in their illuminated manuscripts or their church windows. They also knew that the normal man also likes monsters, and grotesque and fantastic forms, and so they carved gargoyles on the great cathedrals. Both the artists and the public were united in a spirit of wonder, "from the most cunning craftsman who wondered at the thing being carved beautifully, to the most ignorant rustic who wondered at it being carved at all".[13] And Chesterton says this is the right philosophy because it really is a miracle that it should be carved at all. A monkey cannot do it; and when a man does it, he is doing something divine. He is creating. And that is a wonder.

> The real weakness of the best of the new [artists] is that their quaintness does not arise out of a universal world of wonder, but rather out of a world without wonder; it comes not from simplicity, but from satiety.
>
> The shepherds who watched the first sketches of Giotto were surprised that he could draw a face, and therefore still

[12] Ibid. (Emphasis mine.)
[13] Ibid.

more surprised that he could draw a beautiful face. But the modern Giotto is tired of beautiful faces, and feels that there might yet be a surprise of ugly faces.... [But] there is no permanent progress that way; we cannot really be rejuvenated by becoming more and more jaded.[14]

How do we revive a popular interest in art? We cannot assume that everyone can be an artistic genius or that all artists are geniuses or that the most lunatic among them are geniuses. The solution, says Chesterton,

> does not lie in increasing the number of artists who can startle us with complex things, but by increasing the number of people who can be startled by common things. It lies in restoring relish and receptivity to human society; and that is another question and a more important one....
>
> What the modern world wants is religion or something that will create a certain ultimate spirit of humility, of enthusiasm, and of thanks. It is not even to be done merely by educating the people in the artistic virtues of insight and selection. It is to be done much more by educating the artists in the popular virtues of astonishment and enjoyment....
>
> It not only means making more Giottos, but also making more shepherds.[15]

There is a famous saying that there is no disputing about taste. And it is true. But that refers to our relatively minor likes and dislikes that are simply personal preferences and cannot be changed by any argument. But in matters of art, the problem is that there are people who "prefer to dispute about taste, because they do not want their disputes

14 Ibid.
15 Ibid.

settled".[16] They are avoiding the things that *can* be argued about and the things that really are worth arguing about because they do not want to face the consequences of losing those arguments. What they are avoiding is the absolute. And their art reflects it.

Chesterton does not find modern artists particularly revolutionary. Revolting, yes, but revolutionary, no. The only thing "original" about their art is that it pertains to original sin. "The decay of society", he says, is "praised by artists as the decay of a corpse is praised by worms." [17]

> Savages and modern artists are alike strangely driven to create something uglier than themselves. But the artists find it harder.[18]

Chesterton attacks the navel-gazing school of art, the self-obsessed artists who are concerned only with expressing themselves and not with actually communicating something worthwhile. He predicts quite accurately that in the future, "artists who refuse to be anything but artists will go down in history as the embodiment of all the vulgarities and banalities of their time." [19]

The true artist, the artist who transcends time, is driven by an ache to find some sense and some story in the beautiful things he sees; he looks at everything with a careful eye and has a hunger for its secrets; he will not let any tower or tree escape him with its tale untold. Every true artist feels that he is touching truths that transcend the here and now; that his images are shadows of things seen through the veil. He knows that there is something there,

---

[16] *ILN*, December 17, 1927.
[17] *George Bernard Shaw, CW* 11:401.
[18] *ILN*, November 25, 1905.
[19] *William Blake* (London: House of Stratus, 2000), 18–19.

"something behind the clouds or within the trees; and he believes that the pursuit of beauty is the way to find it; that imagination is a sort of incantation that can call it up." [20] But that is not enough. The drive to produce great art is really a manifestation of something else.

> A man cannot have the energy to produce good art without having the energy to wish to pass beyond it. A small artist is content with art; a great artist is content with nothing except everything. [21]

> You never work so well for art's sake as when you are working for something else. [22]

There is no such thing as art for art's sake. Chesterton says, "Philosophy is always present in a work of art." [23] And the artistic philosophy that he subscribes to is Romanticism, as opposed to Realism. Now, "isms" are irritating, and usually difficult to keep track of, so we should know that when Chesterton uses the term "Realism" it is not in reference to highly finished representational renderings, which he admires, but to an artistic philosophy that emphasizes the dark and dirty—and detachment from the eternal. Realism claims to be: Life, warts and all. But what Realism really is, is: Warts as Life. The realists claim to be holding up the mirror to nature, but then they start believing only the mirror, even after they have broken it. [24]

[20] *The Everlasting Man*, *CW* 2:237.

[21] *Heretics*, *CW* 1:198.

[22] *Daily News*, June 25, 1904.

[23] *ILN*, June 15, 1929.

[24] See *The Crimes of England*, *CW* 5:337–38.

Realism, when entirely emptied of romance, becomes utterly unreal.[25]

Realism is simply Romanticism that has lost its reason. . . . It has lost its reason for existing. The old Greeks summoned godlike things to worship their god. The medieval Christians summoned all things to worship theirs, dwarfs and pelicans, monkeys and madmen. The modern realists summon all these million creatures to worship their god; and then have no god for them to worship. . . . Romance means a holy donkey going to the temple. Realism means a lost donkey going nowhere.[26]

Chesterton is a romantic. And so is most any normal person because it is common sense to be a romantic. It has to do with basic loyalties, with deep and universal emotions, and with high ideals that are worth striving for and worth fighting for.

All romances consist of three characters. . . . For the sake of argument they may be called St. George and the Dragon and the Princess. In every romance there must be the twin elements of loving and fighting. In every romance there must be the three characters: there must be the Princess, who is a thing to be loved; there must be the Dragon, who is a thing to be fought; and there must be St. George, who is a thing that both loves and fights. There have been many symptoms of cynicism and decay in our modern civilization. But . . . none [have been] quite so silly or so dangerous as this: that the philosophers of today have started to divide loving from fighting and to put them into opposite camps. [But] the two things imply each other; they implied each other in the old romance and in the old

[25] *ILN*, April 2, 1931.
[26] *Alarms and Discursions* (New York: Dodd, Mead, 1911), 13–14.

religion, which were the two permanent things of humanity. You cannot love a thing without wanting to fight for
it. You cannot fight without something to fight for. To
love a thing without wishing to fight for it is not love at
all; it is lust. It may be an airy, philosophical, and disin-
terested lust ... but it is lust, because it is wholly self-
indulgent.... On the other hand, fighting for a thing
without loving it is not even fighting; it can only be called
a kind of horse-play that is occasionally fatal. Wherever
human nature is human ... there exists this natural kinship between war and wooing, and that natural kinship is
called romance ... and every man who has ever been young
at all has felt, if only for a moment, this ultimate and
poetic paradox. He knows that loving the world is the
same thing as fighting the world.[27]

Inside the word "romantic" is another word. And we have
forgotten that the word "romantic" comes from that word.
That word is "Rome". The City of Fountains has been
the greatest fountain of art the world has ever known.
There is a direct connection between religion and art. And
the modern world has forgotten that connection, just as it
has forgotten the connection between Rome and romantic. Chesterton says that all art is religious art.[28] "The
Arts exist ... to show forth the glory of God; and to
awaken and keep alive the sense of wonder in man."[29]
Certainly all Western art has been directly or indirectly
inspired by the Catholic faith, even when it is only a dim
reflection of it or a direct reaction against it, a frank denial
of it, or a blatant blasphemy of it.

[27] *Appreciations and Criticisms of the Works of Charles Dickens*, CW 15:255.
[28] See *ILN*, June 15, 1929.
[29] *The Thing*, CW 3:173.

All art is born when the temporary touches the eternal.[30]

Now all of our focus to this point has been on the visual arts, but the same ideas can be applied to the literary arts and the performance arts. And it is particularly true of our most vivid art form, the one that essentially combines all the arts: the motion picture. It is the saddest state of artistic affairs that movies today are such a wasted medium, that so much energy and money is poured into producing them, and they are generally empty. Unfortunately, because they are controlled by commercial interests, they are largely commercials. They may be of the highest production qualities, with stunning photography and dazzling special effects and beautiful music, but the problem, as Chesterton says, "is that they are much too good for the meaningless work they serve".[31]

Art has to serve a higher purpose than itself, and certainly a higher purpose than merely making money. It has to serve an eternal purpose. And it has to reflect eternal values, not the world's fugitive values.

Art, like morality, consists of drawing the line somewhere.[32]

It is time we start making some good religious movies.[33] But until then, it is important that we put each movie— like any work of art—to the test: Does it give honor and glory to God? Does it teach us anything eternal? Does it move us to want to change our lives? Does it make us thankful? Does it help us love God better? Does it help us love

[30] *ILN*, July 15, 1922.

[31] *ILN*, July 3, 1909.

[32] *ILN*, May 5, 1928.

[33] I wrote this more than two years before the release of *The Passion of the Christ*. Obviously Mel Gibson took my advice.

our neighbor more? Does it make us want to help our neighbor? If it doesn't do any of these things, it has wasted our time. And that's what hell is: wasted time.

Describing hell and misery and depression is something that too many artists have spent too much time doing, and we've been given quite enough of it, thank you. As Chesterton says, "There are twenty minor poets who can describe fairly impressively an eternity of agony; there are very few even of the eternal poets who can describe ten minutes of satisfaction."[34] Heaven's work is a little harder than hell's work. We have to decide who we are going to work for, whose purpose our art is going to serve. Chesterton does not leave us much wiggle room. He says that when art is not in the service of heaven, it is almost always in the service of hell.[35]

---

[34] *Appreciations*, *CW* 15:311.
[35] See *ILN*, March 11, 1911.

5

The Daily Truth

Have you ever felt like canceling the subscription to your newspaper? I'm speaking, of course, to those of you who haven't already cancelled it. Chances are, you feel like canceling it almost every time you read it. Why is that?

Well, probably because the newspaper has a way of putting you in a bad mood. It puts you in a bad mood for a lot of reasons. Besides the fact that all the news is bad news, the opinions expressed are even worse. When they are not openly offensive, they still manage to defy common sense. And there is no joy, no humor in the paper. We turn to the comic pages for some relief, for a laugh. But even there we are almost always disappointed. There we are greeted by strange drawings of unhappy misfits. And the sports pages—especially if you live in Minnesota as I do—are *really* disappointing. There you will find pages of statistics that are made to look important, but don't matter at all. The business pages are also filled with numbers that strangely lack substance. The only place you can find something that really matters is in the obituaries. But, again, this does not usually contribute to a good mood.

Add to this the fact that you are paying for several pounds of advertisements for things you do not want, things that you did not even know you did not want until they were pointed out to you.

Now the obvious solution to the problem is to cancel your subscription. And while that solves the immediate problem, what do you do about the larger problem of journalism in general, of the modern world in general? And what are you going to read in the morning?

The answer to all those questions is the same. It is the same solution to almost every modern problem: read G. K. Chesterton.

Gilbert Keith Chesterton was a poet, a novelist, a literary critic, a historian, a philosopher, a theologian. But he didn't consider himself any of those things. He considered himself a journalist.

> I could not be a novelist; because I really like to see ideas or notions wrestling naked, as it were, and not dressed up in a masquerade as men and women. But I could be a journalist because I could not help being a controversialist.[1]

A controversialist. A controversy is a fight. A fight about what is right. For Chesterton, there is nothing that is not a fight. But there is a great joy in fighting. It means what is good is being defended and what is bad is being attacked. That is just the way it should be. Chesterton was a fighter, a soldier, and his battleground was the daily newspaper. As a journalist, he was able to take on the whole world. He knew what was wrong with the world—and he also knew what was wrong with the newspapers.

> Modern man is staggering and losing his balance because he is being pelted with little pieces of alleged fact ... which

[1] *Autobiography, CW* 16:277.

are native to the newspapers; and, if they turn out not to
be facts, that is still more native to the newspapers.[2]

Chesterton says that journalism consists of saying "Lord
Jones is Dead" to people who never knew that Lord Jones
was alive.[3] The news is either irrelevant or irreverent. The
great weakness of the news industry is that it "must be a
picture made up entirely of exceptions". The newspapers,
says Chesterton, cannot announce the happiness of mankind at all. They cannot describe all the forks that are not
stolen, or all the marriages that are not dissolved, all the
murders that are not committed. And so they do not give
a normal picture of life at all. "They can only represent
what is unusual." [4]

I can say abnormal things in modern magazines. It is the
normal things that I am not allowed to say.[5]

There is a notion that the press is flashy or trivial because it
is popular, that it is simply giving the public what it wants.
But this, according to Chesterton, is "cold rubbish".[6] The
so-called popular press does not really represent what is popular. There is no popular press, as such. Sometimes the press
is interested in the same things the public is, but it is an
insult to the common man to say that he is as vulgar and
silly as most of the newspapers are. The reason that the
newspapers are vulgar or silly is because the millionaires
who own them are vulgar and silly. Advertisements do not

[2] *ILN*, April 7, 1923.

[3] "The Purple Wig", in *The Penguin Complete Father Brown* (New York:
Penguin Books, 1981), 246.

[4] *The Ball and the Cross*, *CW* 7:73–74.

[5] *A Miscellany of Men* (Norfolk, Va.: IHS Press, 2004), 65.

[6] *Utopia of Usurers*, *CW* 5:500.

come from the great majority; they come from the elite few, from the governing class, the educated class. They are not giving the public what it wants. They are giving the public what it doesn't want, and they are doing it by forcing it upon us.

All newspapers are printed on the back of an advertisement, as it were. Supposedly this is the only way that mass media can be promulgated. The problem is compounded by the fact that not only does crass commercialism pay for the news, but the news itself is crass commercialism. And this commodity called the news is controlled by a very few.

> Knowledge is now a monopoly, and comes through to the citizens in thin and selected streams, exactly as bread might come through to a besieged city. Men must . . . know what is happening, whoever has the privilege of telling them. They must listen to the messenger, even if he is a liar. They must listen to the liar, even if he is a bore.[7]

Chesterton's objection to the press is not that it is exaggerative or overemotional or illiterate, or any of that. His only objection to it is that it tells lies. And this is a real problem. What can we do about it?

> We do not need a censorship of the press. We have a censorship by the press.[8]

> It is not we who silence the press. It is the press that silences us. It is not a case of the Commonwealth settling how much the editors shall say; it is a case of the editors settling how much the Commonwealth shall know. If we attack the Press we shall be rebelling, not repressing.[9]

[7] Ibid., 502.
[8] Orthodoxy, CW 1:321.
[9] ILN, October 19, 1907.

If you attempt an actual argument with a paper of the opposite politics, says Chesterton, "you will have no answer except slanging or silence." [10] Slanging or silence. They will either ignore you or hang one of their poisonous labels on you, a catchword that sums you up and says to the world that you are not worth arguing with.

Chesterton's reference to "a paper of the opposite politics" points out the great fallacy that the press is somehow neutral. This lie is something the media not only tells, but actually believes about itself. The modern myth of the media's "neutrality" has in turn fed the idea that neutrality itself is a great desirable quality, that not taking a stand is somehow admirable, that "tolerance" is the supreme virtue, as opposed to the real virtues, which are the basis of morality. "The whole modern world," says Chesterton, and "the whole modern Press, has a perpetual and consuming terror of plain morals." [11] The press is always attempting to avoid condemning a thing purely and simply on moral grounds.

And we are not only led astray by avoiding morality; Chesterton says we "are twisted out of the path of truth by the very terms" we have to use. "Modern language—scientific, political, and journalistic—is not given to man to conceal his thoughts. It is given to him to conceal his thoughtlessness." [12] We live in an age of journalese. The very language that we are forced to use attacks our traditions, our morals, and our faith. Things that are degenerate and sinful are called "progressive" and "liberating". Good words that were once pure and noble, like "choice" and "gay", now have reprehensible meanings. Everything done inside a house is called

---

[10] *What's Wrong with the World*, CW 4:50.
[11] *ILN*, November 24, 1906.
[12] *ILN*, March 8, 1919.

"drudgery", while anything done inside an office is called "enterprise". Modern doubt, which has engulfed us in the fog of agnosticism, is called bold and broad. Traditional religion, which has given light to millions across the world and across the centuries, is called dull and narrow.

When language is abused, meaning is frustrated and a person cannot even articulate his own thoughts, much less communicate them. It is a grave irresponsibility on the part of the modern press to abuse the language, because it spreads the abuse so widely. But the power of the modern press is matched only by its irresponsibility.

> There never was a power so great as the power of the Press. There never was a belief so superstitious as the universal belief in the Press. It may be that future centuries will call these the Dark Ages, and see a vast mystical delusion spreading its black bats' wings over all our cities.[13]

But while Chesterton was a great critic of the press, he was also a great defender of the press. He was, after all, a journalist. He knew there was great potential for the press to do good in this world. And sometimes it even manages to do it.

Journalism means, literally, daily writing or writing for the daily, writing for the day. Chesterton wrote for some dailies, and he wrote for some weeklies, and he wrote for some monthlies, and for a whole host of other periodicals. He produced an ocean of words. He was always writing, which means he was always thinking, always engaged in a controversy, in a fight. Writing daily is obviously a discipline. Like prayer. Chesterton actually enjoyed writing under a deadline. He said writing quickly means you have to write

[13] *Daily News*, May 28, 1904.

more honestly.[14] And Chesterton's honesty is perhaps the most refreshing thing about him. It is even refreshing and somewhat reassuring to hear from him about what really goes on behind the making of a newspaper:

Nothing looks more neat and regular than a newspaper, with its parallel columns, its mechanical printing, its detailed facts and figures, its responsible, polysyllabic leading articles. Nothing, as a matter of fact, goes every night through more agonies of adventure, more hairbreadth escapes, desperate expedients, crucial councils, random compromises, or barely averted catastrophes. Seen from the outside, it seems to come round as automatically as the clock and as silently as the dawn. Seen from the inside, it gives all its organisers a gasp of relief every morning to see that it has come out at all; that it has come out without the leading article upside down or the Pope congratulated on discovering the North Pole. . . .

I will tell you . . . a story of what journals and journalists really are. A monstrously lazy man[15] . . . writ[es] a column in the Saturday *Daily News*. At the time he usually writes it (which is always at the last moment) his house is unexpectedly invaded by infants of all shapes and sizes. His secretary is called away; and he has to cope with the invading pigmies. Playing with children is a glorious thing; but the journalist in question has never understood why it was considered a soothing or idyllic one. It reminds him, not of watering little budding flowers, but of wrestling for hours with gigantic angels and devils. Moral problems of the most monstrous complexity besiege him incessantly. He has to decide before the awful eyes of innocence, whether, when a sister has knocked down a brother's bricks, in revenge for the brother having taken two sweets out of

[14] See *ILN*, July 20, 1912.
[15] He is referring to himself, of course, as will become evident.

his turn, it is endurable that the brother should retaliate by scribbling on the sister's picture-book, and whether such conduct does not justify the sister in blowing out the brother's unlawfully lighted match.

Just as he is solving this problem upon principles of the highest morality, it occurs to him suddenly that he has not written his Saturday article; and that there is only about an hour to do it in. He wildly calls to somebody (probably the gardener) to telephone to somewhere for a messenger, he barricades himself in another room and tears his hair, wondering what on earth he shall write about. A drumming of fists on the door outside and a cheerful bellowing encourage and clarify his thoughts; and he is able to observe some newspapers and circulars in wrappers lying on the table. One is a dingy book catalogue; the second is a shiny pamphlet about petrol; the third is a paper called *The Christian Commonwealth*. He opens it anyhow, and sees in the middle of a page a sentence with which he honestly disagrees. "Oh, but this won't do. . . ." A stream of images and pictures pour through his head.

He sits down desperately; the messenger rings at the bell; the children drum on the door; the servants run up from time to time to say the messenger is getting bored; and the pencil staggers along, making the world a present of fifteen hundred unimportant words. Then the journalist sends off his copy and turns his attention to the enigma of whether a brother should commandeer a sister's necklace because the sister pinched him. . . . That is how an article is really written.[16]

We might be able to take the newspapers more seriously if they would not take themselves so seriously. If they want to come across as being more honest, they should not be so solemn. Chesterton says, "Honesty is never solemn; it is

[16] *A Miscellany of Men*, 75–76.

only hypocrisy that can be that. Honesty always laughs, because things are so laughable." [17] You find honest opinions in private conversation, but, for some reason, you never find them in print. Chesterton says that when it comes to the matters of truth, "the fact that you don't want to publish something is, nine times out of ten, a proof that you ought to publish it." [18]

Chesterton always wrote under a deadline, and never with the opportunity for a rewrite. When we read his journalism, we are seeing his thoughts as he is thinking them. And the amazing thing is how complete and profound are those ideas as they flow from his pen. Yet he must have been an editor's nightmare. His articles were almost always late and were always controversial. But everything for the newspaper editor is a nightmare. Chesterton says the most familiar emotion to the editor is one of "continuous fear: fear of libel actions, fear of lost advertisements, fear of misprints, fear of the sack". [19]

There is the charge that the press is sensational. But Chesterton says the press is actually quite tame. The press is always trying to play it safe. We only read platitudes in the headlines. They are even more boring when printed in large letters. If the press were really sensational, we would not be so disappointed by our daily newspaper. True sensationalism, says Chesterton, awakens the soul. It takes courage to really surprise someone—especially when you surprise them with the truth. It is like the shock of cold water.

It is precisely that sensationalism that the world really wants and has always wanted. And there was a time in history when there really was some sensational news, news that took the whole world at a rush. It was the news that God had become a man. It was the news that the world had tortured that Divine Man and killed him and buried him and that he rose from the dead. The world has never been the same since the news that death could be conquered, that sin could be conquered, that everything dark and despairing could be conquered by the sensational paradox of Christianity. No wonder it called its message the "Good News", the Gospel. There is an organization that is still trying to get that news out, and trying to spread it across the world. That organization is called the Catholic Church.

But you won't get that news or anything like it in your newspaper.

Why is G. K. Chesterton so important? He was certainly influential on many great writers and thinkers, influential on literature itself, influential on Catholic converts, influential in the very fact that he is actively ignored today in our colleges and universities, that he has to be gotten around in order to teach the dismal ideas that drained all the life out of the twentieth century. He was one of the only widely published journalists who was able to write for the secular press, who always defended Christianity in general and the Catholic Church in particular. That meant taking on the whole world.

But his measurable impact on people and events and history, which is all well and good, is not why he is so important. The reason he is so important is because of what he has to teach us *right now*. He had a prophetic vision, which makes his words still fresh. He saw what we see, but he saw it before it happened. He saw our culture in decline, denying its historical and religious heritage, denying its responsibilities; a culture that is self-absorbed, that is top-heavy with wealth, that is utterly commercialized; a culture of death. He wrote about all these things. But he was not off writing in a hermitage, or in an attic. He was writing all these things in the daily newspapers of his time, and his voice was indeed heard around the world. But, as with so many prophets, it was a voice that was ignored. But, as with so many prophets, it is a voice that still speaks. It is a paradox that timeless truths are always timely, in fact, always urgent.

As we said, Chesterton took on the whole world in the daily newspapers of his time. He still does. There are not many journalists who last longer than their own day. They usually fade like an old newspaper. But pick up a volume of the *Illustrated London News* essays by G.K. Chesterton that were written eighty or ninety years ago; turn to any one of them, and you will find that it is as vibrant and witty and relevant as if it were written today. That is the great advantage of writing the truth. It does not go out of date.

So, help lead the revolt. Cancel your daily newspaper. Unless the press reforms, the only reason to read the newspaper is to find out what the enemy is up to. But why start the day in a bad mood? Read G.K. Chesterton instead, and be refreshed, and be ready to take on the whole world.

6

Words about Words

Suppose you were to embark on a journey, an adventure to an exotic land unlike any place you have ever been. You might go alone, and that would be fine. But you would probably rather have a guide with you, someone who has an intimate knowledge of the place, someone who can not only help you find your way, but give you the best possible experience while you are there, showing you where the surprises are, pointing out things that you might not otherwise see, explaining their significance. You also want a guide who will protect you and tell you what to avoid and why to avoid it. And you would want your guide to be "colorful". A good guide can be as interesting as the adventure itself.

When you open a good book, you set off on a kind of journey. A great work of literature is an interior adventure. It is full of amazing twists and turns. There is always something around the corner. And there are plenty of wonderful things that you miss because you are looking for something else. Or because you are just plain lost. To find your way into that world of words, or even to find your way back out of it, it is helpful to have a good guide. That is what a literary critic is.

We tend to think of critics as negative. And most of them are. Part of the problem is that there is so much bad literature that the critic has no choice but to point out how bad it is. But another reason why criticism is so negative is that, in addition to so much bad literature, there are so many bad critics, some of whom have lost the ability to recognize good literature. As guides, they are lost. They have no reference points.

G. K. Chesterton began as a journalist, and his beginning as a journalist was as a book reviewer. He was inspired by the fact that so few ever read the literary pages in a newspaper. He used his reviews of books by other writers as an excuse to write about his own ideas. Soon people started reading the literary pages just to read his reviews, because they were so enamored with his writing and fascinated by his ideas. It led to his own regular column in many newspapers and magazines. He wrote about everything, of course, but he would still write occasional book reviews. However, instead of reviewing new books, he took the opportunity to review old books: the classics. He led his readers on thrilling expeditions into the world's great literature.

While the adventurer who journeys into the jungle tries to capture extraordinary creatures, the literary critic ventures into great literature trying to capture extraordinary ideas and bring them home to us. Chesterton spent his whole life trying to capture ideas with words, trying to coax huge and unwieldy ideas into the manageable and comfortable confines of words—words that we would understand. He was always trying to connect with his reading audience. Art, he said, is only successful when "the work has passed from mind to mind".[1] Chesterton used words

[1] *ILN*, November 27, 1926.

to do all the things that words can do. He excelled in all literary forms: prose and poetry, praise and polemics. As a creative writer, he was a unique genius in his own right. But some of his most exhilarating and astonishing writing is what he wrote about other writers. Words about words, is how he defined literary criticism.[2] He proved to be an exciting guide, as good as any book he wrote about.

Chesterton did not consider himself a scholar. And he did not want anyone else to consider him a scholar, either. Just as he thought that philosophy and theology were too important to be left to philosophers and theologians, so he thought that literature was for everyone, not just for literary critics. We should not need a diploma to study a book or a poem as a chemist might need one to study the imminent explosion in his laboratory. Literature is about life, which entitles everyone to comment on it—not just the higher critics.

> The higher critics are wholly deficient in the highest form of criticism, which is self-criticism.[3]

Chesterton is the critics' critic. The first thing he goes after is their incessant criticism, that is, their negativity.

> Praise, which was recognised in the Bible as the universal thing, is almost always right; it is always better criticism to admire a snake for having all the colours of the rainbow than to despise it for not having two legs. Critics would almost always be right if they would only refrain from being critical.[4]

[2] See *The Everlasting Man, CW* 2:341.
[3] *Nash's Pall Mall Magazine*, April 1935.
[4] *Daily News*, June 26, 1901.

Modern critics do not only attack literature; they attack the audience who likes the literature that the critics have deemed as bad. Chesterton defends the audience against the critics.

> The public does not like bad literature. The public likes a certain kind of literature and likes that kind of literature even when it is bad better than another kind of literature even when it is good. Nor is this unreasonable; for the line between different types of literature is as real as the line between tears and laughter; and to tell people who can only get bad comedy that you have some first-class tragedy is as irrational as comforting a man who is shivering over weak, warm coffee by offering him a really superior sort of ice. Ordinary people dislike the delicate modern work, not because it is good or because it is bad, but because it is not the thing that they asked for.[5]

As a literary critic, Chesterton is our advocate. He represents the reader. In fact, when Chesterton was asked to testify at a parliamentary hearing on censorship in 1909, he agreed to testify, but he said he was not appearing as an author, but rather as a member of the audience. Chesterton represents the common man and common sense. He represents the truth we all know to be true, even when literature lies to us; but more importantly, as a great literary critic, he represents the truth when it is told so beautifully that we do not see it. Chesterton says, "Anything beautiful always means more than it says."[6] And, "Pleasure in the beautiful is a sacred thing."[7]

It is interesting that many people's door to the world of Chesterton is through his literary criticism. Non-Christians

[5] *Charles Dickens, CW* 15:98.

[6] *Robert Louis Stevenson, CW* 18:118.

[7] *A Handful of Authors* (New York: Sheed and Ward, 1953), 84.

who have absolutely no interest in picking up a book like *Orthodoxy* or *The Everlasting Man* will discover Chesterton through his books on Charles Dickens, Robert Browning, Robert Louis Stevenson, and Chaucer, as well as his various essays on Shakespeare, Samuel Johnson, Jane Austen, and a host of other authors. They get hooked on Chesterton because he not only provides stunning new insights, but he has an incomparable way of bringing everything together.

But first he has to turn everything around. He says there is nothing stranger today than "the importance of unimportant things. Except, of course, the unimportance of important things." [8] We have everything backwards. We think marriage and the family is something boring and prosaic, even though the home is where most of life's exciting and dramatic things happen. We turn our attention to bizarre and jarring events that happen to those who live on the fringe of life, even though these things are disappointing and sometimes diabolical.

It is easy to be artistic about what is unimportant, and think of all the great artistic effort that is wasted on things like television commercials. But it is difficult for art to capture what is really important, and that is why there are so few really great works of art. For instance, marriage and the family, says Chesterton, "are essential and sacred things," but it is "exactly for those reasons that [they] cannot be adequately expressed in art at all; for all art is a thing of glimpses, and marriage is a thing of continuity. Dramas, however realistic, deal with events. But monogamy is not merely a good event; it is a good habit." [9] It continues day after day, and it cannot be portrayed; it can only be lived.

[8] *ILN*, January 3, 1914.
[9] *A Handful of Authors*, 141.

Modern artists are obsessed with trying to be "original". But the claim to originality, says Chesterton, "is really a claim to absolute unsociability: a claim to absolute loneliness".[10]

> There is no clearer sign of the absence of originality among modern poets than their disposition to find new themes. Really original poets write poems about the spring. They are always fresh, just as the spring is always fresh. Men wholly without originality write poems about torture, or new religions, or some perversion of obscenity, hoping that the mere sting of the subject may speak for them.[11]

In 1998, some self-accredited literary clique put out a list that ranked the twentieth century's top one hundred novels in the English language. Lists of this kind are of course useful for starting arguments, and arguments of course are wonderful pastimes; but it is especially interesting to see what those who consider themselves in-the-know considered to be the best novels of our previous hundred years. (It is not worth mentioning that Chesterton did not make the list, so I won't mention it.) A quick look at the list reveals that what passes for great literature in the last century not only isn't read; it really can't be read. This fact is epitomized by the novel that landed on the top of the heap: *Ulysses* by James Joyce. How many people have actually read *Ulysses*?

According to Chesterton, the strangest thing about Joyce's *Ulysses* is the title. The title, and the book itself, is based on Homer's epic poem of the same name, but, as Chesterton points out, if you compare the two, Homer "manages to be very pure in very plain language, while Joyce manages to

---

[10] *Appreciations and Criticisms of the Works of Charles Dickens, CW* 15:262.
[11] Ibid., 244.

be very coarse in very esoteric language".[12] Classic literature, the kind that survives for centuries, is popular because it is the voice of the common man speaking to the ears of the common man. But, as Chesterton says, we do not feel that James Joyce ever speaks for anybody except James Joyce. And that is the problem with most modern literature. The audience has not merely been ignored, but scorned.

The whole modern revolution in literature, says Chesterton, began way back when men demanded that the Scriptures be translated into English. Ironically, it has ended when nobody dares to demand that English writers be translated into English.[13]

> In expressing confused ideas, the moderns have great subtlety and sympathy. It is in expressing clear ideas that they generally find their limitations.[14]

Every great work of literature is universal: "*The Iliad* is great because all life is a battle, *The Odyssey* because all life is a journey, *The Book of Job* because all life is a riddle."[15]

Shakespeare is universal because he deals in the universals of life and love, of sin and suffering and redemption. *Hamlet* is not a pessimistic piece about a dark skeptic. It is a transcendent story about a noble soul who survives his moods and struggles to maintain his faith in something beyond himself. *Macbeth* is a tragedy that teaches us that a good man can be as bad as he chooses to be. *Midsummer Night's Dream* is a comedy that teaches us that an absurd character like Bottom the Weaver, who has no brains, is still so richly human and bursting with life that he can eat

---

[12] *Sidelights on New London and Newer York*, *CW* 21:608.
[13] See *ILN*, June 6, 1931.
[14] *ILN*, September 12, 1931.
[15] *The Defendant* (London: J. M. Dent, 1907), 47.

great men for breakfast. Chesterton exalts comic characters because they teach us how to suffer fools gladly, and his emphasis is always on the gladly rather than on the suffering.

Another great fool whom Chesterton gets us to suffer gladly is Charles Dickens' character Pickwick of *The Pickwick Papers*. Chesterton points out that it is always the fool, the greenhorn, the innocent, who has the great adventures, who gets the most out of life. The one who is gullible, who is "taken in", as it were, is the one who gets to see the inside of everything, while the skeptic is kept out. Pickwick's servant is the streetwise Sam Weller. Sam Weller represents knowledge; Pickwick represents innocence. "Knowledge and innocence are both excellent things," says Chesterton, "and they are both very funny. But it is right that knowledge should be the servant and innocence the master." [16]

In the great books, as in everything else, Chesterton gets us to see something that we did not see before, no matter how well we think we know a thing.

He shows how Daniel Defoe's novel *Robinson Crusoe* is not merely about a man stranded on an island; it is about the whole human race. [17] We have all been saved from a shipwreck, and everything we have is a gift. Life is always precious.

He shows how the moral of Robert Louis Stevenson's *Dr. Jekyll and Mr. Hyde* is always misunderstood. It is not that man can be split into two creatures—one evil, one good—but that he cannot. Evil does not care about good, but good still cares about evil. "Man cannot escape from God." [18] Man's good conscience, planted in him by God, will rip him apart if he tries to give free reign to evil.

---

[16] *Appreciations*, 251.
[17] See *Orthodoxy, CW* 1:267–68.
[18] *The Victorian Age in Literature, CW* 15:528.

Chesterton is a good and sure guide because he knows where the reference points are. And they are eternal reference points. What makes a great work of literature interesting is that it is always about the state of a person's soul. It is about life at the crossroads. What choice will the character make? We cheer him on, hoping he will make the right decision. We want him to defeat the evil enemy. We want him to win the love of the woman he desires. Modern literature has become boring and unreadable because it has left out the eternal drama of the soul. It has forgotten about life, especially eternal life. The modern world is shortsighted and fragmented and self-indulgent. So is its literature. It glorifies death and destruction and the dark underside of things.

Chesterton says, the streets are not life. The cities are not life. Even faces are not life. Life is that mysterious thing on the inside. Even our meals and our manners and our clothes are only symbols of life. "Literature has to do with the soul, the unknown quantity in man." [19] Nothing is important except the fate of the soul. The only thing that redeems literature from "utter triviality" is the fact that it describes not the world around us or the things we merely see, "but some condition to which the human soul can come".[20]

We are trying to get to heaven. That's what life is about, and that's what any good story is about. Every story begins with Creation and ends with the Last Judgment. Every author is trying to achieve the Incarnation, trying to make the Word into flesh. Every author puts his characters to the test. There is always an adversary that has to be overcome. Evil will

[19] *Daily News*, March 1, 1901.
[20] Ibid.

always seem to have the upper hand and will appear to triumph. Ultimately, however, good will prevail, but not without sacrifice. The object of Incarnation is Crucifixion. The object of Crucifixion is Resurrection. But you cannot get to Easter morning unless you go through the Agony in the Garden and the Death on the Cross. Every author who has mastered the craft of storytelling will give us a taste, a hint of these eternal truths. All art touches the eternal.

There are two things we all share, and great literature will always bring out those two things: tears and laughter. Both are things that overcome us. "Tragedy", says Chesterton, "is the point when things are left to God and men can do no more." [21] But, he says, "The comedy of man survives the tragedy of man." [22] Laughter means "self-abandonment and humility". [23] It is "the power of uproarious reaction against ourselves and our own incongruities". [24] It is "the one indestructible brotherhood, the one undeniably social thing". [25]

> Everything human must have in it both joy and sorrow; the only matter of interest is the manner in which the two things are balanced or divided. . . . The mass of men have been forced to be [happy] about the little things, but sad about the big ones. . . . [But] man is more himself, man is more manlike, when joy is the fundamental thing in him, and grief the superficial. Melancholy should be an innocent interlude, a tender and fugitive frame of mind; praise should be the permanent pulsation of the soul. Pessimism is at best an emotional half-holiday; joy is the uproarious labour

[21] *A Handful of Authors*, 66.
[22] *ILN*, February 10, 1906.
[23] *Heretics*, *CW* 1:170.
[24] *ILN*, September 9, 1922.
[25] *A Handful of Authors*, 28–29.

by which all things live.... In Christianity ... joy is something gigantic and sadness something special and small. The vault above us is not deaf because the universe is an idiot; the silence is not the heartless silence of an endless and aimless world. Rather the silence around us is a small and pitiful stillness like the prompt stillness in a sick-room. We are perhaps permitted tragedy as a sort of merciful comedy: because the frantic energy of divine things would knock us down like a drunken farce. We can take our own tears more lightly than we could take the tremendous levities of the angels. So we sit perhaps in a starry chamber of silence, while the laughter of the heavens is too loud for us to hear.[26]

Chesterton says that the best thing we can get out of an interest in literature is a finer interest in life.[27] A good book is not a means of escape from the world, but rather it gives us fresh eyes with which to see how amazing the world is. The writer is successful if he gets us to think this is a "strange world", when we have no other world with which to compare it! This is, as Chesterton says, "the best of all impossible worlds".[28] Likewise, a good book is not an escape from life, but a means of bringing life closer and making what is already precious even sweeter and dearer. In a way, a great author—and Chesterton is one—does the same thing that Jesus does: he comes that we may have life, and have it more abundantly.[29]

---

[26] *Orthodoxy, CW* 1:365.
[27] See *ILN,* October 9, 1920.
[28] *Charles Dickens, CW* 15:203.
[29] See John 10:10.

7

Talking in Rhyme

Most modern poetry can be described as variations on a
suicide note. It is one long cry of despair, dark and depressing and demoralizing. The poets are angry at lovers, angry
at the world, angry at existence. They are angry at God for
making this mess, or, if they don't believe in him, they are
angry at God for not existing. Their poems are odes to
destruction, decay, and death. In fact, the rarest of all poetry
written in the last century would be a poem about *not* committing suicide.

But there was one poet who *did* write such a poem:

> The gallows in my garden, people say,
> Is new and neat and adequately tall.
> I tie the noose on in a knowing way
> As one that knots his necktie for a ball;
> But just as all the neighbours—on the wall—
> Are drawing a long breath to shout "Hurray!"
> The strangest whim has seized me.... After all
> I think I will not hang myself today.[1]

---

[1] "A Ballad of Suicide", in *The Collected Poems of G. K. Chesterton* (New
York: Dodd, Mead, 1949), 180.

Only G. K. Chesterton could write a line like, "I think I will not hang myself today."

The people who read Chesterton are usually drawn to him by his timely and quotable essays, his social and literary criticism, his eloquent defense of the Christian faith, or, if none of that does the trick, his detective fiction. But Chesterton also published several volumes of poetry during his life. In fact, his first two books, both published in 1900, were books of poetry. And when he died in 1936, many of his obituaries predicted that G. K. Chesterton would be best remembered as a poet.

So far that prediction has been wrong. Part of the problem is that hardly anyone is remembered as a poet these days. Not much poetry gets read. And not much gets written either. What the poets have passed off on us for the last hundred years does not much resemble poetry. They freed themselves from form, and in the process freed themselves from the ability to say anything worth remembering, or at least worth memorizing. Modern poetry just doesn't dance. Modern poets, with all their freedom, have pretty much locked themselves out of writing poems that rhyme.

Chesterton says that rhyming is one of our first pleasures, learned in the nursery, where all the important things are learned, and learned, "in every sense, by heart".[2] Rhyming is a skill everyone can learn, but one must take the trouble to learn it, like playing the piano or throwing a ball or riding a bike, and only a few ever learn it very well. But those who do learn it well give the rest of us a pleasure that is both great and subtle, which is why poetry is enjoyed by both children and even some critics. There is in rhyme the

[2] *Fancies Versus Fads* (London: Methuen, 1923), 2.

sense of returning to the same place, like a homecoming. It must be exact, because home is a specific place. Our ears want the rhyme just as we want completeness and balance and fulfillment.

> We should all like to speak poetry at the moment when we truly live, and if we do not speak it, it is because we have an impediment in our speech. It is not song that is the narrow or artificial thing, it is conversation that is a broken and stammering attempt at song. When we see men in a spiritual extravaganza ... speaking in rhyme, it is not our language disguised or distorted, but our language rounded and made whole. Rhymes answer each other as the sexes in flowers and in humanity answer each other.[3]

For Chesterton there is nothing artistically revolutionary about free verse, because there is nothing creative about leaving rhyme behind—and all the other poetic forms that have been left behind with it. The new artist "does not invent anything, but only abolishes something".[4] Chesterton argues that the rejection of rhyme came in a rebellion led by snobs and aristocrats who had no love of common things or of the common man. Rhyme—along with rhythm and meter—has been frozen out of modern poetry, and he says, "The freezing process began after the Reformation with a search for finer yet freer forms; today it has ended in formlessness."[5]

Ironically, it is now far more daring and original for a poet to defend conventional poetic forms than to defend "a cart-load of revolutions".[6]

---

[3] *Twelve Types* (Norfolk, Va.: IHS Press, 2003), 42.

[4] *Fancies Versus Fads*, 18.

[5] Ibid., 16.

[6] *Varied Types* (New York: Dodd, Mead, 1905), 255.

> We talk of art as something artificial in comparison with life. But I sometimes fancy that the very highest art is more real than life itself.... As passions become real they become poetical; the lover is always trying to be the poet. All real energy is an attempt at harmony and a high swing of rhythm; and if we were only real enough we should all talk in rhyme.[7]

One of Chesterton's fictional characters echoes this idea when he says that he always had a notion that a real poet would never talk prose.[8] Chesterton says that rhyme goes with reason, "since the aim of both is to bring things to an end".[9] But rhyming is hard work. One of the problems is that our language is fallen, just like the rest of the fallen world we live in. Chesterton says that we are struggling and entangled in this fallen language, "like men in the folds of a fallen tent".[10]

But there are good things that seem beyond all speech or figure of speech, and we have a perpetual desire to try to express them.[11] We are always trying to make the word into flesh. It is part of our nature. We are creators, because we are made in the image of the Creator. And no creature has a truer sense of the divine task of making the word into flesh than the poet.

And G. K. Chesterton rises to this divine task over and over again. Let's take a look at some of his poetry. And let's

---

[7] *Lunacy and Letters* (New York: Sheed and Ward, 1958), 144.

[8] See Gabriel Gale in *The Poet and the Lunatics* (New York: Sheed and Ward, 1955), 203.

[9] *The Victorian Age in Literature*, *CW* 15:431.

[10] *ILN*, December 24, 1910.

[11] See "The Mystagogue", in *A Miscellany of Men* (Norfolk, Va.: IHS Press, 2004).

begin with his most famous poem, a poem every child should memorize: "The Donkey".

> When fishes flew and forests walked
> And figs grew upon thorn
> Some moment when the moon was blood
> Then surely I was born.
>
> With monstrous head and sickening cry
> And ears like errant wings
> The devil's walking parody
> On all four-footed things.
>
> The tattered outlaw of the earth,
> Of ancient crooked will;
> Starve, scourge, deride me: I am dumb,
> I keep my secret still.
>
> Fools! For I also had my hour;
> One far fierce hour and sweet:
> There was a shout about my ears,
> And palms before my feet.[12]

"The Donkey" is a microcosm of Chesterton and his philosophy. It is an early poem but it contains all the elements that would fill his writing for the rest of his life: paradox, humor, humility, wonder, the defense of the poor and the simple, the rebuke of the rich and worldly wise. The other recurrent theme, seen in everything from his Father Brown stories to his public debates, is the presentation of a character we would at first dismiss, but who surprises us by being in direct contact with the very embodiment

---

[12] *Collected Poetry*, *CW* 10, Part 1:134.

of Truth. Be careful before you call someone an ass: he may be carrying Christ.

Chesterton says, "The language of poetry is simpler than that of prose ... and, being simpler, it is also truer, and being truer, it is also fiercer." [13]

But his fierceness can be funny. In his "Song of the Strange Ascetic" he muses on the irony of joyless millionaires who think like pagans, but live like puritans.

> If I had been a Heathen,
> I'd have praised the purple vine,
> My slaves should dig the vineyards,
> And I would drink the wine.
> But Higgins is a Heathen,
> And his slaves grow lean and grey,
> That he may drink some tepid milk
> Exactly twice a day.
>
> If I had been a Heathen,
> I'd have crowned Neaera's curls,
> And filled my life with love affairs,
> My house with dancing girls;
> But Higgins is a Heathen,
> And to lecture rooms is forced,
> Where his aunts, who are not married,
> Demand to be divorced.
>
> If I had been a Heathen,
> I'd have sent my armies forth,
> And dragged behind my chariots
> The Chieftains of the North.
> But Higgins is a Heathen,

[13] *Utopia of Usurers, CW* 5:506.

And he drives the dreary quill,
To lend the poor that funny cash
That makes them poorer still.

If I had been a Heathen,
I'd have piled my pyre on high,
And in a great red whirlwind
Gone roaring to the sky;
But Higgins is a Heathen,
And a richer man than I:
And they put him in an oven,
Just as if he were a pie.

Now who that runs can read it,
The riddle that I write,
Of why this poor old sinner,
Should sin without delight—
But I, I cannot read it
(Although I run and run),
Of them that do not have the faith,
And will not have the fun.[14]

The fierceness of his poetry comes in his *Lepanto*, a powerful poem about the battle where Christian forces ultimately turned back the Muslim advance into Europe in the sixteenth century. It was a time when Christendom was not only being attacked from the outside by Muslim warriors, but from the inside by Protestant rebels. All of Western civilization was threatened. Chesterton captured the idea in this poem, a poem that was shouted in the trenches in World War I.

[14] *Collected Poetry, CW* 10, Part 1:523.

Dim drums throbbing, in the hills half heard,
Where only on a nameless throne a crownless prince has
    stirred,
    Where, risen from a doubtful seat and half-attainted stall,
    The last knight of Europe takes weapons from the wall,
The last and lingering troubadour to whom the bird has
    sung,
That once went singing southward when all the world was
    young,
    In that enormous silence, tiny and unafraid,
    Comes up along a winding road the noise of the
    Crusade.
Strong gongs groaning as the guns boom far,
Don John of Austria is going to the war,
    Stiff flags straining in the night-blasts cold
    In the gloom black-purple, in the glint old-gold,
Torchlight crimson on the copper kettle-drums,
Then the tuckets, then the trumpets, then the cannon, and
    he comes.
Don John laughing in the brave beard curled,
Spurning of his stirrups like the thrones of all the world,
    Holding his head up for a flag of all the free.
Love-light of Spain—hurrah!
Death-light of Africa!
Don John of Austria
    Is riding to the sea.[15]

Sometimes the power of poetry is in the plainness of
its words. Chesterton says, "A plain word always covers an

infinite mystery." [16] But words can be misused by poets and drained of their power. "Words are deeds", [17] says Chesterton, and poets have a responsibility to speak the truth and speak it beautifully, to point to the truth and point artfully.

> Pride and a little scratching pen
> Have dried and split the hearts of men. [18]

Those lines are from the opening Dedication of one of Chesterton's greatest poems, and what is perhaps the last great epic poem in the English language, a marvelous achievement that not only deserves to be appreciated, but studied in depth and discussed at length: *The Ballad of the White Horse*. Like *Lepanto*, this is another poem about a battle. It is the story of the English King Alfred, who fought the Danes in the year 878. But it is also the story of Christianity battling against the destructive forces of nihilism and heathenism. It is the battle we are still fighting.

At the beginning of the poem, the Blessed Virgin appears to King Alfred, and he asks her if he is going to win the upcoming battle. Her reply is not what he expects:

> The gates of heaven are lightly locked,
>   We do not guard our gold,
> Men may uproot where worlds begin,
> Or read the name of the nameless sin;
> But if he fail or if he win
>   To no good man is told.

---

[16] *Appreciations*, *CW* 15:374.

[17] *ILN*, February 2, 1907.

[18] *The Ballad of the White Horse*, with notes by Sister Bernadette Sheridan (San Francisco: Ignatius Press, 2001), Dedication, lines 80–81. (Hereafter, *BWH*, followed by book and line numbers.)

The men of the East may spell the stars,
   And times and triumphs mark,
But the men signed of the cross of Christ
   Go gaily in the dark.

The men of the East may search the scrolls
   For sure fates and fame,
But the men that drink the blood of God
   Go singing to their shame.

The wise men know what wicked things
   Are written on the sky,
They trim sad lamps, they touch sad strings,
Hearing the heavy purple wings,
Where the forgotten seraph kings
   Still plot how God shall die.

The wise men know all evil things
   Under the twisted trees,
Where the perverse in pleasure pine
And men are weary of green wine
   And sick of crimson seas.

But you and all the kind of Christ
   Are ignorant and brave,
And you have wars you hardly win
   And souls you hardly save.

I tell you naught for your comfort,
   Yea, naught for your desire,
Save that the sky grows darker yet
   And the sea rises higher.

Night shall be thrice night over you,
   And heaven an iron cope.

> Do you have joy without a cause,
> Yea, faith without a hope?[19]

We are not guaranteed victory—even if we fight for what is right. The Church teaches that the two sins against hope are presumption and despair. We must not be either triumphalist or defeatist. We must not be either smug or suicidal. We do not know the outcome of the battle. And yet it is still up to us to choose the right side, even if it might not be the winning side. It is enough to know what we are fighting for. That is the meaning of faith and hope. That is the meaning of going "gaily in the dark". Alfred gets no encouraging words from Mary. And yet, strangely enough, he is encouraged. He gets naught for his comfort and naught for his desire, yet he is comforted, and emboldened in his desire to fight the foe. It is like the story of Job, who refuses to be satisfied until God answers his questions. But when God does appear to Job, he gives him none of the answers he had sought. Yet Job is satisfied. His trust in God is stronger than ever.

King Alfred goes off to recruit an army and fight the Danes. He also goes undercover into the Danish camp, dressed as a wandering minstrel. He sits by the enemy fire with his harp and hears from their own lips their empty and dangerous philosophy, a truth that "is cold to tell", that "the soul is like a lost bird", and "the body a broken shell". When he returns to his own camp, still in disguise, he learns a much more important lesson about himself. He is stopped by an old woman who is roasting cakes over a fire. She tells him to watch the cakes while she goes about some other task. Alfred sits philosophizing about the menial role of this

---

[19] *BWH* I:225–261.

woman and, naturally, lets the cakes burn. The woman comes and strikes the king across the face, leaving a red scar. But Alfred is struck by something else: the idea of humility. He stands up and laughs and realizes that he who "is struck for an ill servant/Should be a kind lord".

> He that has been a servant
>   Knows more than priests and kings,
> But he that has been an ill servant,
>   He knows all earthly things.
>
> Pride flings frail palaces at the sky,
>   As a man flings up sand,
> But the firm feet of humility
>   Take hold of heavy land.
>
> Pride juggles with her toppling towers,
>   They strike the sun and cease,
> But the firm feet of humility
>   They grip the ground like trees.[20]

And now Alfred is ready for battle, vowing to return the blow he has received, not at the old woman, of course, but at the enemy. And he and his army charge into combat to fight a fight that does not seem winnable. And yet they win.

But after his great victory, Alfred, who calls himself "a common king", prophesies that the heathen shall return.

> They shall not come with warships,
>   They shall not waste with brands,
> But books be all their eating,
>   And ink be on their hands.

[20] BWH IV:252–264.

Not with the humour of hunters
   Or savage skill in war,
But ordering all things with dead words,
Strings shall they make of beasts and birds,
   And wheels of wind and star ...

They shall come mild as monkish clerks,
   With many a scroll and pen;
And backward shall ye turn and gaze,
   Desiring one of Alfred's days,
When pagans still were men ...[21]

By this sign you shall know them,
   The breaking of the sword,
And man no more a free knight,
   That loves or hates his lord.

Yea, this shall be the sign of them,
   The sign of the dying fire;
And Man made like a half-wit,
   That knows not of his sire.

What though they come with scroll and pen,
   And grave as a shaven clerk,
By this sign you shall know them,
   That they ruin and make dark;

By all men bond to Nothing,
   Being slaves without a lord,
By one blind idiot world obeyed,
   Too blind to be abhorred;

By terror and the cruel tales
   Of curse in bone and kin,

[21] *BWH* VIII:248–267.

By weird and weakness winning,
Accursed from the beginning,
By detail of the sinning,
   And denial of the sin.[22]

Sin is a weed. It starts out small and subtle. But left unattended it becomes an infestation and covers everything—which brings us to the image of the White Horse.

High on a Berkshire hill overlooking the valley where Alfred fought the Danes, is an ancient image of a White Horse. The silhouette was formed long ago by removing the turf covering the underlying chalk and setting off a distinct white outline against a green background. Because the grass and weeds always strive to creep across the chalky ground again, the ancient form would be erased by the pressure of the elements if people had not continually cleared the outline century after century. Alfred's first act after defeating the Danes at Ethandune is to gather his people together and scour the White Horse again, which the barbarians had left to be overgrown by weeds. It is because of this "act of will and intelligence" against the natural elements, that we still see the silhouette of the horse as it was seen in King Alfred's time.

Chesterton uses this mysterious image as a symbol of the traditions that preserve mankind. Our parents have taught us certain truths, certain commandments; we, in turn, teach them to our children. If we do not teach them, soon comes "the detail of the sinning and the denial of the sin". The moral tradition of the human race is never secure. It is active, hard work. We can never take it for granted. As the Russian Chesterton scholar Ekaterina Volokhonskaia says, "If

[22] *BWH* VIII:273–94.

we do not clear the outline of the White Horse with unwearying care, grass will very soon choke it and we will lose it forever. It is not the moral tradition that keeps us, it is we who keep (or do not keep) it." [23]

Words are deeds.
Sins are weeds.

[23] Ekaterina Volokhonskaia, "A Russian Perspective of Chesterton", in *The Gift of Wonder: The Many Sides of G. K. Chesterton*, Dale Ahlquist, ed., (Minneapolis: American Chesterton Society/JC Graphics, 2001), 79.

8

Uneducating the Educated

What is the point of sending our children to school? If you put this question to the children themselves, they would probably answer that there is no point. Unfortunately, considering the present state of our educational system, that is probably the right answer. And one child who never grew up, G. K. Chesterton, thought it was the right answer a long time ago. In his view, "The purpose of Compulsory Education is to deprive the common people of their common sense." [1]

What common sense through the ages tells us is that most people have this simple basic desire: to have a happy family and a happy home. Chesterton says that "just now there is a tendency to forget that the school is only a preparation for the home, and not the home a mere jumping off place for the school". [2]

As is so often the case in the modern world, we have things exactly backward. In the process of turning our children over to the public education system, we have turned our backs on the home and the family. And we have somehow mislaid the primary purpose of going to school.

[1] *ILN*, September 7, 1929.
[2] "The Best Toy in the World", *Merry-Go-Round*, June 1924.

The one thing that is never taught by any chance in the atmosphere of public schools is this: that there is a whole truth of things, and that in knowing it and speaking it we are happy.[3]

According to Chesterton, the whole point of education is that it should give a person a set of standards, eternal standards that can be used to judge fugitive standards.[4] We have this backward, too. Our schools change their standards more often than they change the light bulbs. The modern mind cannot make up its mind. It has no eternal philosophy, no eternal reference point. But the irony is that the more doubtful we are about the value of philosophy, the more certain we are about the value of education. This is the same thing as saying that "the more doubtful we are about whether we have any truth, the more certain we are (apparently) that we can teach it to children. The smaller our faith in doctrine, the larger our faith in doctors".[5]

It is the great paradox of the modern world that at the very time when the world decided that people should not be coerced about their form of religion, it also decided that they should be coerced about their form of education.[6]

I think our coercive popular education has been uncommonly near a complete failure.[7]

Every education teaches a philosophy; if not by dogma then by suggestion, by implication, by atmosphere. Every part of that education has a connection with every other part. If it

[3] ILN, August 11, 1906.
[4] See ILN, March 29, 1930.
[5] ILN, January 26, 1907.
[6] ILN, August 8, 1925.
[7] ILN, January 31, 1914.

does not all combine to convey some general view of life, it is not an education at all.[8]

The truth is that the modern world has committed itself to two totally different and inconsistent conceptions about education. It is always trying to expand the scope of education; and always trying to exclude from it all religion and philosophy. But this is sheer nonsense.[9]

It is perfectly obvious—it is common sense—that we cannot have a system that claims to provide a complete education, and then leave out theology and religion. But that is precisely what we have. We pour money into education because education is the answer to everything. The more education the better, except, of course, if it includes theology.

Chesterton claims that this idea of "infinite education" arose among the wealthy classes where it was natural enough for a fashionable lady to leave her little daughter to be taught by five different governesses, while that same fashionable lady was out demanding more rights for women. It was that mentality, more or less, that became the basis for our modern public education, the idea of entrusting a child to specialists, while the parents go off and do something else, which in most cases meant working in a factory. By turning public education over to "the experts", we have undermined the natural authority of the family. Chesterton says that the man in the street is wholly at the mercy of an "academic priesthood".[10] But there is a further problem with this system because it does not have the same advantages as the fashionable lady with her five governesses. As

[8] *The Common Man* (New York: Sheed and Ward, 1950), 167.
[9] Ibid., 168–69.
[10] *The Superstitions of the Sceptic* (Cambridge: W. Hefner and Sons, 1925), 27.

Chesterton points out, "among poorer people there cannot
be five teachers to one pupil. Generally there are about
fifty pupils to one teacher. There it is impossible to cut up
the soul of a single child and distribute it among specialists." [11] Instead we tear in pieces the soul of a single school-
teacher and distribute it in rags and scraps to a whole mob
of children.

> In the case of comparative poverty, which is the common
> lot of mankind, we come back to a general parental respon-
> sibility, which is the common sense of mankind. We also
> come back to the parent as the person in charge of educa-
> tion. . . . If you exalt education, you must exalt the parental
> power with it. If you deprecate the parental power, you
> must deprecate education with it. . . . Private education really
> is universal. Public education can be comparatively narrow.
> The mother dealing with her own daughters in her own
> home does literally have to deal with all sides of a single
> human soul. [12]

"The human house", says Chesterton, "is a paradox for it
is larger inside than out." [13] When we step out of the home,
when we pass from private life to public life, we are passing
from a greater work to a smaller one, and from a harder
work to an easier one. And that is why most modern people wish to pass from the great domestic task to the smaller
and easier commercial one. They would rather be in the
business world serving the minor needs of a hundred different people than meeting all the major needs of just one
person, which includes serving meals, conversation, and moral
support. They would rather teach a course in trigonometry

[11] *Fancies Versus Fads* (London: Methuen, 1923), 196.
[12] Ibid., 196–97.
[13] Ibid., 198.

to a hundred children than struggle with the whole human character of one child. Chesterton says that anyone "who makes himself responsible for one small baby, as a whole, will soon find that he is wrestling with gigantic angels and demons".[14]

While public education suffers from the conflicting problem of not enough teachers and yet too many specialists, the result is a lack of results. Children actually keep learning less and less. They cannot even get a basic education.

> To say that the moderns are half-educated may be too complimentary by half.[15]

> I have nothing but general information; but it is fairly general. What surprises me in people younger, brighter, and more progressively educated than myself is that their general information is very sketchy.[16]

The schools are painfully aware of the decline in education. And so they scramble to try new things, new theories, new ways to teach. Chesterton says that most educational theories are not as old as the children being taught. We are not educating students any more; we are desperately educating the educators and then giving them a group of students on which to experiment with the latest techniques of teaching. Chesterton says, "Our schools are swept nowadays with wave after wave of scientific speculation; by fad after fad and fashion after fashion." [17] There is an utter rejection of tradition, of the truths that built our civilization, the truths that were handed down through the generations.

[14] Ibid., 202.
[15] *ILN*, June 2, 1928.
[16] *ILN*, June 18, 1932.
[17] "The Inefficiency of Science", *North American Review*, November 1929.

The prevailing ideas in modern education from nursery school to graduate school defy common sense and insult the common man. Worse still, they oppress the common man.

> There are two ways of dealing with nonsense in this world. One way is to put nonsense in the right place; as when people put nonsense into nursery rhymes. The other is to put nonsense in the wrong place; as when they put it into educational addresses, psychological criticisms, and complaints against nursery rhymes.[18]

What makes it even worse is that everyone knows that education is in serious disarray. Everyone is upset about the schools. But as Chesterton says, the people who try to escape from the system are found and punished; the people who cannot be found anywhere are those who are happy with the system.

> It is rare to come across anyone enthusiastic for our system of elementary instruction. It is not common to find anyone who is even free from grave misgivings about it. Nobody seems very keen about education—least of all the educators. I have a huge personal respect for the teachers in the Church and State schools, in regard to their untiring cheerfulness, industry, and courage. But I never met one of them who seemed at all certain that the system was doing any good.[19]

The basic cause of all the problems in modern education can be summarized in three words: Darwin, Marx, and Freud. The theories of these three men have pervaded all of modern thought. Their ideas are much alike in that they are narrow, materialistic, fatalistic, and utterly anti-Christian.

[18] *ILN*, October 15, 1921.
[19] *ILN*, August 24, 1912.

Their influence has been felt far beyond their limited fields. Darwin's ideas have contributed to a blind belief in progress. They have also served as the justification for cut-throat capitalism and the survival-of-the-fittest mentality in our commercial and political relations. Marx's ideas plunged half the world into darkness for most of the last century, but in the other half of the world they have served as the justification for the extended growth of the State and the loss of the authority of the family and the centrality of the home. And Freud's ideas have led to an overemphasis on sex and have served as the justification for the normalizing of the abnormal, and the pervasive decline in morality. The academic community's utter sellout to these three figures has elevated science, economics, and psychology above religion. In fact, all of these three have been invoked to explain away religion.

Chesterton says that the primary public duty before us today is "not to educate the uneducated but to uneducate the educated".[20] We could start this process, the process of bringing common sense back to education, by tossing out Darwin, Marx, and Freud, and all their minions, or studying them solely for the purpose of finding out what the enemy is up to.

Chesterton does not say there is absolutely no truth in Darwin, Marx, and Freud; he says that the minor truths that they got hold of, they stated entirely out of proportion to a thousand other truths.

Each of them took not so much a half-truth as a hundredth part of a truth, and then offered it not merely as something, but as everything. Having never done

[20] *ILN*, November 8, 1913.

anything except split hairs, [each of them] hangs the whole
world on a single hair [whether it be biology, economics,
or psychology]. . . . It is yet another mark of this sort of
agnostic that he is ready to assert his absolute knowledge
of everything to the verge of a contradiction in terms.
Just as he will always try to write a history of prehistoric
man, so he will always struggle to be conscious of his
own unconsciousness. . . . Just as it is the latest fad to prove
that everything is sexual, so it was the last fad to prove
that everything was economic. The Marxist notion, called
the materialist theory of history, had the same sort of stupid self-confidence in its very insufficient materialism. As
the one fad conceives everything about the bird to be
connected with mating, so the other conceived everything
connected with it to consist of catching worms. . . . These
fads fade very fast, and it may seem hardly worth while to
prick bubbles that will burst of themselves. Nevertheless,
there is one consideration that makes it worth while. It is
a character of all these manias that they cannot really convince the mind, but they do cloud it. Above all, they do
darken it. All these tremendous and rather temporary discoveries have had the singular fascination that they were
not merely degrading, but were also depressing. Each in
turn leaves no trace on the true and serious conclusions
of the world. But each in turn may leave very deep and
disastrous wounds and dislocations in the mentality of the
individual man.[21]

Darwinism was embraced by its first great proponents,
Thomas Huxley and Herbert Spencer, because they were
agnostics who used Darwin to support their own skepticism about religion. Chesterton says, "It would have been
better if they had cultivated a little more agnosticism about

[21] "The Game of Psychoanalysis", *Century Magazine*, May 1923.

Darwinism." [22] The problem is not that they opened the evolutionary question, but that they closed it. Evolution is no longer a subject for debate.

> The Darwinian will not condescend to argue with you. He will inform you of your ignorance; he will not enlighten your ignorance. [23]

Chesterton points out any number of weaknesses in Darwin's theory, including the rather remarkable lack of fossil evidence. He says, "They continue to demonstrate the Darwinian theory from the geological record, by means of all the fossils that ought to be found in it." [24] And, indeed, the gaping holes in the fossil record continue to be as problematic as they have always been. The missing link is still missing. Chesterton says, "If there were a missing link in a real chain, it would not be called a chain at all." [25]

But the real problem with Darwinism has not been its implications for science, but its implications for everything else. Chesterton argues that Darwin's theory is directly related to the rise of industrialism in the nineteenth century and the mass of human oppression that went along with it. It is also largely responsible for our modern-day cult of progress, or what Chesterton calls "The absurd necessity for maintaining that everything is always getting better." [26] It has other implications as well.

> The Declaration of Independence dogmatically bases all rights on the fact that God created all men equal; and it is right;

[22] *ILN*, February 2, 1935.
[23] *ILN*, July 17, 1920.
[24] *The Well and the Shallows*, *CW* 3:358.
[25] *ILN*, April 8, 1922.
[26] *ILN*, December 21, 1912.

for if they were not created equal, they ... certainly evolved unequal. There is no basis for democracy except in a dogma about the divine origin of man.[27]

Even if the evolutionary theory *is* true, it is totally useless for human affairs. "It is enormous, but irrelevant. Like the solar system, it is a colossal trifle." [28]

What I complain of is a vague popular philosophy which supposes itself to be scientific when it's really nothing but a sort of new religion and an uncommonly nasty one. When people talked about the fall of man they knew they were talking about a mystery, a thing they didn't understand. Now that they talk about the survival of the fittest they think they do understand it, [but] they have ... no notion of what the words mean.[29]

Darwinism failed as a true philosophy, says Chesterton, but it has succeeded as a false religion.[30] It has become ingrained in our thinking. And we have gone, he says, from talking unphilosophically about philosophy to talking unscientifically about science.[31]

I want to make it clear that science itself is not the villain. Science, as Chesterton says, is either a tool or a toy.[32] If we make it into something more than that, it has dire consequences in all other phases of our lives. Putting science up on a pedestal and putting our trust in it, giving it a primary function instead of a secondary one, causes us to neglect our responsibilities, our moral and artistic standards, and our ability to think for ourselves. We end up

[27] *What I Saw in America*, *CW* 21:261.
[28] *ILN*, September 18, 1909.
[29] *The Club of Queer Trades*, *CW* 6:192.
[30] See *ILN*, May 29, 1920.
[31] See *The Club of Queer Trades*, *CW* 6:194.
[32] See *ILN*, October 9, 1909.

using our choices to lose our choices, to enslave ourselves, and then we put our hope in science to set us free. We expect science to take care of us, to watch over us, to make our future safe. We stand up and *demand* a cure for a disease, when it is our own immoral behavior that has caused the epidemic. We try to cure every troublesome behavior with chemical concoctions rather than change that behavior by making good decisions. We ask science to control us instead of making a conscious effort to control ourselves.

This is faith in the material to the utter neglect of the spiritual. And it is nothing less than idolatry, plain and simple, the most rampant and condemned sin of the Old Testament: creating and setting up our own ultimate authority, believing our own remarkable fabrications, bowing down to our own accomplishments, relying only on what we can see and touch. It is ironic that we have put all our faith in science and then claim to be autonomous and supreme. We have intoxicated ourselves with self-esteem. And at what cost? At the considerable cost of our souls. We have taken government and turned it into a surrogate parent, even a surrogate self, as we let regulation replace conscience. We have taken economics, which should be nothing but a minor nuisance three times a day, and we've made it into an all-powerful, all-consuming force. We have put the comforts of the body above the care of the soul. We've scorned religion as something backward, even dangerous, and we proceed on the presumption that the answers to all questions not only can be found through our own searching, but can be quantified and distributed within a system of our own making. But the system no longer serves us. We serve it.

There is just a little space left in this chapter to dispense with Marx and Freud—which is probably more space than they deserve.

While Marxism as a whole has been completely discredited after doing untold damage to the world, there remain elements of it that still have influence, such as the idea that everything can be explained in terms of economics, that the events of history are inevitable, and that the State is the absolute authority. In terms of education, it is this last one that is most damaging, for with State-sponsored compulsory education, the State has used its power to replace the authority of religion, of the family, and of individual conscience—which brings us to Freud.

> The wild and credulous worship of Psychology seems to be especially common in America. As we have seen a new republic of Russia founded entirely upon Marx, perhaps we may eventually see a new republic of America founded entirely upon Freud.[33]

As with Darwin and Marx, the conjectures of Freud have passed from being a hypothesis and have hardened into a dogma. Chesterton says, "The student of Freud is forbidden to forget sex",[34] and will "remember everything about the unconscious mind except that it is unconscious."[35]

It was Freud and his theory of psychoanalysis that led to the incredible rise of the counseling industry and psychological therapy. The worst part of this legacy is that it has replaced the confessional. So instead of finding forgiveness for our sins, sins that we committed through our own fault, we get the most amazing psycho-babble, wrapped in the mantle of science, which explains that our sins are not sins, and whatever it was we did, it wasn't our fault. It was our parent's fault, or our teacher's fault, or simply nature's fault.

[33] *ILN*, December 21, 1929.
[34] *Fancies Versus Fads*, v.
[35] *ILN*, May 29, 1920.

The evil perpetuated by this sort of counseling is twofold: we become less responsible for our sinful actions even while we long for a forgiveness that never comes. It is the marriage of Freud and Darwin, of one pseudo-science to another.

> The eager use of ... scientific terms is but a part of our evasion of responsibility and our dark adoration of fate.[36]

> The mere word "Science" is already used as a sacred and mystical word in many matters of politics and ethics. It is already used vaguely to threaten the most vital traditions of civilization—the family and the freedom of the citizen.[37]

And the word "science" is especially used to eliminate anything that might be considered supernatural, as "natural" explanation is used to explain everything. But Chesterton says, "Take away the supernatural and what remains is the unnatural."[38] Darwin, Marx, and Freud, each of whom rejected Christianity, gave us theories that have been used to promote some of history's most unnatural and degrading attacks against human dignity. If we want to rescue education—and our society—we can start by kicking these three bad boys out of school, and letting God back in. We need to take away the State's power and give it back to the parents. And we need to get rid of the fads and fashions in education and start teaching the permanent things. As Chesterton says, "Teach, to the young, men's enduring truths, and let the learned amuse themselves with their passing errors."[39]

[36] ILN, August 13, 1910.
[37] ILN, October 9, 1920.
[38] Heretics, CW 1:88.
[39] ILN, October 15, 1910.

9

Science and Secondary Things

The subject of science, which we touched upon in the last chapter, is rather large and potentially cumbersome, but it is only as large as the universe. And that is an important point: the realm of science is limited. The problem is that there are those who do not recognize its limits, and that is what we are going to talk about in this chapter.

In order to have a complete view of the universe, you have to have a view that is larger than the universe. A complete view of the universe involves the natural and the supernatural. The "natural" is the realm of science: the physical or "natural" world, we might even say the mechanical world. We could certainly say that nature is like a machine, and science looks after the machine, studying it, trying to understand how it works, trying to use it, even trying to take care of it. Science, then, is purely practical, which is to say, it is not philosophical. G. K. Chesterton says physical science is like simple addition. It either works or it doesn't work.[1] It either adds up or it doesn't. We can use science to predict how the physical world will behave. But we cannot use it to predict how we will behave, or *if* we will behave. Science simply cannot account for free will, nor

[1] See *ILN*, September 28, 1907.

should it attempt to. As Chesterton points out, it's up to my private physician to tell me which food will kill me. But it's up to my private philosopher to tell me whether I ought to be killed.[2]

This should be obvious. It is common sense. But we have to point it out because somewhere in the history of scientific inquiry, something went wrong. Chesterton could already see, almost a century ago, that science had moved beyond its realm. He observed that the mere word "science" was being used as a sacred and mystical word in education and ethics and politics.[3] It still is. It is used to add legitimacy to any rumor or fashionable fiction.

> Let anyone run his eye over any average newspaper or popular magazine, and note the number of positive assertions made in the name of popular science, without the least pretence of scientific proof, or even of any adequate scientific authority.[4]

People will claim that "science" says this or that, but they don't know if an actual scientist has actually said something, or what kind of scientist, or, most importantly, what philosophy that scientist has. The word "science" is used as an authority on everything, but a vague authority that is always invoked yet can never be pinned down. And since we have made science this great authority, we now look to science to solve all our troubles. We expect physical solutions to spiritual problems.

> What we have suffered from in the modern world is not . . . physical knowledge itself, but simply a stupid mistake about

[2] Ibid.
[3] See *ILN*, October 9, 1920.
[4] *ILN*, July 12, 1930.

what physical knowledge is and what it can do. It is quite as obvious that physical knowledge may make a man comfortable as it is that it cannot make a man happy. It is as certain that there are such things as drugs as that there are no such things as love-potions. Physical science is a thing on the outskirts of human life; adventurous, exciting, and essentially fanciful. It has nothing to do with the centre of human life at all. Telephones, flying-ships, radium, the North Pole are not in the ultimate sense good, but neither are they bad. Physical science is always one of two things; it is either a tool or a toy. At its highest and noblest, of course, it is a toy. A toy is a thing of far greater philosophical grandeur than a tool; for the very simple reason that a toy is valued for itself and a tool only for something else. A tool is a means, a toy is an end. You use a hammer to make a doll's house; if you tried to use a doll's house to make a hammer you would soon be convinced that you had selected a somewhat clumsy instrument. When we look through a fieldglass at the German forces invading England we are using science as a tool. When we look through a telescope at the tremendous planets and the remote systems, we are using science as a toy. When science tells me that there is a house in Ealing that I can communicate with by telephone, I am interested; when science says there is a star in Sirius I can communicate with by telescope, I am amused. But in neither case can science be anything else except a tool or a toy. It can never be the man using the tool. It can never be the child playing with the toy. It can never, in short, be the thing that has natural authority over toy and tool. For the child has the kingdom of heaven, and the man has the kingdom of the earth.[5]

Science can never be anything other than a tool or a toy. Chesterton associates the toy with children, who are the kingdom of heaven, while the tool is for adults, who are

[5] *ILN*, October 9, 1909.

the kingdom of earth. One of his most wonderful lines is, "Earth is a task-garden; heaven is a playground."[6] This is good theology. Play is an end in itself, so is heaven. Work is a means to an end, so is earth. But work is not only labor, that is, it is not only punishment. Another word for work is "stewardship", which means responsibility, and responsibility means free will. The kingdom of earth is our responsibility, and, paradoxically, children are our responsibility, even though they are the kingdom of heaven. Our work is a kind of divine responsibility. Another word that means work is "liturgy". That is good theology, too. Work should be a form of worship. Earth is seeking heaven. The natural is seeking the supernatural. That is what we do when we worship. That is the right relationship between the natural and the supernatural. When the natural is avoiding the supernatural, something is wrong.

Our religion should not contradict our science, because our religion should not contradict anything in our lives. Religion is what keeps everything in its proper place. That has always been its role. Chesterton says that once we admit there is a God, "the Cosmos begins to know its place". And its place is second place. The "Cosmos falls down before Him".[7] The main problem with science today is that it needs to be kept in its right place.

> Science must not impose any philosophy, any more than the telephone must tell us what to say.[8]

In his book *What's Wrong with the World* Chesterton introduces us to two characters, Hudge and Gudge. Hudge

[6] *ILN*, August 17, 1907.
[7] *A Miscellany of Men* (Norfolk, Va.: IHS Press, 2004), 73.
[8] *ILN*, October 9, 1909.

represents big government, and Gudge, big business. These
two characters conspire together to deprive the common
man of his freedom and dignity. Well, I think we should
add a third character. I would like to introduce Sludge.
Professor Sludge. He represents big science. Professor Sludge
is not a scientist per se because it's not really science that
he cares about. It's *scientism*—or "The mistake about science", the misconception that science can be used for something more than the study of secondary causes. Professor
Sludge simply wants to use science to impose his philosophy. He is a materialist and an agnostic, and is not shy
about it. Even though the word "agnostic" literally means
"ignorant", Professor Sludge is pretty smart. And even
though "agnostic" is supposed to imply impartiality, Sludge
is very biased. He is biased against religion. As Chesterton
says, "People who pretend to be impartial are always par-
tial." [9] Professor Sludge believes that the material world is
all there is, which means, of course, that he does not accept
Christianity. But he cannot avoid Christianity, and he is
always trying to dance around it. He can never decide if
he wants to be more pessimistic or more optimistic than
Christianity.

The Christian worldview is that God created the world
and it was good. Man sinned, and the good world was tainted
by sin. Then God provided Redemption. Professor Sludge
always falls on either side of that idea. On the one hand, he
looks only at that good creation. On other hand, he looks
only at the sin, or rather only at the tainted creation. In
neither case does he acknowledge the Creator, neither the
Creator who made the good world nor the Creator who
has been sinned against. On the one hand, the optimistic

[9] *ILN*, February 14, 1914.

Happy Sludge thinks everything natural is good. And so he starts the environmentalist movement, which is aimed at preserving nature because nature is good. But the environmentalists, led by Happy Sludge, see man as violating nature, interfering with it, abusing it, and just not fitting in. So Professor Sludge introduces the idea of population control as a way to protect the environment, in other words, killing people in order to save the world.

On the other hand, the pessimistic Sad Sludge sees that nature is heartless, and everything is hopeless. We are defeated already. We are the unintended byproduct of a mindless process; we are "a disease of the dust".[10] We can look forward to rotting. We are dispensable because the whole world is dispensable. Not only can the world not be saved, it's not worth saving. So let's just grab what we can and try to stay comfortable for as long as we can.

Whether Sludge is happy or sad, whether he's in a good mood or bad, his philosophy leads to the same end: to what Chesterton calls "the most hopeless and inhuman extremes of destructive thought".[11] When we stop caring about God, we stop caring about those who were made in the image of God.

Sludge's complete disregard for mankind is evident in his rejection of free will. He really believes that every decision we make, every act we do, is a result of a mechanical, natural process. He gives every human act a scientific name, and we readily accept that term as some sort of explanation for our behavior.

The stupidest or the wickedest action is supposed to become reasonable or respectable, not by having found a reason in

[10] *ILN*, April 20, 1907.
[11] *The Victorian Age in Literature, CW* 15:512.

scientific fact, but merely by having found any sort of excuse in scientific language.[12]

Chesterton says that science is dangerous not because it encourages doubt, but, on the contrary, because it is so easily and universally believed. We always trust in new technologies, in the scientific proposals for helping mankind, but these things always seem to operate behind our backs. Professor Sludge has us right where he wants us, because each time we trust his proposals, we are giving up more of our freedom. The sin, as Chesterton says, is not that engines are mechanical, but that men are mechanical. Sludge wants to create the best "environment", the best "conditions" so that we somehow improve without knowing it. We are always lured by the word "progress". We can look at science and can certainly see great progress. But can we see progress when we look anywhere else? Especially when we look inside ourselves?

> It is instinctive to dwell on those airy matters of science in which we have progressed so much rather than on those solid matters of morals in which it is highly doubtful if we have progressed at all. It is pleasanter to reflect on the mind of man bridging the starry abysses and dissecting the atoms of the ultimate, rather than to remember that the heart of man is still mysterious and barbaric, deceitful above all things, and desperately wicked.... It cannot be disputed that our age ... is marked by an advance in this ruthless and rigid accuracy, this sharp and polished dexterity of the sciences and the machines. Whether a man detests it ... or accepts it ... there can be no ... dispute about the existence of practical science, about its strength, or about its precision. This being so, a grave difficulty

[12] *ILN*, September 29, 1923.

follows. We are now confronted with the colossal and really terrifying responsibility of doing things that we can really do. As long as people only dreamed of flying or tried to bridge the sea, they were as innocent as any other fancies of the intellect; but dreams that come true are very dreadful things.... Science has always shown a capacity ... in the creation of cruel and destructive things. It stands to reason that a person who knows enough about the body to help it, knows enough about it to hurt it; and it would be a delicate question to decide whether science has turned out more pills or more cannon-balls.[13]

Over a hundred years ago, at the dawn of the twentieth century, Chesterton said, "We are learning to do a great many clever things.... The next great task will be to learn not to do them." [14] But Sludge has no interest in not doing them. It is one of Sludge's dogmas that progress must never be stopped. But the dogma he has not defined is: Progress toward what?

Unlike the good pagans of ancient Athens, today's agnostics do not worship the Unknown God; they simply worship the unknown.

What we are fighting is a new and false religion.... It may almost be called a religion of irreligion. It trusts itself utterly to the anarchy of the unknown; and, unless civilisation can sober it with a shock of disappointment, it will be for ever inexhaustible in novelties of perversion and pride.[15]

Now, we could say, "Forgive them for they know not what they do." We could. But I have this sneaking suspicion that they do know what they're doing. And I suspect

[13] *ILN*, August 20, 1910.
[14] *Varied Types* (New York: Dodd, Mead, 1903), 228.
[15] *ILN*, June 24, 1916.

that Chesterton suspected the same thing. He says that the problem with the man of modern science is not that he is trying to know what he does not know, but that he is "pretending not to know what he does know".[16]

And what is it that he pretends not to know? Well, it has something to do with those three words, "In the beginning ..."

Professor Sludge exposes himself as a fraud, when he calls on science to do what science cannot do: to describe what never was observed and what never can be observed; to explain that the formation of matter and of all known physical laws of the universe, of life, of consciousness, of music, of laughter, of prayer, can all be accounted for by the process of nothing becoming something and then becoming something else. Sludge hangs his hat on a primal event he calls the Big Bang, which is creation without a creator, and he uses it to explain everything. This is not science. It is either the height of presumption or the height of dishonesty. I'm not sure which is worse: one is arrogant, the other, devious.

It would be nice to be able to talk about science without having to bring up evolution, but we can never seem to do it. Although Sludge has effectively shut down the debate on this matter, many problems remain even though Sludge has declared the problems are not there. But regardless of how that theory may apply to the development of life, the main problem is how it applies to the origin of life. And it doesn't apply, for the simple reason that as an explanation it doesn't explain anything.

> Evolution as an explanation ... of the cause of living things, is still faced with the problem of producing rabbits out of

[16] *ILN*, February 27, 1926.

an empty hat; a process commonly involving some hint of design.[17]

Evolutionists continually use the phrase "the purpose of Nature", but "nature" is a purposely vague word, and purpose naturally implies an act of the will. Chesterton says, "To talk of the purpose of Nature is to make a vain attempt to avoid being anthropomorphic, merely by being feminist. It is believing in a goddess because you are too sceptical to believe in a god."[18] He says nature is not our mother, but our sister, for we both have the same father.[19] And the beauty of the world "is not a work of nature, but a work of art", and if it's a work of art, "then it involves an artist".[20] And so, says Chesterton, "What we call Nature, the wiser of us call Creation."[21]

But Sludge has kept the Creator out of the discussion. We have lost our balance because the role of science is out of proportion in our society. We need to put science back in its place because in its rightful place, science can do a great deal of good, instead of adding to the confusion and doubt of the modern world. Chesterton says, "Science is a splendid thing; if you tell it where to go."[22] But the only thing that can put science in its proper place is religion. Only the supernatural can give the proper context to the natural.

You can already imagine the editorials, sputtering with outrage at such a suggestion. They will say that religion

[17] *Chaucer, CW* 18:172.

[18] *The Superstition of Divorce, CW* 4:253.

[19] See *Orthodoxy, CW* 1:317.

[20] Ibid., 319.

[21] "A Note on Rousseau", in *The Chesterton Review*, vol. 19, no. 4, November 1993.

[22] *ILN*, October 9, 1909.

will persecute science or inhibit scientific progress. After all, look at how the Church persecuted Galileo! Chesterton says that the name "Galileo" has become "imbedded in journalese and preserved there like a fossil".[23] You cannot read an article on science and religion without seeing the name "Galileo". Chesterton suggests that a tax be put on the word "Galileo", which would force young journalists to come up with some other example of a scientist who has been persecuted by the Church. It would force them to do some research and perhaps learn something about history. They might even learn that Galileo's "persecution" was pretty minor, if you can even call it persecution. "Every leader-writer who thunders 'Galileo' at us assumes that we know even less about Galileo than he does."[24] And, of course, Galileo's idea about the earth going around the sun was not Galileo's idea. It was first suggested by a Catholic priest from Poland named Copernicus, who was never persecuted for his idea but was always held in the greatest esteem by the Church. (Chesterton also points out that "long before even Copernicus stated it, it had been suggested in the very middle of the Middle Ages by Cusa: and that the persecuting Church proceeded to persecute him by making him a Cardinal."[25]) The heliocentric theory is called the Copernican Revolution and not the Galilean Revolution. But, according to Chesterton, the most important point is that the discovery by Copernicus and Galileo really doesn't matter. As he says, the Solar System is a colossal trifle.[26] It is irrelevant to

[23] *ILN*, December 18, 1920.
[24] *The Thing*, *CW* 3:199.
[25] "A Politician on Purgatory", in *The Chesterton Review*, vol. 3, no. 1, fall–winter, 1976–1977.
[26] See *ILN*, September 18, 1909.

human affairs. Looking through the telescope is only an amusement. The telescope is a toy. The Solar System doesn't matter. What matters is our souls. What matters is feeding the hungry and relieving the suffering of those who hurt. The Solar System doesn't matter to them. Neither does the Neanderthal Man.

Science is a tool or a toy. When it is a tool, the real issue is, whose tool is it and what is it being used for? In our complicated, lop-sided society, science is an expensive tool and is funded by big government and big business. The only time that the common man can use science as a tool or a toy is when he does so as a consumer. Hudge and Gudge are in cahoots with Sludge.

And as for the tired argument about Galileo, the question needs to be updated. Is the Church obstructing science? Or is science obstructing the Church? Who is being persecuted now? Whose creed is taught in the schools, fully underwritten by the government? Whose creed is silenced under penalty of law?

> The thing that is really trying to tyrannize through government is Science. The thing that really does use the secular arm is Science. And the creed that is really levying tithes and capturing schools, the creed that really is enforced by fine and imprisonment, the creed that really is proclaimed not in sermons but in statutes, and spread not by pilgrims but by policemen—that creed is the great but disputed system of thought which began with Evolution and has ended in Eugenics. Materialism is really our established church; for the Government will really help it to persecute the heretics.[27]

[27] *Eugenics and Other Evils, CW* 4:345.

We need to put science back in its place. One of the best ways to make that happen would be for everyone to read G. K. Chesterton. Once we understand that science is merely a tool or merely a toy, the conclusion is simple and obvious. Work and play. Let's use the tools to help build the Kingdom of God. And let's have fun with the toys. I'll see you at the playground.

10

A Short History of History

G. K. Chesterton says that many people are largely out of touch with the present because they are entirely out of touch with the past. Someone who doesn't know history, he says, is "in the literal sense half-witted . . . He does not know what half his own words mean, or what half his own actions signify." [1]

As we know, Chesterton is not afraid to use paradox occasionally to make a point. He has a way of showing that things are not what they seem, not what we expect, not what we have been led to believe. And so it is only natural that his approach to history would be to turn it on its head. But with the way history has been studied, that is pretty easy to do because our modern historians have not given us a very reliable version of the story of our civilization. Chesterton says that historians do the one thing that God himself cannot do: they change the past.[2] Because they succumb to current fashions, they revise history according to the prevailing politics of the day. When they call up the past, they choose to emphasize certain trivialities and utterly neglect certain enormities.

[1] *ILN*, December 5, 1925.
[2] See *ILN*, March 2, 1935.

History is not science. There are historians who have tried to claim otherwise, and they have certainly tried to make history textbooks as boring as science textbooks, the idea being that if a book is dull and unreadable it will sound true.[3] But human events cannot be forced into dry scientific theorems. While there are things in the universe that do repeat themselves, history is not one of them. And history is not inevitable. Just because something happened, doesn't mean it had to have happened. History is not a system, not a machine. It is a story, a story filled with characters who have that slippery variable called free will, which means we never know when we will see surprising courage, unbelievable charity, or unimaginable malice.

> In every historical event, I feel the thrill of uncertainty and the suspense of human choice.[4]

> One of the most necessary and most neglected points about the story called history, is the fact that the story is not finished.[5]

The purpose of studying history is to follow the events that lead to where we are now, and to see how the present could just as easily have been quite different. "The highest use of the imagination", says Chesterton, "is to learn from what never happened."[6]

> We do not realize what the past has been until we also realize what it might have been.[7]

[3] See *ILN*, June 23, 1923.
[4] *ILN*, June 4, 1932.
[5] *Chaucer, CW* 18:174.
[6] *G. K.'s Weekly: A Miscellany* (London: Rich and Cowan, 1934), 191.
[7] *The Resurrection of Rome, CW* 21:329.

In one sense the past is more important than the present, simply because there is more of it. Chesterton says, "To compare the present and the past is like comparing a drop of water and the sea." [8] And yet we often take a condescending attitude toward the past, rather than the humble attitude that would allow the past to be our teacher.

> The historian has a habit of saying of people in the past: "I think they may well be considered worthy of praise, allowing for the ideas of their time." There will never be really good history until the historian says, "I think they were worthy of praise, allowing for the ideas of my time." [9]

> I am not urging a lop-sided idolatry of the past; I am protesting against ... [a] lop-sided idolatry of the present. [10]

> We cannot fling ourselves into the blank future; we can only call up images from the past. This being so, the important principle follows, that how many images we have largely depends on how much past we have. Even new ideas will depend on whether we have enough history to forget. [11]

Though it is a cliché to say it, it is a cliché Chesterton would repeat: history is more than just names and dates. And Chesterton certainly demonstrates the truth of this cliché—he wrote a whole book on the history of England that has no dates in it. He says dates "are occasionally useful", [12] but the point is that we are not supposed to test things by a calendar that records whether they have

[8] *ILN*, September 7, 1912.
[9] *ILN*, August 15, 1925.
[10] *ILN*, September 5, 1925.
[11] *ILN*, October 4, 1924.
[12] *ILN*, January 3, 1931.

happened, but by a creed that decides whether they ought to have happened.[13]

According to Chesterton, *understanding* the facts is more important than *knowing* the facts. But this is not to say that Chesterton doesn't know the facts. His grasp of facts and names and even dates is astounding. He could quote from memory whole passages from medieval documents in the original Old English. He could connect characters and events that most of us have never heard of and would be hard-pressed even to find in a standard book of reference. And yet there is an amazing irony about Chesterton: in spite of his mastery of the material, he has a reputation for not getting his facts right. There are probably two reasons for this. First, Chesterton was absent-minded in his day-to-day affairs, and apparently some people feel this carried over into his writing. This simply is not true. It was precisely *because* he was such a clear and focused thinker on paper, that he occasionally forgot to get on a train in real life or finish getting himself dressed. The other thing that contributed to his reputation of being careless with the facts is that one notable critic said that one of Chesterton's first books, his biography of Robert Browning, is worthless as a biography because it has so few biographical facts in it and most of those are wrong. This critic did untold damage to the reputation of G. K. Chesterton, portraying him as slovenly and careless and inaccurate about names and dates and facts and figures. But we should point out that this critic *was* G. K. Chesterton.

Most people who study a lot of Chesterton have reached quite a contrary conclusion. They agree that he is very, very trustworthy—except when he writes about himself.

[13] See *ILN*, October 30, 1920.

On this particular subject, he is blinded by his humility. When he says what a poor historian he is, he cannot be believed. If he does have a weakness as an artist, it is in his self-portraits. If he has a weakness as a writer, it is directly connected to his strength: his intensity to carry out an idea, to complete a thought, which means he writes without stopping, without looking anything up. He relies only on what he calls "the vast uncatalogued library" of his own mind. He did indeed misquote Browning, because he was quoting from memory (though many critics have pointed out that the misquotes were an improvement on the original!).

Chesterton, of course, would never call himself a historian. He admits that his knowledge of history is rudimentary and that most other people know more details about history than he does. But he also says that while they know the details, they don't know the rudiments. They don't know the "basic alphabet of history".[14] And part of the alphabet of history is the legends and the traditions that make history understandable. Legend is precisely the element that historians try to remove from history to make it more "historical", or more "scientific". But, Chesterton says, "History will be wholly false unless it is helped by legend."[15] There are important events and important characters who have managed to elude written history at a time when there was very little written history, and that is where the traditions of a people are probably more trustworthy than "written evidence when there is not enough of it".[16]

[14] *ILN*, March 22, 1919.
[15] *ILN*, September 12, 1908.
[16] *Short History of England*, *CW* 20:442.

> The vulgar rumor is nearly always much nearer the historical truth than the "educated" opinion of today; for tradition is truer than fashion.[17]

> It is quite easy to see why a legend is treated, and ought to be treated, more respectfully than a book of history. The legend is generally made by the majority of people in the village, who are sane. The book is generally written by the one man in the village who is mad.[18]

> All modern historians are divided into two classes—those who tell half the truth . . . and those who tell none of the truth.[19]

> There are two quite distinct purposes of history; the superior purpose, which is its use for children; and the secondary or inferior purpose, which is its use for historians.[20]

History is the story of civilization. That means that history begins with civilization. We cannot really talk about prehistory, and yet we do. In fact that is the only thing some people talk about. They try to explain everything about mankind by what happened before mankind, even though we have no record of that. This is another example of what Chesterton calls the art of missing the point.

> Now the special trouble with modern philosophy has been that it is either prehistoric or post-historic. It is either concerned with the past of which we know very little, or else with the future of which we know nothing at all. . . . The danger for the modern man of genius is that between these things lies something rather large; the real history of humanity. When he happens to hit that, or stumble over it, he

[17] Ibid., 468–69.
[18] *Orthodoxy, CW* 1:251.
[19] *Lunacy and Letters* (New York: Sheed and Ward, 1958), 129–30.
[20] *ILN*, October 8, 1910.

will get into trouble.... The trouble comes, when they leave
off bothering about barbaric memories or prophetic visions;
and try to grapple with the historic creed that created their
own civilization.[21]

The creed that created our civilization, Western civilization, is the Catholic Creed: "It is a popular proverb that all
roads lead to Rome. It is a historic and literal fact that all
roads come from Rome." [22] Our civilization was built on
Roman civilization. And while a famous historian named
Edward Gibbon wrote *The Decline and Fall of the Roman
Empire*, Chesterton says what Gibbon doesn't understand is
that there is one element that came out of Rome that did
the opposite of decline and is still with us to this hour.[23] It
is the Catholic Church. The *Roman* Catholic Church.

There are modern historians, from Gibbon onward, who
claim it was the Church that kept us in the Dark Ages. But
Chesterton says the Church was the only thing that brought
us out of the Dark Ages. The Church was the only light in
the Dark Ages. Historians do not want to admit this. That
is because, as Chesterton says, "History is every bit as controversial as theology." [24]

The Catholic Church rose to its greatest prominence in
the Middle Ages. Most people do not know anything about
medieval history. Or what they do know is wrong.

Now the ordinary version of ... history that most moder-
ately educated people have absorbed from childhood is
something like this. That we emerged slowly from a semi-
barbarism in which all the power and wealth were in the

[21] *G. K.'s Weekly*, July 26, 1934.
[22] *ILN*, March 22, 1919.
[23] See *Resurrection of Rome, CW* 21:455.
[24] *ILN*, June 12, 1920.

hands of kings and a few nobles, that the king's power was broken first and then in due time that of the nobles, that this piece-meal improvement was brought about by one class after another waking up to a sense of citizenship and demanding a place in the national councils, frequently by riot or violence; and that in consequence of such menacing popular action, the franchise was granted to one class after another and used more and more to improve the social conditions of those classes, until we practically became a democracy, save for such exceptions as that of women. I do not think anyone will deny that something like that is the general idea of the educated man who reads a newspaper and of the newspaper that he reads. That is the view current at public schools and colleges; it is part of the culture of all the classes that count for much in government; *and there is not one word of truth in it from beginning to end.*[25]

The Medieval Age was a time of a united and devout faith. It was "the most purely vigorous time in history".[26] The Middle Ages were a "rich civilisation, creative and systematic, with fruitful sciences and masterful arts".[27] And there was greater liberty and distribution of property and power in the Middle Ages than in the present age. Monasteries were places where men of poor origins could not only be educated, but could be influential in culture and society. Guilds were places where men could learn a craft and work for themselves and not for a plant manager. Women had freedom and power and creativity in running the basic unit of society—the home—and thus were more influential in building a society of people with integrity and faith. Small shops formed a line of defense against big shops. These things

---

[25] *Utopia of Usurers, CW* 5:450–51. (Emphasis mine.)
[26] *Tremendous Trifles* (New York: Sheed and Ward, 1955), 156.
[27] *ILN*, May 20, 1911.

did not decay. They were murdered—ravaged and looted by an alliance between the ruling aristocrats and the rich manufacturers, an alliance that rules us still.

The word "medieval" is generally used as a term of abuse. Chesterton says there is an automatic assumption that it must always mean "throwing mud at a thing to call it a relic of medievalism".[28] Well, here are some of the relics of medievalism: Dante, Chaucer, Giotto, Oxford, Cambridge, Paris, St. Thomas Aquinas, St. Francis of Assisi, hospitals, trade unions, the printing press, the press, parliament. Many of the so-called relics of medievalism are the basis for common sense, that is, they are the things our civilization has in common. We can find them if we look at the Middle Ages. The Middle Ages, while not perfect, were, according to Chesterton, the high point of civilization. So far.

> If the medieval world did not establish peace, I am not sure the modern world has been a roaring success at it.[29]

Chesterton readily admits there was a cruel side to the Middle Ages. But he insists this was only one side. There may have been more cruelty but there was also more courage. He says, "When we think of our ancestors as the men who inflicted tortures, we ought sometimes to think of them as the men who defied them."[30]

Generally speaking, when people talk about the cruelty of the Medieval Ages, they do so either because they don't know what they are talking about or because they have a clear motive. They want to reinforce the modern impression that the Catholic Church was something cruel and

[28] *ILN*, March 12, 1932.
[29] *The Listener*, February 6, 1935.
[30] *Short History of England*, *CW* 20:483.

barbaric. They ignore the fact that it was the Catholic Church
that fought off the barbarians or, in an even more stunning
development, converted them. They ignore the much more
prominent fact that it is the modern culture, the one that
rejected the Catholic Church, that has been cruel, and it
has been the Catholic Church—and whatever was borrowed from the Catholic Church—that has been humane.
It was the Church that founded hospitals and universities
and fed the poor and defended the weak. It was the culture
that rejected the Church, the culture that triumphed in the
twentieth century, that tortured and killed more people than
the rest of history combined.

The key turning point in modern history? The thing that
could have and should have been different? Chesterton says
it is the meeting of Voltaire and Frederick the Great. That
is what dragged down the Holy Roman Empire, transfer-
ring the crown of the old Catholic princes to a Protestant
prince, who was not even a Christian. He calls Frederick
the Great the "soulless soulmate of Voltaire".[31] Their philosophical alliance led to the rise of a new Protestant empire
in the North, built on the ruin of the old Catholic empire
in the South. These two empires have been warring ever
since. It was their battle that led to a couple of recent events
known as World War I and World War II. The philosophical battle between secularism and Christianity continues
today.

> Just as all Christian history begins with the happy recon-
> ciliation of Herod and Pilate, so all modern history in the
> recent revolutionary sense, begins with that strange friend
> ship [of Voltaire and Frederick the Great]. . . . Between them,
> [they] were to shake the world to pieces. From Voltaire the

[31] *The End of The Armistice, CW* 5:583.

Latins were to learn a raging scepticism. From Frederick the Teutons were to learn a raging pride. The root of both perversions is in the common ground of atheist irresponsibility.... There was nothing to stop him from interpreting liberty as the infinite license of tyranny. The spiritual zero of Christendom was at that freezing instant when two dry, thin, hatchet-faced men looked in each other's hollow eyes and saw the sneer that was as eternal as the smile of the skull. Between them, they have nearly killed the thing by which we live.[32]

The thing by which we live. What is "the thing by which we live"? The Christian faith. Chesterton says, "There is no intelligible history without a religion."[33] He says that most of the history now taught in schools and colleges "is made windy and barren by the narrow notion of leaving out the theological theories.... Historians seem to have completely forgotten two facts—first, that men act from ideas; and second, that it might, therefore, be as well to discover which ideas."[34]

As we said earlier, history is a story. It is a story with a main character. Jesus Christ. In Chesterton's great book *The Everlasting Man* he allows the reader no escape from the fact that everything before Christ specifically anticipates him, and everything after Christ rests on and refers to him. Chesterton goes so far as to say that the Crucifixion and the death of Jesus was "the end of a very great thing called human history, the history that was merely human".[35] A new story began with the Resurrection of Christ. Those visiting the tomb on Easter morning "were

[32] *ILN*, November 25, 1933.
[33] *ILN*, November 19, 1910.
[34] *ILN*, May 13, 1911.
[35] *The Everlasting Man*, *CW* 2:345.

looking at the first day of creation".[36] If names and dates are important to you, then here indeed are the most important, in fact, the only ones you need to know: B.C. and A.D., Before Christ and Anno Domini, respectively. Every year that you and I live in is indeed "The Year of Our Lord". Of course, now historians are even trying to do away with that designation.

We can study history, we can study philosophy, we can study art and literature, but Chesterton says, "There is only one subject."[37]

> We do not need the learned man to teach us the important things. We all know the important things, though we all violate and neglect them.[38]

When we look into the past, the main thing to know is "the terrible secret that men are men—which is another way of saying that they are brothers. For every man knows the inmost core of every other man."[39]

Current events are related to historical events, but that is not because history repeats itself. It is because new movements are connected to old movements. Truth is always under attack. But truth does not change.

> An imbecile habit has arisen in modern controversy of saying that such and such a creed was credible in the twelfth century but is not credible in the twentieth. You might as well say that a certain philosophy can be believed on Mondays but cannot be believed on Tuesdays.[40]

[36] Ibid.
[37] *ILN*, February 17, 1906.
[38] *ILN*, October 8, 1910.
[39] Ibid.
[40] *Orthodoxy, CW* 1:278.

The truth that we really need to study and really need to know is not in recent but in remote events. "If you want the last lesson of politics, it is that if you forget far-off things, your sons and grandsons will remember them and rise up against you." [41]

[41] *The Listener*, February 6, 1935.

11

Feminism and Other Fads

Do you know what "communal kitchens" are? Neither do I. But we are about to hear an argument against them. It should not be necessary to argue against fads that are now forgotten. But then, it should not be necessary to argue against any fad. And yet that is precisely what we always have to do. The temporary things are always attacking the permanent things. In one of Chesterton's most popular essays, he takes on communal kitchens. The fact that this essay about a now long lost fad is still being reprinted in anthologies demonstrates that Chesterton is still timely even when his opponents are horribly out of date:

> A correspondent has written me an ... interesting letter in the matter of some allusions of mine to the subject of communal kitchens. He defends communal kitchens.... He knows it would be cheaper if a number of us ate at the same time, so as to use the same table. So it would. It would also be cheaper if a number of us slept at different times, so as to use the same pair of trousers. But the question is not how cheap are we buying a thing, but what are we buying? It is cheap to own a slave. And it is cheaper still to be a slave.

My correspondent also says that the habit of dining out in restaurants, etc., is growing. So, I believe, is the habit of committing suicide. I do not desire to connect the two facts together. It seems fairly clear that a man could not dine at a restaurant because he had just committed suicide; and it would be extreme perhaps, to suggest that he commits suicide because he has just dined at a restaurant. But the two cases when put side by side, are enough to indicate the falsity ... of this eternal modern argument from what is in fashion. The question for brave men is not whether a certain thing is increasing; the question is whether we are increasing it. I dine very often in restaurants because the nature of my trade makes it convenient: but if I thought that by dining in restaurants I was working for the creation of communal meals, I would never enter a restaurant again; I would carry bread and cheese in my pocket or eat chocolate out of automatic machines. For the personal element in some things is sacred. . . .

My correspondent says, "Would not our women be spared the drudgery of cooking and all its attendant worries, leaving them free for higher culture?". . . If my correspondent can find any way of preventing women from worrying, he will indeed be a remarkable man. I think the matter is a much deeper one. First of all, my correspondent overlooks a distinction which is elementary in our human nature. Theoretically, I suppose, every one would like to be freed from worries. But nobody in the world would always like to be freed from worrying occupations. I should very much like (as far as my feelings at the moment go) to be free from the consuming nuisance of writing this article. But it does not follow that I should like to be free from the consuming nuisance of being a journalist. Because we are worried about a thing, it does not follow that we are not interested in it. The truth is the other way. If we are not interested, why on earth should we be worried? Women are worried about housekeeping, but those that are most interested are the most worried. Women are still more worried about their husbands and their children. And I suppose if we strangled the children and poleaxed the husbands it would leave women free for higher culture. That is, it would leave them free to begin to worry about that. For women would worry about higher culture as much as they worry about everything else.

I believe this way of talking about women and their higher culture is almost entirely a growth of the classes which (unlike the journalistic class to which I belong) have always a reasonable amount of money. One odd thing I especially notice. Those who write like this seem entirely to forget the existence of the working and wage-earning classes. They say eternally, like my correspondent, that the ordinary woman is always a drudge. And what, in the name of the Nine Gods, is the ordinary man? These people seem to think that the ordinary man is a Cabinet Minister. They are always talking about man going forth to wield power, to carve his own way, to stamp his individuality on the world, to command and to be obeyed. This may be true of a certain class. Dukes, perhaps, are not drudges; but, then, neither are Duchesses. The Ladies and Gentlemen of the Smart Set are quite free for the higher culture, which consists chiefly of motoring and Bridge. But the ordinary man who typifies and constitutes the millions that make up our civilisation is no more free for the higher culture than his wife is.

Indeed, he is not so free. Of the two sexes the woman is in the more powerful position. For the average woman is at the head of something with which she can do as she likes; the average man has to obey orders and do nothing else. He has to put one dull brick on another dull brick, and do nothing else; he has to add one dull figure to another dull figure, and do nothing else. The woman's world is a small one, perhaps, but she can alter it. The woman can tell the tradesman with whom she deals some realistic things about himself. The clerk who does this to the manager generally gets the sack, or shall we say (to avoid the vulgarism), finds himself free for higher culture. Above all ... the woman does work which is in some small degree creative and individual. She can put the flowers or the furniture in fancy arrangements of her own. I fear the bricklayer cannot put the bricks in fancy arrangements of his own, without disaster to himself and others. If the woman is only putting a patch into a carpet, she can choose the thing with regard to colour. I fear it would not do for the office boy dispatching a parcel to choose his stamps with a view to colour; to prefer the tender mauve of the sixpenny to the crude scarlet of the penny stamp. A woman cooking may not always cook artistically; still she can cook artistically. She can introduce a personal and imperceptible alteration into the composition of a soup. The clerk is not encouraged to introduce a personal and imperceptible alteration into the figures in a ledger. . . .

And then the higher culture. I know that culture. I would not set any man free for it if I could help it. . . . The higher culture is sad, cheap, impudent, unkind, without honesty and without ease. In short, it is "high.". . . Do not ask them now to sink so low as the higher culture.[1]

Chesterton says that a fad is like a heresy. It is the exaltation of something that, even if it is true, is secondary or temporary. And it is set against the things that are essential and eternal.[2]

Our society is plagued with one fad or fashion after another. They are usually recognized by how short-lived they are. Like leisure suits. Or pet rocks. But some fads

[1] *ILN*, April 7, 1906, and later reprinted as "Woman", in *All Things Considered* and anthologized many times since.

[2] See *William Blake* (London: House of Stratus, 2000), 47.

have slightly deeper roots and hang on longer, like a pernicious sort of weed. They are still temporary even if they are long-lived. How can they can be recognized? Because they attack or undermine or mock the permanent things. And one of the permanent things is the family. It is the basic unit of any solid society. Chesterton defends the sacred walls of the home against all the fashionable ideas that attempt to beat them down. He is constantly trying to get us to see past the contemporary trends that seem so urgent, and to look at first principles, which are far more important.

> We shall never return to social sanity till we begin at the beginning. We must start where all history starts, with a man and a woman, and a child, and with the province of liberty and property which these need for their full humanity. As it is, we begin where history ends.... We judge everything by the particular muddle of the moment.[3]

There are few fads that typify the "muddle of the moment" more than feminism. Feminists seize on a few tiny truths—the fact that men in general have greater professional opportunities than women, the fact that some women have certainly been used and abused by some men—and they emphasize these all out of proportion. They talk about "how far" women have come, even while they rail that they "have not come far enough". How far they expect to go is never quite made clear. Equality is sometimes the obscure goal mentioned, with the ideal apparently being that women should play football.

Chesterton says that it may be sensational for a woman to discover the North Pole, even after it has already been

[3] *ILN*, May 3, 1919.

discovered,[4] and for women to succeed in all the exotic professions that have traditionally been dominated by men, but apart from the sensationalism, which bulks big in the newspapers, the fact remains: the vast majority of *men* don't succeed at those things either. Most women who are "freed" from domestic life are wage earners in shops and factories and office buildings, just like most men. "Our present civilization", says Chesterton, "is far too much a civilization of clerks and office stools." [5] In any case, it is really no great accomplishment for a woman to do what a man can do. It is fairly obvious that a woman has always been able to do all the things a man can do. But what is much more obvious—and much more ignored, the way common sense is ignored—is that there is one thing a woman can do that a man cannot do: be a mother. And that seems to be the main complaint of feminists: that women are mothers and men aren't. As Chesterton says, they "support what is feminist against what is feminine." [6]

The feminists claim they want the woman to have more influence in society, and then they take her away from the place where she has the greatest of all influence in society: the home. They exalt public, professional life over private, domestic life. But fads are what fill public life: glitter and fuss and an emphasis on all the things that are false. Public life is fragmented, narrow, and temporary. Private life—that is, family life—is full and universal and even a reflection of eternity.[7]

There could not be a community in which the average woman was in command of a ship. But there can be a

[4] See *ILN*, December 18, 1926.
[5] *ILN*, September 4, 1920.
[6] *ILN*, August 5, 1922.
[7] See *ILN*, August 12, 1922.

community in which the average woman is in command of
a house. To take a hundred women out of a hundred houses
and give them a hundred ships would be obviously impossible. To take the hundred women out of a hundred houses
and put them on two ships is obviously to increase the number of servants and decrease the number of mistresses [or
lady captains]. . . . The principle applies as much to a shop
as to a ship. A shop or factory must consist of a very large
majority of servants; and one of the few human institutions
in which there need be no such enormous majority of servants is the human household. . . .

The place where babies are born, where men die, where
the daily drama of mortal life is acted, is not an office or
shop or a bureau. It is something much smaller in size, yet
much larger in scope. And while nobody would be such a
fool as to pretend that the home is the only place where
people should work, or even the only place where women
should work, it has a character of unity and universality
that is not found in any of the fragmentary experiences of
the office or the shop or the bureau.[8]

In our society, we hear endless talk about the importance
of education. But we somehow manage to forget that the
primary place of education is the home. Chesterton says,
"If education is the largest thing in the world, what is
the sense of talking about a woman being liberated from
the largest thing in the world?"[9] In other words, if
education is really as important as we say it is, then certainly domestic life is more important than we currently
make it out to be, and everything else, especially public
life and commercial life, is less important than we hold it
up to be.

[8] *ILN*, December 18, 1926.
[9] *ILN*, August 5, 1922.

Human culture is handed down in the customs of countless households; it is the only way in which human culture can remain fully human. The households are right to confess a common loyalty to some king or republic. But the king cannot be the nurse in every nursery, and the government cannot become the governess in every schoolroom.[10]

The main legacy of feminism has been the breakup of the family (and the growth of government and commercial enterprises, which have swept in to replace the family). In truth, there is an almost direct connection between the rise of feminism and the rise of what is called "the nanny state": as women retreat from the family, the government intrudes into it. As women indict men, government seeks to usurp the place of men. Government has insinuated itself into every aspect of private life, most especially and most insidiously into the lives of our children. Hardly anything compares with the rapid growth of the day-care industry, or, as some observers have called it, "day orphanages".

And who benefits? Women? Of course not. Most women, just like most men, are working in servile jobs, largely separated from their families. Only the elite classes benefit. In government, an elite class stays in power by pandering to the feminist voting block. In industry, an elite class of big business owners can pay lower wages because women are competing for the same jobs as men, either because they are single parents or because both parents are compelled to work, or at least feel compelled to work—or at least manage to convince themselves that they both must work.

Too many of us take all this for granted today. We assume it is part of the permanent landscape. And yet it really is a fad, and no fad is permanent. Most fads are foisted on us

[10] *Sidelights, CW* 21:519.

by powerful commercial interests. Chesterton says that an industrial society cannot create customs, only fashions.[11] This is a sign of instability and discontent in a culture. Because every fashion flees. Every fashion is a failure. We brag about a "free market economy", but the fact is that we can only buy what we are told to buy, not what we might actually want to buy. And this is true not only of clothes and candy and the things that fill our bodies, but especially true of music and movies and the things that fill our heads.

There is no excuse for the utter garbage that is being produced and promoted by our entertainment industry. Chesterton says, "There is a real sin in being as bad as your society; but it is not the same sin as that of being deliberately worse than your society." [12] When the chief purveyor of fads is the entertainment industry, it creates a downward spiral when it deliberately tries to be worse than the society it is constantly making worse.

Chesterton's understanding of the power of motion pictures is, well, visionary. But it is a deeper insight as well that goes beyond merely what is on the screen.

> The just and reasonable criticism of the cinema is not a criticism of the cinema, but of the whole of the diseased industrial society that produces it.[13]

Cinema prevails over our private entertainments not because it is great art but because it is big business. And we all know that. But rather than keeping us away from the theaters, it seems that is what pulls us in. Chesterton says prophetically, "Many modern people have a sort of

[11] See *ILN*, June 26, 1926.
[12] *ILN*, March 14, 1908.
[13] *ILN*, June 19, 1920.

imaginative reverence for a thing not only because a lot of money is got out of it, but merely because a lot of money is put into it." [14] And he says we will not be free so long as we depend on a magic machine for the emotional thrills it gives us of watching other people fall off precipices or rescuing brides from burning houses. Freedom means a citizen takes an interest in his own wife and in his own home. "A free man will fall off his own private precipice." [15]

The whole concept of entertainment being an "industry" shows how far we have strayed from being a healthy and self-sufficient society.

> Men in a state of decadence employ professionals to fight for them, professionals to dance for them, and a professional to rule them. [16]

We have become incapable of entertaining ourselves. And so we must be entertained. And incapable of governing ourselves, we must be governed. And incapable of thinking for ourselves, Chesterton says, we rely on "a class of men richer and more cunning and more scientific" than ourselves. [17]

When we become passive, we lose our freedom. Freedom is something active and alive. And it means standing up and opposing the fads and fashions that would sweep us away. As Chesterton says, "A dead thing can go with the stream, but only a living thing can go against it." [18]

[14] *ILN*, October 8, 1921.
[15] *ILN*, June 19, 1920.
[16] *Twelve Types* (Norfolk, Va.: IHS Press, 2003), 49.
[17] *ILN*, June 19, 1920.
[18] *The Everlasting Man*, *CW* 2:388.

It is the traditional things, the permanent things, that have always kept men free. Family and faith and friends. Chesterton says, tradition is the truth of the common people. It is always distrusted by snobs.[19]

It is the snobs who sneer at our values and at our common sense. For instance, in the past few years we have seen an open conspiracy among the elites in the entertainment industry to portray homosexuality as something normal and natural. This is in absolute defiance of the common sense of common people.

> Decadents may like living in a dream which they can alter at any moment to suit themselves, in which they can create causes without creating consequences, in which they can pervert the future or unmake the past. But I think a decent working man of any class, whether he is working at cube roots or cabbage roots, ought to be glad that, as he sows, so shall he surely reap.[20]

The homosexual fad—and yes, it is a fad—is another attack on the family, and it has to do with the same argument about feminism. There is a difference between men and women and there is a reason for that difference. They have distinct roles, even while our society tries to muddle what those distinct roles are. The problem today, says Chesterton, is that each sex is trying to be both sexes at once; "and the result is a confusion more untruthful than any conventions".[21]

Not only are the differences between men and women obvious and elemental; they are, well, necessary. If Chesterton exaggerates the differences between men and women,

[19] See *ILN*, September 18, 1926.
[20] *ILN*, March 21, 1914.
[21] *The Victorian Age in Literature*, *CW* 15:468.

it is because only the truth can be exaggerated. Nothing else, he says, can stand the strain.[22] So Chesterton emphasizes those amazing differences between men and women as being quite necessary for true romantic love.

> The differences between a man and a woman are at best so obstinate and exasperating that they practically cannot be got over unless there is an atmosphere of exaggerated tenderness and mutual interest. To put the matter in one metaphor, the sexes are two stubborn pieces of iron; if they are to be welded together, it must be while they are red-hot. Every woman has to find out that her husband is a selfish beast, because every man is a selfish beast by the standard of a woman. But let her find out the best while they are both still in the story of "Beauty and the Beast." Every man has to find out that his wife is cross—that is to say, sensitive to the point of madness; for every woman is mad by the masculine standard. But let him find out that she is mad while her madness is more worth considering than anyone else's sanity.[23]

Worldly wisdom is narrow and limited, and it passes away.[24] But fads and fashions have also found their way into the place that should be least susceptible to such fleeting phenomena: the Church. There are always attempts to "update" the Faith, as if eternal truth can somehow go out of date. These schemes always have secular sources. They are always an attempt to get the Church to follow the world, not the other way around.

> The new theologians often say that the old creeds need re-statement; but though they say it, they do not mean it.

---

[22] See *Charles Dickens*, *CW* 15:145.

[23] *The Common Man* (New York: Sheed and Ward, 1950), 142–43.

[24] See *ILN*, August 7, 1920.

They mean exactly the opposite. They do not mean that
we should find new words to express the exact meaning of
the old doctrines. They mean that we should say old words,
but agree they mean something entirely different.[25]

Chesterton says, "There will be no end to the weary debates
about liberalising theology, until people face the fact that
the only liberal part of it is really the dogmatic part."[26]
The liberalizing dogma is that God created creatures with
free will, that we are really responsible for our actions and
can make the right choices if we want to. The liberalizing
dogma is that God became a man and died for our sins.
The liberalizing dogma is that we can know the truth. And
it is only the truth that can set us free.

---

[25] *ILN*, July 3, 1920.
[26] *The Everlasting Man*, *CW* 2:373.

12

The "D" Word

G. K. Chesterton loved to argue politics. Once, when he was a young man, he and a friend went out canvassing during an election, and each agreed to work one side of a street, going to each house and asking the residents to vote for a particular candidate. His friend went to all the houses on his side of the street and realized that Chesterton had not kept pace, so he crossed the street and started working his way back up the other side, figuring he would soon meet Chesterton. He didn't find him until he reached the very first house, where Chesterton was still arguing politics with the person who lived there.

If we open any of his books, we are surprised to find that Chesterton is still arguing about politics. He is still defending democracy, and still reminding us that just as Christianity means more than just going to church, so democracy means more than just going to vote. Democracy means that people should truly have the opportunity to govern their own affairs. The reason he is a great defender of democracy is that he is a great defender of the common man—and common sense. He says that when someone says that democracy is false because most people are stupid, the best and most philosophical response "is to hit him smartly and with precision on the exact tip of the nose".[1] Chesterton believes that the common sense of the common man is more trustworthy, more practical, and more just than any system run by "the corrupt and evasive muddlers who are called practical politicians".[2] "A democracy", he says, "is a strange sort of place, where politics could be conducted even without politicians." [3]

> The essence of democracy is very simple and, as Jefferson said, self-evident. If ten men are wrecked together on a desert island, the community consists of those ten men, their welfare is the social object, and normally their will is the social law. If they have not a natural claim to rule themselves, which of them has a natural claim to rule the rest? To say that the cleverest or boldest will rule is to beg the moral question. If his talents are used for the community, in planning voyages or distilling water, then he is the servant of the community; which is, in that sense, his sovereign. If his talents are used against the community by stealing rum or poisoning water, why should the community submit to him? and is it in the least likely that it will? In such a simple case as that, everybody can see the popular basis of the thing, and the advantage of government by consent. The trouble with democracy is that it has never, in modern times, had to do with such a simple case as that. In other words, the trouble with democracy is not democracy. It is certain artificial anti-democratic things that have, in fact, thrust themselves into the modern world to thwart and destroy democracy.[4]

[1] *Alarms and Discursions* (New York: Dodd, Mead, 1911), 76.
[2] *The Well and the Shallows*, *CW* 3:496.
[3] *ILN*, November 17, 1923.
[4] *ILN*, July 16, 1932.

All government, says Chesterton, is an "ugly necessity".[5]
And so is commerce. But if either of these two ugly neces-
sities grow too large, they become enemies of democracy.
The people no longer control them; they control the people.

Most of us are all too familiar with the problems caused
by excessive government. Chesterton says the problem with
government is that it has become ungovernable; "it cannot
leave off governing. Law has become lawless; it cannot see
where laws should stop. The chief feature of our time is
the meekness of the mob and the madness of the government."[6] The growth of governmental power has really gone
beyond our ability to comprehend it. For instance, nothing
compares with the power the State has when it controls
what can and cannot be taught to our children.

> The State did not own men so entirely, even when it could
> send them to the stake, as it sometimes does now where it
> can send them to the elementary school.[7]

As for big business, Chesterton admits that in all normal
civilizations the trader existed and must exist. "But," he
says, "in all normal civilisations the trader was the exception; certainly he was never the rule; and most certainly he
was never the ruler. The predominance he has gained in
the modern world is the cause of all the disasters of the
modern world."[8]

While we have rightly understood communism to be an
enemy of democracy, we have been far too quick to assume
that capitalism is necessarily the friend of democracy. Democracy has to do with how we govern ourselves, not how we

[5] *A Short History of England*, *CW* 20:483.
[6] *Eugenics and Other Evils*, *CW* 4:349.
[7] *The Well and the Shallows*, *CW* 3:507.
[8] Ibid., 497–98.

earn a living—or how a few of us create wealth. Now, the basic philosophy of capitalism is based on the writings of Adam Smith, whose main idea is that self-interest and virtue are not necessarily in conflict. Karl Marx rejected capitalism, and, in doing so, he tried to throw out both self-interest and virtue. Chesterton, however, simply points out that the weakness of capitalism is that you cannot have a virtuous system that is based on a vice, and the weakness of both the systems of Adam Smith and Karl Marx is that they reduce all of human behavior to a totally materialistic explanation. Both capitalism and communism manipulate the masses and disregard that key factor that is not only the great variable, but is also the essence of human dignity: free will. Chesterton says, "The Capitalists praise competition while they create monopoly and the Socialists urge a strike," just so that they can turn every working man into a state official.[9]

Chesterton points out that many of the things we call democracy are not democracy. Machinery is not democracy; the surrender of everything to trade and commerce is not democracy; capitalism is not democracy; and plutocracy by definition is not democracy. He suggests that the democratic ideal may be too idealist to succeed and that, in fact, democracy has had everything against it in practice, and that very fact may be something against it in theory. But he insists that the problem with democracy is not that it has human life against it, but that it has modern life against it.

There are many men now beginning to say that the democratic ideal is no longer in touch with the modern spirit.

[9] *The New Jerusalem, CW* 20:196.

I strongly agree ... except that I prefer the democratic ideal
to the modern spirit.... It is the cranks who are hastening
to shed the democratic ideal. They go so far as to say, "The
voice of the people is commonly the voice of Satan." The
truth is that these Liberals never did really believe in popular government, any more than in anything else that was
popular, such as pubs or the Dublin Sweepstakes. They did
not believe in the democracy they invoked against kings
and priests. But I did believe in it; and I do believe in it,
though I much preferred to invoke it against prigs and fad-
dists. I still believe it would be the most human sort of
government, if it could be once more attempted in a more
human time.

Unfortunately, humanitarianism has been the mark of an
inhuman time. And by inhumanity I do not mean merely
cruelty; I mean the condition in which even cruelty ceases
to be human. I mean the condition in which the rich man,
instead of hanging six or seven of his enemies because he
hates them, merely beggars and starves to death six or seven
thousand people whom he does not hate, and has never
seen, because they live at the other side of the world. I
mean the condition in which the courtier ... of the rich
man, instead of excitedly mixing a rare, original poison for
the Borgias ... works monotonously in a factory turning
out a small type of screw, which will fit into a plate he will
never see; to form part of a gun he will never see; to be
used in a battle he will never see.[10]

The problem with industrialism, according to Chesterton,
is its complexity and indirection; "the fact that nothing is
straightforward; that all its ways are crooked even when they
are meant to be straight. Into this most indirect of all systems we tried to fit the most direct of all ideas, Democracy,

[10] *ILN*, July 16, 1932.

an ideal which is simple to excess", but which has been applied to a society "which is complex to the point of craziness".[11] He understands how in this environment, the vision of democracy has faded. But he still likes the vision.

The maxim of democracy is *Vox Populi Vox Dei*: The Voice of the People is the Voice of God. To Chesterton, this is not a maxim we have ever been in any danger of overdoing, because, quite frankly, we have profoundly lost faith in both entities. But he says, "There is one sense in which the voice of the people is really like the voice of God; and that is that most of us take precious little notice of it."[12]

When we say "the People", what do we mean? It is important to understand that the basic unit of society is the family. The enemies of democracy are the enemies of the family. The enemies of democracy use democracy as a catchword, but they emphasize "individual rights", not "family rights", and individual rights do nothing but atomize society, isolating each person from one another and then regrouping them according to interests that are usually limited or strange but always secondary and always against the primary interests of the family. Chesterton says, "Without the family we are helpless before the state."[13]

If we elevate individual rights over the family, we end up giving all the power in a society to government and to industry because the individual will be dependent on one or both of those entities and will ironically lose all his independence and liberty, even while affirming his so-called rights. For democracy to work, the family must be recognized as the primary unit of society and the primary focus

[11] Ibid.
[12] *ILN*, September 9, 1911.
[13] *The Superstition of Divorce, CW* 4:242.

of society. Anything "for the good of society" means for the good of the family—for that unit of husband and wife and children, for their home and their happiness. If the family is subordinate to any other interest, we do not have a democracy. This great insight of Chesterton is something that Adam Smith never grasped and Karl Marx openly warred against.

Chesterton, of course, does not deny that we also have a responsibility to our next-door neighbors and our community. With them we share a mutual interest in the maintenance of local rights and liberties. From there interests widen to the outer circles of regional, national, and foreign affairs. But the pivotal point is the home. The home is the "true dominion, the true symbol of authority" [14] for the whole State. In other words, democracy is bottom up, not top down.

> Politicians now think they have to educate the electorate and explain to them what is good for them. Gone are the days when the electorate educated their representatives . . . with the certainty that if no result were forthcoming . . . neither would any further votes be forthcoming.[15]

Democracy can work only in those places where the population is not dependent on a huge governmental machine or on a huge industrial machine. The majority of the people have to be self-employed, not wage slaves. As Chesterton says, "The alternative to employment is not unemployment, but independence." [16] That is what freedom is: independence, which brings with it responsibility, just as self-employment brings

[14] *G. K.'s Weekly*, March 30, 1933.
[15] Ibid.
[16] *G. K.'s Weekly*, February 2, 1929.

responsibility. Responsibility requires self-control. An economy *should* be based on self-control. The very word "economy" has to do with thriftiness. Chesterton says, "Self-denial is the test and definition of self-government." [17] And, of course, the literal meaning of the word "economy" is to manage or look after a house. Modern economics has utterly lost sight of this fundamental idea.

> The old order has been reversed. The people, instead of surveying the world from their doorsteps, survey their mortgaged doorsteps through a vague and hazy mental screen compounded by international misunderstanding and national mistrust. . . .
> The disintegration of rational society started in the drift from the hearth and the family; the solution must be a drift back. [18]

Self-government begins by thinking for ourselves and acting for ourselves: doing the basic things like writing our own love letters and blowing our own noses. There are some things that simply should not be done by someone else. If we let the specialists do these things, if we lose our self-reliance, we lose democracy. One of Chesterton's best examples of direct democracy in action, that is, of not trusting the specialist with fundamental things, is the jury system:

> Our civilization has decided, and very justly decided, that determining the guilt or innocence of men is a thing too important to be trusted to trained men. If it wishes for light upon that awful matter, it asks men who know no more law than I know. . . . When it wants a library catalogued, or the solar system discovered, or any trifles of that kind, it

[17] *Alarms and Discursions*, 193.
[18] *G. K.'s Weekly*, March 30, 1933.

uses up its specialists. But when it wishes anything done
which is really serious, it collects twelve of the ordinary
men standing round. The same thing was done, if I remember right, by the Founder of Christianity.[19]

One of Chesterton's most famous and most misunderstood
(and misapplied) lines is, "A thing worth doing is worth
doing badly." [20] The point he is trying to make is that an
amateur does something because he loves to do it, not necessarily because he is the best at doing it. The professional
may be better, but the professional is doing it for money,
not for love. The larger point is that the rise of the specialist coincides with the demise of democracy and the demise
of the family. By not doing things for ourselves we lose
control over our lives, we lose our freedom. We become
passive and weak and out of control. When that happens
we are then controlled by big outside forces, by the dem-
agogues of big government and big business who play to
our weaknesses, our passions, and our fears. Chesterton would
much rather see what he unhesitatingly calls "mob rule".
Mob rule, he says, is democracy in its purest form.

> I believe that the people can rule, and that when they do
> rule, they do so better than any of their rulers. Even where
> they are unjustly forbidden to rule, and appear only to dis-
> solve and destroy, I am disposed to defend them; I believe
> no human institution in history has really so little to be
> ashamed of as the mob.[21]

The reason we do not have mob rule is because there is no
mob. We have been successfully isolated from one another

[19] *Tremendous Trifles* (New York: Sheed and Ward, 1955), 58.
[20] *What's Wrong with the World*, *CW* 4:199.
[21] *North American Review*, April, 1918.

(and from our past). In general, we don't trust the common man to govern himself because we don't trust ourselves to govern ourselves. We have delegated the responsibility to others: to experts, to bureaucrats, to professors and politicians, to fashions and to fools. Common sense has come under attack by uncommon nonsense. We have lost common sense because we have lost what we once held in common. We have cut ourselves off from our common heritage, and from each other. It has left us passive about things that matter (like our family and our faith), and left us passionate about things that don't matter (like entertainment and sports and money).

Democracy is possible only if people are directly involved in the things that most concern their lives. If there is widespread ownership of property and of production and of capital, then there is little opportunity for outside control or oppression from outside forces. There is no foothold for the twin enemies of democracy: big government and big business.

But we live by the wage. Whether we work for the government or for a huge corporation, we live by the wage. This is not to be confused with freedom. Wage slavery is still slavery. It may provide a few creature comforts, but a wage slave is even more disposable than a slave. Wage slavery creates a huge class of people that are utterly dependent on big business for employment and on the government for supplemental support. This system is what Chesterton's friend Hilaire Belloc calls "The Servile State". And Chesterton argues that such a system "is totally inconsistent with the free family and is bound to destroy it".[22] I suppose another way of saying it is that the sin of wages is death.

[22] *What's Wrong with the World*, *CW* 4:214.

In order for democracy actually to work, or, as Chesterton says, if actual political power is to pass to the ordinary citizen, then land and capital must pass to the ordinary citizen.[23] In other words—and you may have been expecting this—the D word is also Distributism. Chesterton says, Property is the art of democracy.[24] Property is the positive form of liberty. Nowadays many of us think only of the negative form of liberty. Freedom "against" or freedom "from", instead of freedom "for". Freedom "for" means that a person has the *means* to live a normal, healthy life, unencumbered by bureaucrat or corporate control, but, more importantly, not dependent on those twin taskmasters.

> Our society is so abnormal that the normal man never dreams of having the normal occupation of looking after his own property. When he chooses a trade, he chooses one of the ten thousand trades that involve looking after other people's property.[25]

We have seen a steady decline of craftsmanship and a steady rise of the "service" industry. Chesterton says this is "like so many modern notions, it is an idolatry of the intermediate, to the oblivion of the ultimate.... All these silly words like Service and Efficiency and Practicality and the rest fail because they worship the means and not the end."[26] And what is the end? In politics and economics, the goal, quite simply, is human happiness. Chesterton says, "There is no obligation on us to be richer, or busier, or more efficient, or more productive, or progressive, or in

---

[23] See *ILN*, July 5, 1924.
[24] See *What's Wrong with the World*, CW 4:66.
[25] *Commonweal*, October 12, 1932.
[26] *The Thing*, CW 3:139–40.

any way worldlier or wealthier if it does not make us happier." [27]

> An honest man falls in love with an honest woman; he wishes, therefore, to marry her, to be the father of her children, to secure her and himself. All systems of government should be tested by whether he can do this. If any system— feudal, servile, or barbaric—does, in fact, give him so large a cabbage-field that he can do it, there is the essence of liberty and justice. If any system—Republican, mercantile, or Eugenist—does, in fact, give him so small a salary that he can't do it, there is the essence of eternal tyranny and shame. [28]

A society can only continue to decline when it is so indifferent to the consequences of wage slavery, to the incredible gaps between the rich and the poor, and so willing to create a welfare state that it encourages the destruction of families. Such a society has forgotten first principles, namely that the family is more important than the State, but also more important than the factory or the office. Chesterton says that "the iron of frustration" has entered people's souls:

> They nourish grievances yet no one will stand up and demand the rational remedy of a return to rational first principles. [29]

G. K. Chesterton devoted a great part of his life, especially in his later years when time was very precious, to trying to bring social and economic justice to the world. And his emphasis was always on trying to get people to think clearly, to see first principles. And Chesterton understands that

---

[27] *The Outline of Sanity, CW* 5:145.
[28] *ILN*, March 25, 1911.
[29] *G. K.'s Weekly*, March 30, 1933.

ultimately every political question is also a theological question. He seeks to define these things clearly because, as he says, "We cannot be vague about what we believe in, what we are willing to fight for, and to die for." [30]

Democracy, he admits, is always difficult, but only a Christian society has the fixed principles to face those difficulties.[31] To make a democracy work, we have to face honestly the problems of injustice. Chesterton reminds us very pointedly: "God Himself will not help us ignore evil, but only to defy and to defeat it." [32]

There are some people who are very concerned about politics and insist that religion doesn't matter, just as there are some who are very concerned about religion and insist that politics don't matter. But both matter. Just like both of the two great commandments matter and must always go together: love God and love your neighbor.

---

[30] *Daily News*, September 28, 1907.
[31] Ibid.
[32] *ILN*, April 14, 1917.

13

Puritans and Pagans

There are two kinds of people: those who divide people into two categories, and those who do not. G. K. Chesterton is in the first group. The two basic categories he divides people into are those who get things right, and those who do not. But the people who get things wrong he also divides into two categories, because generally they get things wrong for opposite reasons. For instance, the optimist and pessimist. Chesterton says the optimist thinks everything is good except the pessimist, and the pessimist thinks everything is bad except himself.[1]

> No man would be tempted to be a pessimist except by the optimist. Neither of the terms corresponds to any clear thought. But as things are at present, the pessimist is a man who thinks little and thinks wrong, and the optimist a man who refuses to think at all.[2]

Another false dichotomy between two groups of people who both get things wrong, but who have pitted themselves against each other, are the liberals and the conservatives.

[1] See *Orthodoxy, CW* 1:269.
[2] *ILN*, May 20, 1922.

The liberals call themselves "progressive" but cannot say what they are progressing toward, and neither can the conservatives say exactly what it is they are conserving.

> The whole modern world has divided itself into Conservatives and Progressives. The business of Progressives is to go on making mistakes. The business of the Conservatives is to prevent the mistakes being corrected.[3]

Similarly, the socialists and the capitalists are against each other, but both are against what is right, albeit for opposite reasons. Both are against the widespread ownership of property, and therefore widespread liberty and independence. Though they claim to be different, in the end, says Chesterton, big government and big business are exactly alike—especially big business.[4]

The problem, as Chesterton explains, is that when a society breaks up, as Christendom broke up at the Reformation, two things happen. The vices run wild and do damage, but, also, the virtues run wild and do even more damage, "because they are isolated from each other and are wandering alone". Thus truth is separated from justice, and there are the people on the right who care only for truth, and their truth is pitiless, and there are those on the left who care only for pity, and their pity is untruthful.[5]

There is another group of people who can be divided into two categories, who think they are against each other, when, in fact, both are against what is right. They are the puritans and the pagans. Chesterton deals extensively with

[3] *ILN*, April 19, 1924.
[4] See *G. K.'s Weekly*, April 10, 1926.
[5] See *Orthodoxy*, *CW* 1:233.

both of them throughout his writings because their errors are fundamental and pervasive in our society.

Puritanism is indignation about the things that don't matter.[6] Paganism is a devotion to things that don't matter. Puritanism is legalism. Paganism is license. Both lack the balance of common sense. The puritan tries to make innocent things seem guilty; the pagan tries to make guilty things seem innocent. What they have in common is that they are both reactions against the wholeness of the Catholic Faith, which is the only creed that protects both truth and liberty and keeps the proper balance between the two.

> A man's minor actions ought to be free, flexible, creative; the things that should be unchangeable are his principles, his ideals. But with us, the reverse is true; our views change constantly, but our lunch does not change.[7]

> What the wreckers of the medieval system really did, practically and in the long run, was to let loose some of the vices on the excuse of exterminating the others. After the Renaissance, the Pagans went in for unlimited lust and the Puritans for unlimited avarice; on the excuse that at least neither of them was being guilty of sloth.[8]

Let's take paganism first. There are two kinds of paganism: the ancient and the modern.

> It is often said by the critics of Christian origins that certain ritual feasts, processions or dances are really of pagan origin. They might as well say that our legs are of pagan origin. Nobody ever disputed that humanity was human

---

[6] Or, as Chesterton says, "righteous indignation about the wrong things". *New York Times*, November 21, 1930.

[7] *Tremendous Trifles* (New York: Sheed and Ward, 1955), 52.

[8] *Chaucer, CW* 18:330.

before it was Christian; and no Church manufactured the
legs with which men walked or danced, either in a pil-
grimage or a ballet. What can be maintained ... is this: that
where [the] church has existed it has *preserved* not only the
processions but the dances; not only the cathedral but the
carnival. One of the chief claims of Christian civilisation is
to have preserved things of pagan origin. In short, in the
old religious countries men *continue* to dance; while in the
new scientific cities they are content to drudge....

[W]hen this saner view of history is realized, there does
remain something more mystical and difficult to define. Even
heathen things are Christian when they have been preserved by Christianity.[9]

The heathen things preserved by Christianity include
chivalry, fidelity, charity, virtue, patriotism, the nature of
a vow. Christianity "christened" a pagan world, christened its temples and its traditions. There are cynics (and
puritans) who try to claim that Christmas and Easter are
of pagan origin, because pagans had midwinter feasts
and spring festivals. But Christmas and Easter are precisely
the things that changed paganism forever and why the
world can never return to the ancient form of paganism.
Christianity changed all that.[10] The modern form of paganism is a rejection of Christianity and can even be seen as
an attempt to return to a pre-Christian understanding of
the world, but that is impossible. The world can never be
pre-Christian again.

When G. K. Chesterton stood in the city of Rome, he
looked around him and saw quite clearly the distinctive connection between paganism and Christianity: it was not that

[9] *The Superstition of Divorce, CW* 4:264.
[10] See *ILN*, December 24, 1921.

paganism led to Christianity, but that paganism ended in
Christianity.

> What is to be done with the dingy and inky little people
> who laboriously prove to us that Christianity (if they are
> atheists) or Catholicism (if they are Protestants) is "only" a
> rehash of Paganism or borrowed its ideas from the Pagans?
> A man standing here in Rome is reduced to silence; he can
> only answer that such stupidity is stupefying. It is rather as
> if somebody said that Science may pretend to be indepen-
> dent, but it has really stolen all its facts from Nature; or
> that Protestants professed to be Christians, and yet filched
> things from the sacred books of the Jews. Science boasts of
> being based on Nature; and Protestants, when they were
> Protestants, boasted of being based on the Bible. Christian
> Rome boasts of being built on Pagan Rome; of surmount-
> ing and transcending, but also of preserving it.[11]

The new paganism is not a return but a decline, a deca-
dence.[12] The old pagans had clear ideas that could be stated
as a connected train of thought. The moderns who call
themselves pagans have no connected theory of life that
can be explained.[13] The old pagans had a reverence for nature
and understood that there was some great force behind it.
They were, as Chesterton says, among the few people who
could really "take Nature naturally".[14] The new pagans, however, worship nature itself, apart from God. But "take away
the supernatural and what remains is the unnatural".[15] The
old pagans may have had an emphasis on sex, but at least it

[11] *The Resurrection of Rome, CW* 21:357.
[12] See "A Century of Emancipation", in *The Well and the Shallows, CW* 3.
[13] See *ILN*, September 13, 1930.
[14] *Victorian Age in Literature, CW* 15:481.
[15] *Heretics, CW* 1:88.

was connected to fertility, which is natural. The new pagan "exalts lust, but forbids fertility", which is very unnatural.[16]

How did this happen? The old pagans were not atheists. They felt the presence of some power and they guessed about its personality. Chesterton says it was "an attempt to reach the divine reality through the imagination alone".[17] It was religion unconnected to reason.

It is natural to worship. But if we do not worship the true God, we will worship something else. The new pagan, with his nature worship, is always in danger of worshipping something unnatural, including the most unnatural thing of all: the devil.[18] In reflecting on the famous Gospel story about Jesus casting out a demon, Chesterton says that in the modern world, "we have left out nothing except the Redeemer, we have kept the devils and the swine."[19]

Men will eventually do the most disgusting thing they can think of, such as cannibalism or sexual perversion. Why? Chesterton says, "They are not doing it because they do not think it wrong, but precisely because they do think it wrong."[20]

> Pessimism is not in being tired of evil but in being tired of good. Despair does not lie in being weary of suffering, but in being weary of joy. It is when for some reason or other the good things in a society no longer work that the society begins to decline; when its food does not feed, when its cures do not cure, when its blessings refuse to bless. . . . The weaknesses in nature-worship and mere mythology . . . produced a perversion among the Greeks. . . . Just as they

[16] *The Well and the Shallows, CW* 3:502.
[17] *The Everlasting Man, CW* 2:242.
[18] See *ILN*, October 29, 1921.
[19] *The New Jerusalem, CW* 20:328.
[20] *The Everlasting Man, CW* 2:251.

became unnatural by worshipping nature, so they actually became unmanly by worshipping man.[21]

I do not believe that mythology must begin with eroticism. But I do believe that mythology must end in it. I am quite certain that mythology did end in it. Moreover, not only did the poetry grow more immoral, but the immorality grew more indefensible. Greek vices, oriental vices, hints of the old horrors of the Semitic demons, began to fill the fancies of decaying Rome, swarming like flies on a dungheap. The psychology of it is really human enough, to anyone who will try that experiment of seeing history from the inside. There comes an hour in the afternoon when the child is tired of "pretending"; when he is weary of being a robber or a Red Indian. It is then that he torments the cat. There comes a time in the routine of an ordered civilisation when the man is tired at playing at mythology and pretending that a tree is a maiden or that the moon made love to a man. The effect of this staleness is the same everywhere; it is seen in all drug-taking and dram-drinking and every form of the tendency to increase the dose. Men seek stranger sins or more startling obscenities as stimulants to their jaded sense. They seek after mad oriental religions for the same reason. They try to stab their nerves to life, if it were with the knives of the priests of Baal. They are walking in their sleep and try to wake themselves up with nightmares.[22]

The good thing about the old paganism, as noted earlier, is that it led to Christianity. But the new paganism leads nowhere. It represents a world without God, the world we make for ourselves if left to ourselves. It is not a paradise of

[21] Ibid, 285–86.
[22] Ibid, 291. Yes, the latter part of this passage was in chapter 2. Though Chesterton wrote millions of words without repeating himself, I cannot write a few hundred without repeating Chesterton.

pleasure that the new pagans would like to think it is. As Chesterton says, "Pleasure-seeking is not pleasure-finding." [23] The world we make for ourselves without God is something dark and dreadful and doomed. It lacks faith, it lacks hope, it lacks charity.

Now there are two reactions against paganism: a right one and a wrong one. Let's talk about the wrong one. Let's talk about puritanism. The problem with the puritans is that they attack the pleasures of the pagans, which are only the pleasures of all mankind, good things that can be abused like all the good things that God created. It was the abuse of those pleasures that led to puritanism. But it was not a principled response; it was simply a mood. Chesterton says it was "an honourable mood ... a noble fad". But it was a mistake, even if it was "a highly creditable mistake".[24]

Chesterton compares puritanism with Manicheanism, which was a heresy attacked by St. Thomas Aquinas among others. The Manichees, much like the puritans, tried to portray the physical world as evil. It is the opposite mistake of the pagans, who worship nature and become unnatural. The puritans begin by denouncing everything natural as unnatural. They start by denouncing beer and tobacco and soon denounce tea and coffee. Chesterton imagines them eventually denouncing salt and pepper—and mustard, and any other "unnatural stimulants". The puritan is a "man whose mind has no holidays".[25]

We could say, no holy days. Chesterton does not attack puritans for their faith. He actually respects puritans for being

---

[23] *ILN*, December 9, 1922.
[24] *William Blake* (London: House of Stratus, 2000), 48.
[25] *George Bernard Shaw*, *CW* 11:378.

dogmatic, but he says puritanism is an enemy of righteousness, or, more subtly, a rival of righteousness.[26] "The puritan substituted a God who wished to damn people for a
God who wished to save them."[27] Puritans destroyed saints
but encouraged belief in witches.[28] Their conscious Christianity is nearly always some "shallow business about whether
there are any cigarettes in the Bible, but their unconscious
Christianity is not shallow but very deep indeed."[29] Deep,
but not very broad. It is a great narrowing and a diminish-
ing of the wholeness of the Catholic Faith.

Chesterton says that the puritan believes it is better to
worship in a barn than in a cathedral for the specific reason
that the cathedral is beautiful. Physical beauty is regarded as
a false and sensual symbol coming in between the intellect
and the object of its intellectual worship. This is the essential puritan idea, that God can be praised with only your
brain; it is wicked to praise him with your passions or your
physical habits or your gestures or your instincts of beauty.
Therefore it is wicked to worship by singing or dancing or
drinking sacramental wines or building beautiful churches
or repeating magnificent prayers. We must not worship by
dancing, drinking, building, or singing; we can only worship by thinking. Our heads can praise God, but never our
hands and feet. That is the true impulse of puritanism, and
there is a great deal to be said for it.[30] It is a bleak, but
blazing truth. But it doesn't relax. It is pure austerity. Asceticism without joy. It is not something positive; it is only a
negation. The difference between a puritan and a Catholic

---

[26] See *ILN*, August 6, 1921.
[27] *Sidelights*, *CW* 21:563.
[28] See *ILN*, August 20, 1921.
[29] *Sidelights*, *CW* 21:567.
[30] See "The Puritan", in *George Bernard Shaw*, *CW* 11:374–83.

is that a Catholic gives something up not because it is bad, but because it is good. That is why virginity and celibacy are positive, good things. That is why our Lenten sacrifices are good for us. A sacrifice is a gift of something good. And we are blessed in the giving of it.

Now, just as there are two kinds of people, and two kinds of pagans, there are, of course, two kinds of puritans. There are the old puritans and the new puritans. The old puritans were Christian, the new puritans are not. The new puritans worship the God of Health and Hygiene.

Chesterton warns, "Mere pursuit of health always leads to something unhealthy." [31] The new puritans examine everything under a microscope, "in which microbes look much larger than men".[32] Looking at everything microscopically of course leads to a loss of perspective, "the sacrificing of the normal to the abnormal".[33] The secular puritan attacks the tobacco industry but supports the abortion industry. "Quality of life" suddenly becomes more important than life. It throws out the baby, but keeps the bath water.

The old puritans may have been accused of setting up a restrictive society, but Chesterton argues that the new abstinence is more intolerant than the old abstinence. It becomes a "health-care issue" and a "social issue" and simple basic freedoms come under attack from media onslaught, government regulation, and industrial coercion. The new puritans not only attack the old standbys such as beer and wine and tobacco, but also basic things like meat. And even more basic things like chocolate! They want to do away with simple pleasures such as traditional toys and games and nursery

---

[31] *Orthodoxy, CW* 1:280.
[32] *ILN*, February 8, 1913.
[33] Ibid.

rhymes. They attack words. They are always ready to release the dogs of Prohibition.

> Idolatry is committed, not merely by setting up false gods, but also by setting up false devils; by making men afraid of war or alcohol, or economic law, when they should be afraid of spiritual corruption and cowardice.[34]

> Sin is in a man's soul, not in his tools or his toys.[35]

Chesterton says that we "wreck the tribunal of truth" when we pronounce the innocent guilty, just as much as when we pronounce the guilty innocent. We destroy all innocence when we make people detest an innocent practice. And he warns that if we begin with a heresy in morals, whether it be a prohibition or a permission, it will end in the worst and wildest license.[36]

He knew firsthand what he was talking about. He saw that in Catholic Europe there was historically a healthy and normal attitude toward wine and beer, drinking without drunkenness. But in America, there was the puritanical idea that drinking itself was evil. The reaction to that false idea was a false emphasis on drinking. That eventually led to Prohibition, which in turn led to the rise of the cocktail generation, and a continued problem with alcoholism that afflicts us still today.

Chesterton defends wine and beer as good things that are liable to be abused like any other good thing.[37] He says, "Drink because you are happy, but never because you are

[34] *ILN*, September 11, 1909.

[35] *ILN*, June 5, 1920.

[36] See *True Temperance Quarterly*, May 1933.

[37] See *ILN*, November 26, 1921.

miserable." [38] Every pleasure should be an event, not a habit. Every pleasure is a kind of exception, which is what helps keep it a pleasure.

> Modern men have lost the joy of life. They have to put up with the miserable substitutes for the joys of life. And even these they seem less and less able to enjoy. Unless we can make ordinary men interested in ordinary life, we are under the vulgar despotism of those who cannot interest them but can at least amuse them. [39]

The problem of paganism and puritanism is partly a problem of pleasure. The old paganism degenerated into the mere pursuit of pleasure. The old puritans reacted against it by the deliberate and elaborate avoidance of pleasure. The new pagans reacted against the old puritans. The new puritans reacted against the new pagans. Reactions against reactions, all missing the point. Both puritanism and paganism misunderstand pleasure. But, more importantly, both misunderstand what is good. The pagans emphasize the physical to the neglect of the spiritual. The puritans emphasize the spiritual to the neglect of the physical. Both miss the point of the Incarnation. God created a physical world and said it was good. He created us in his image. We are both spiritual and physical beings. And though we have taken a good world and misused it, though we are sinners, God himself redeemed us by becoming flesh.

Chesterton says, "The trend of good is always towards Incarnation." [40] And this is why Chesterton battled against both paganism and puritanism, because both were trying to

---

[38] *Heretics*, *CW* 1:92.
[39] BBC talk, 1934.
[40] *A Miscellany of Men* (Norfolk, Va.: IHS Press, 2004), 98.

rob the Incarnation of something. Just as God came to meet us, so we have to go and meet the rest of the world.

> Each human soul has in a sense to enact for itself the gigantic humility of the Incarnation. Every man must descend into the flesh to meet mankind.[41]

The Incarnation is a paradox. It is the spirit made flesh. But Chesterton says that the moral atmosphere of the Incarnation is common sense.[42] The two extremes of paganism and puritanism lack the balance and common sense of the Catholic Church. Paganism was pre-Catholic; puritanism is post-Catholic (that is, post-Reformation). Chesterton says that after the world tried being more puritan than the Christian tradition, it then tried being more pagan than the Christian tradition.[43] Neither worked. The only thing that will work is true reform, a return to form, a return to the normal. That is what the Church offers: the normal. The perfect balance of purity and pleasure, the perfect combination of the flesh and the spirit. Reform means admitting that we have strayed from the form, that we need to return. Chesterton says, "A reform is a repentance, and the point of all repentance is beginning afresh." [44] Christ offered one of the greatest pleasures and greatest paradoxes of all when he said that we can start over. He called it being born again.

---

[41] *What's Wrong with the World, CW* 4:93–94.
[42] See *Orthodoxy, CW* 1:347.
[43] See *ILN*, September 4, 1920.
[44] Ibid.

14

The Art of Defending the Christian Faith

In Matthew 10:16, when Jesus sends out his disciples to preach the Gospel, he tells them to be "as wise as serpents and as innocent as doves". Wisdom and innocence. Perhaps more than any Christian writer in the twentieth century, G. K. Chesterton truly embodies these two virtues. Wisdom is about not compromising truth. And innocence means not compromising goodness. As a man and a writer, Chesterton never compromises either. His life and work beautifully convey both truth and goodness. His wisdom is evident in all his books and essays and poems, but it is also his goodness that makes him such a good writer, and what draws us to him.

But goodness should not be confused with something soft and passive. Defending the truth means fighting for the truth. And Chesterton says, "One of the best things is a good fight." [1] When he looked back on his life, he realized that he was always arguing. Not that he never did anything else, but he did find that he was always doing that, and that he seldom did anything else so well or worth doing.

[1] "In the Days of My Youth", uncollected manuscript.

I remember once arguing with an honest young atheist, who was very much shocked at my disputing some of the assumptions which were absolute sanctities to him ... and he at length fell back upon this question, which he delivered with an honourable heat of defiance and indignation: "Well, can you tell me any man of intellect, great in science or philosophy, who accepted the miraculous?" I said, "With pleasure. Descartes, Dr. Johnson, Newton, Faraday, Newman, Gladstone, Pasteur, Browning, Brunetière—as many more as you please." To which that admirable young man made this astonishing reply—"Oh, but of course they had to say that; they were Christians." First he challenged me to find a black swan, and then he ruled out all my swans because they were black. The fact that all these great intellects had come to the Christian view was somehow or other a proof either that they were not great intellects or that they had not really come to that view.[2]

It was almost a disappointment to Chesterton that the modern world "has far too little argument of the real sort". Avoiding the "real" argument is a way of avoiding the truth. But "the aim of any public-spirited person" should be to find out what the truth is, and finding it, to defend it. Why? Well, there's the slight matter of eternity, but there is also that thing that always seems of more immediate concern: the here and now. Chesterton says, without "a stable statement of truth",[3] we have nothing upon which to build a solid society. Truth is not merely a religious ideal; it is quite useful for other things, too. In fact, he says, "Theology is a product far more practical than chemistry."[4]

[2] *ILN*, May 4, 1907.
[3] "In the Days of My Youth".
[4] "Why I Believe in Christianity", in *The Blatchford Controversies*, *CW* 1:383.

Truth touches everything, which is exactly why it is attacked from all sides. And so defending the Faith means being able to talk about everything. Chesterton says, "Things can be irrelevant to the proposition that Christianity is false, but nothing can be irrelevant to the proposition that Christianity is true."[5] No matter what you talk about, he says, "You cannot evade the issue of God", which of course is exactly the thing that our society tries to do, especially in public.

> Religious liberty is supposed to mean a man is free to discuss his faith, in practice it means he is hardly allowed to mention it.[6]

So, the first step in defending the faith is to insist that we have to talk about God. And there should be nothing unnatural about talking about God. Believing in God is more normal than not believing in God. "Atheism", says Chesterton, "is abnormality."[7] It goes against what every normal person believes, namely, "that there is a meaning and a direction in the world".[8] Religion, he says, is merely "the sense of ultimate reality",[9] and so everybody is religious because everybody has an ultimate view of things. Most people have not taken the time or trouble to articulate it. And if they did they might be troubled by how incomplete a view of things they have, which is why they too often say, "It doesn't matter what you believe." Because they are hoping that what they believe *doesn't* matter, since they have given so little thought to it. Still, they believe something,

[5] *Daily News*, December 12, 1903.
[6] *Autobiography*, CW 16:225.
[7] *The Everlasting Man*, CW 2:294.
[8] Ibid.
[9] *ILN*, June 15, 1929.

even if they seriously believe that what they believe doesn't matter.

One of Chesterton's basic points is that man is a creature of faith. Man is a religious animal. Man is an animal who makes dogmas. Trees, he says, have no dogmas, and turnips are also quite broad-minded.[10]

> If a man wishes to remain in perfect mental breadth and freedom, he had better not think at all. Thinking is a narrowing process. It leads to what people call dogma. A man who thinks hard about any subject for several years is in a horrible danger of discovering the truth about it. . . . It is a terrible thing when a man really finds that his mind was given him to use, and not to play with; or, in other words, that the gods gave him a great ugly mouth with which to answer questions, and not merely to ask them.[11]

Chesterton disposes of atheists more easily than atheists dispose of God. He says, "If there is no God, there would be no atheists."[12] But he actually has more respect for an atheist than he does for an agnostic. An atheist has at least made up his mind. The agnostic takes great pride in the fact that he cannot make up his mind. The agnostic tries to pass himself off as impartial, but the word "agnostic" doesn't mean impartial; it merely means ignorant.

What the atheist and the agnostic refuse to accept is that there is an absolute Truth and that it is something outside of ourselves and larger than ourselves. This takes some humility to acknowledge, but also common sense.

[10] See *Heretics, CW* 1:197.
[11] *ILN*, September 16, 1909.
[12] *Where All Roads Lead, CW* 3:38.

> I do not ... believe that a baby gets his best physical food
> by sucking his thumb; nor that a man gets his best moral
> food by sucking his soul, and denying its dependence on
> God or other good things.[13]

The skeptic does not contribute anything to a religious discussion, except doubt. The skeptic always begins the conversation by telling us what he does not believe. So the
best defense in this case is attack: simply to turn it around
and ask, "What *do* you believe?" Most enemies of the faith
can be skewered with their own ideas. One of Chesterton's
simplest and most effective devices is simply to restate his
opponent's argument in a way that makes it sound ridicu-
lous, which is what it usually is. He has the ability to slay
his opponents with their own swords. Cordially, of course.
The reason he stumbled upon this technique is worth not-
ing: it was listening to the arguments *against* Christianity
that led him to become a Christian.

> The more I saw of the merely abstract arguments against
> the Christian cosmology the less I thought of them. I found
> the moral atmosphere of the Incarnation to be common
> sense, I then looked at the established intellectual argu-
> ments against the Incarnation and found them to be com-
> mon nonsense.... If I am asked, as a purely intellectual
> question, why I believe in Christianity, I can only answer,
> "For the same reason that an intelligent agnostic disbelieves
> in Christianity."[14]

There are, according to Chesterton, three typical arguments that the skeptic offers against Christianity: first, that
humans are mere animals, just a variation on the same

[13] *A Short History of England*, *CW* 20:463.
[14] *Orthodoxy*, *CW* 1:347.

biology shared by the rest of the animal kingdom; second, that religion originally arose out of ignorance and fear; third, that organized religion has ruined societies with bitterness and gloom. He says, these three anti-Christian arguments "are very different; but they are all quite logical and legitimate; and they all converge." And upon consideration, his only objection to them is that they are all untrue.[15]

To the first argument, Chesterton says that if you really look at beasts and men, the startling thing is not how much men are like beasts but how different they are. Apes may have hands, but they don't do much with them. They don't play the violin or eat with a knife and fork. Elephants don't build ivory temples, even in a primitive style. Camels don't paint pictures. In beehives there are no statues of the "gorgeous queens of old". And so on. Chesterton says, "We talk of wild animals; but man is the only wild animal. It is man that has broken out. All other animals are tame ... following the ... tribe or type."[16] Only man can be unpredictable and act against type. Only man can be a criminal or a monk.

As for the second argument, that religion began in some darkness and terror, Chesterton says that when we examine the foundations of this modern idea we find there are no foundations. All the legends of mankind point back not to prehistoric fear but to paradise. The idea of a lost paradise is precisely the opposite idea of evolutionary progress.

The whole human race has a tradition of the Fall. Amusingly enough, the very dissemination of this idea is used against its authenticity. Learned men literally say that this

[15] Ibid., 348.
[16] Ibid., 349.

pre-historic calamity cannot be true because every race of mankind remembers it.[17]

And then the third argument, that priests and organized religion darken and embitter the world. A compelling argument, except for the fact that it just isn't true. The places where there is a rich culture of art and music and creativity are exactly the places where the Church has been most prominent. Chesterton says the countries that are "still influenced by priests are exactly the countries where there is still singing and dancing and coloured dresses and art in the open-air".[18]

> The most absurd thing that could be said of the Church is the thing we have all heard said of it ... that the Church wishes to bring us back into the Dark Ages.... The Church was the only thing that ever brought us out of them.[19]

Chesterton turns the arguments around. *He* challenges the skeptic to give an explanation: first, of why man towers over the brutes; second, why there is a vast human tradition of some ancient happiness; and third, of why there are such joyous and colorful customs in those countries of Catholic culture.

We can do the same thing with all the other arguments that come from the skeptics. When they say, for instance, that Christianity can't be true because there are many myths from other cultures that closely parallel the Christian story, we can respond: if Christianity is true, if Jesus really is the Son of God, isn't it perfectly natural that other cultures would have some hint of this great fact? Wouldn't there be other

[17] Ibid., 349–50.
[18] Ibid., 350.
[19] Ibid., 352.

myths that mirror Christianity, and pagans who dream of the Son of God?

When the skeptics say that Christians have invented God simply to fill a psychological need, we can respond first by reminding them that the word "psyche" means soul, and, yes, the soul does have a hunger for God, which, if there is a God, would be quite natural, and no more disproves the existence of God than the hunger in the stomach disproves the existence of food.

When the skeptics say that Christianity has been an ascetic and gloomy thing—look at those miserable saints who gave up home and happiness because of their ferocious single-mindedness—we can respond: the saints indeed suffered, but the odd thing about them is that they were not miserable. Why wouldn't they surrender themselves to something true and actual and solid; why wouldn't they give up all other pleasures for one surpassing spiritual pleasure? How does it prove that the hope for heaven is false, just because that hope actually does sustain people?

And of course Christianity has been accused of hypocrisy and cruelty and loads of other not nice things. And all these are offered up as evidence that Christianity is false. But Chesterton says the world in fact pays the highest compliment to the Church when the world is intolerant of the Church's failures, the same failures that the world tolerates everywhere else.[20] The world thinks we are fools for trying to be true to our faith, but then condemns us when we are not. But either we are fools because Christianity is not true, or else we are hypocrites because it is true. We cannot be both.

[20] See *The Thing*, *CW* 3:275.

But to call Christianity false because it has been a failure is not only bad logic; it is a bad assessment of history. Chesterton says that Christianity has never been enough of a success to properly be called a failure.[21]

> The Christian ideal has not been tried and found wanting. It has been found difficult and left untried.[22]

The claim that Christianity is true may be hard to accept, but that is because in general the truth is harder to accept than a lie, because lies are designed to be accepted.

> Truth must of necessity be stranger than fiction, for we have made fiction to suit ourselves.[23]

Miracles are strange things, for instance, which is probably why they are called miracles. "The most incredible thing about miracles", says Chesterton in a Father Brown story, "is that they happen."[24] And Chesterton says the reason he believes in miracles is because there is evidence for them.[25] The reason skeptics do not believe in miracles is because they will not accept the evidence, and the reason they will not accept the evidence is because they have a dogma against miracles. A materialist, after all, is not free to believe in miracles. There must always be some naturalistic explanation. But these naturalistic explanations are often more unbelievable than the miraculous ones. And nowhere is this more evident than when it comes to the miracle of the

---

[21] See *ILN*, July 5, 1919.

[22] *What's Wrong with the World*, *CW* 4:61.

[23] *Heretics*, *CW* 1:66–67.

[24] "The Blue Cross", *The Penguin Complete Father Brown* (New York: Penguin Books, 1981), 11.

[25] See "Miracles and Modern Civilisation", in *The Blatchford Controversies*, *CW* 1:388.

Incarnation, the central claim of Christianity—that Jesus Christ is indeed God in the Flesh.

> If we look at Jesus as he appears in the New Testament; not as he appears to a believer, but as he appears to anybody; as he appeared to me when I was an agnostic; as He appeared and still appears to pagans when they first read about Him, the first thing that strikes us is that he is not at all what [the modern critics] claim Him to be. [They contend] that when we look through the four windows of the evangelists at this mysterious figure, we can see there a recognizable Jew of the first century, with the traceable limitations of such a man. Now this is exactly what we do not see.... What we see is this: an extraordinary being who would certainly have seemed as mad in one century as another, who makes a vague and vast claim to divinity, who constantly contradicts himself, who imposes impossible commands, who where he seems wrong to us would certainly have seemed quite as wrong to anybody else, who where he seems right to us is often in tune with matters not ancient but modern.... From some of his utterances men might fairly call him a maniac; for others, men long centuries afterwards might justly call him a prophet. But what nobody can possibly call him is a Galilean of the time of Tiberius. That was not how he appeared to his own family who tried to lock him up as a lunatic. That is not how he appeared to his own nation, who lynched him, still shuddering at his earth-shaking blasphemies.... The thing to say about Jesus, if you do not like Him, is that He was a megalomaniac ... or a mystagogue.... But whether or not He was small, it is plain that the Gospels are too small for Him. Whether or not he is large, He is too large for the stage....
>
> If I take it for granted (as most modern people do) that Jesus of Nazareth was one of the ordinary teachers of men, then I find Him splendid and suggestive indeed, but full

of riddles and outrageous demands.... But ... suppose
the Divine did really walk and talk upon the earth, what
would we be likely to think of it? ... I think we should
see in such a being exactly the perplexities that we see in
the central figure of the Gospels: I think he would seem
to us extreme and violent; because he would see ... the
virtue which would be for us untried. I think he would
seem to us to contradict himself; because, looking down
on life like a map, he would see a connection between
things which to us are disconnected. I think, however,
that he would always ring true to our own sense of right,
but ring (so to speak) too loud and too clear. He would
be too good but never too bad for us.... I think there
would be, in the nature of things, some tragic collision
between him and the humanity he had created, culminat-
ing in something that would be at once a crime and an
expiation. I think he would be blamed as a hard prophet
for dragging down the haughty, and blamed also as a weak
sentimentalist for loving the things that cling in corners,
children or beggars. I think, in short, that he would give
us a sensation that he was turning all our standards upside
down, and yet also a sensation that he had undeniably put
them the right way up.[26]

The Christian explanation of Christ is the only complete
explanation. And besides that, the Christian explanation of
the world is the only complete explanation. We are in a
fallen state and we need the redemption that only Christ
can bring. Chesterton says this may seem a complicated sort
of solution, but the problem is complicated, the world is
complicated. A lock is a complicated thing, and so is a key.
But if a key fits the lock, you know it is the right key. He

[26] *Hibbert Journal*, July 1909.

says, you know your religion is true not when something proves it, but when everything proves it.[27]

Chesterton is a master of logic. He not only points out what is illogical in the attacks on Christianity; he also shows what happens if any worldly philosophy is taken to its logical conclusion. In every case, the result is madness and self-destruction. He argues prophetically that modern ideas will lead to a culture of death. Modern art and literature is full of pessimism and despair. There is no wonder at existence or joy at the gift of life. Instead we find new ways to kill our children, to kill our parents, and ultimately to kill ourselves. The modern world portrays these various forms of death as freedom, just as it portrays the destruction of marriage as a form of freedom. Chesterton says that in a dreary time we listen to two counsels of despair: the freedom from life and the freedom from love.[28] In contrast to this is the good news of Jesus Christ, who says, "I have come that they may have life and have it more abundantly."[29]

The reason the Church is against the modern trends and barren fads of divorce and birth control and abortion and homosexuality is that, for one thing, they are not new and the Church has always been against them. As Chesterton says, "A new philosophy generally means in practice the praise of some old vice."[30] But more importantly, these so-called freedoms do not make people happy; they make people miserable.

Chesterton is an ardent defender of the truth because only the truth can set us free.[31] And ultimately only the

---

[27] See *Orthodoxy, CW* 1:287.
[28] See *The Superstition of Divorce, CW* 4:265–70.
[29] John 10:10.
[30] *ILN,* January 6, 1906.
[31] See John 8:32.

truth can make us happy. Perhaps the greatest evidence for the truth of Chesterton's philosophy is the great joy it gave him, a profound joy that overflowed from him and swept over everyone around him. One person close to him said that to know him was a benediction. G. K. Chesterton lived his faith. He demonstrated not only the mere art of speaking the truth, but the holy art of speaking the truth in love. One of the really remarkable things about him is that he not only loved his enemies, but his enemies could not help loving him. His philosophical opponents did not merely like him; they loved him. He was always generous but honest to his enemies. He says, "Most mistaken people mean well, and all mistaken people mean something. There is something to be said for every error; but, whatever may be said for it, the most important thing to be said about it is that it is erroneous." [32] That statement is typical of how Chesterton does not compromise either truth or goodness. In his life as well as in his writing, Chesterton shows that it is truth that answers error, but also that it is humility that answers arrogance. It is kindness that answers cruelty. It is gentleness that answers wrath. And just as it is goodness that answers a lack of goodness, it is humor that answers— this is important—a distinct lack of humor. Chesterton points out that the opposite of funny is not serious, the opposite of funny is not funny. "Whether a man chooses to tell the truth in long sentences or short jokes", he says, is the same "as whether he chooses to tell the truth in German or French." [33]

When Chesterton defends Christianity, his great gift is to laugh and make us laugh. He says, "It is the test of a

---

[32] *ILN*, April 25, 1931.
[33] *Heretics*, *CW* 1:160.

good religion whether you can joke about it." [34] Those who knew him said that Chesterton always had a highly developed sense of humor, but also a sense of beauty and a sense of reverence. It is a combination of these things that make for happiness. And Chesterton's happiness continues to be a light in this dark age, in this culture of death.

[34] *ILN*, June 9, 1906.

15

The Art of Defending the Catholic Faith

G. K. Chesterton is one of the great ecumenical writers of the twentieth century. He is widely quoted and held in great esteem by both Catholics and Protestants—and even non-Christians. And while Chesterton's wit and wisdom have been called upon again and again to defend Christianity, any serious reader of Chesterton soon realizes that Chesterton doesn't just defend the Christian faith in general; he defends the Catholic Faith in particular. When I was an Evangelical Protestant who had become quite smitten with Chesterton's writings, it was something that I tried for the longest time to get around. Finally I had to face the fact that not only is the Catholic Faith central to Chesterton's thinking; it is central to everything else. It was, for me, a glorious defeat.

The institution of the Catholic Church is attacked for many things. One of the first things it is attacked for is the fact that it is an institution. Some people insist on avoiding an institution because they claim to be afraid of confining themselves, of becoming narrow. They say they want a belief that is broad and unrestricted. The New

Improved Religion, says Chesterton, always promises that there will be a better and broader belief, however, "it seldom touches on the belief but only on the broadness."[1]

> It is the fashion to talk of institutions as cold and cramping things. The truth is that when people are in exceptionally high spirits, really wild with freedom and invention, they always must, and they always do, create institutions. When men are weary they fall into anarchy; but while they are [happy] and vigorous they invariably make rules. This, which is true of all the churches and republics of history, is also true of the most trivial parlour game or the most unsophisticated meadow romp. We are never free until some institution frees us, and liberty cannot exist till it is declared by authority.[2]

When Chesterton defends the Faith, he is always fair to his opponents. He always considers their arguments carefully, so carefully that he can usually state their argument better than they can state it themselves. But the most beautiful thing about his debating technique is that he always begins by finding something in their argument that he agrees with, even if it is the thinnest shred of truth, so that he can start on common ground with them. He then proceeds to show how their ideas are not so much wrong, as merely incomplete.

Defending the Faith against atheists and agnostics and skeptics and so-called freethinkers is for Chesterton almost effortless because the barrenness of their thinking is so quickly apparent. It is the challenge presented by Protestantism, in all its various forms, that is more complicated and requires more work. Both the strength and weakness

---

[1] *The Thing, CW* 3:182.
[2] *Manalive, CW* 7:286.

of Protestantism is that it has borrowed its truths from the Catholic Church, but not the whole truth.

As we have explained elsewhere, a heresy is at best a half-truth.[3] It is usually less than half, but the point is, it is a belief that has seized on some truth taken from the wholeness of the Catholic Faith and has left out the rest. For example:

> It is true to insist upon God's knowledge, but heretical to insist on it as Calvin did at the expense of his Love; it is true to desire a simple life, but heretical to desire it at the expense of good feeling and good manners. The heretic (who is also the fanatic) is not a man who loves truth too much; no man can love truth too much. The heretic is a man who loves his truth more than truth itself. He prefers the half-truth that he has found to the whole truth which humanity has found.[4]

Every heresy, as we said, leaves out part of the truth, but it usually doesn't stop there. It soon attacks the truth it leaves out, which, in effect, attacks the whole truth. Almost every heresy is an attack on the Incarnation, on the Person of Jesus Christ, fully God and fully Man. Every heresy at some point either rejects something of Christ's divinity or something of his humanity. But there is a corollary to these attacks on Christ. Almost every heresy is also an attack on the priesthood. As explained in the Epistle to the Hebrews, Jesus Christ is the High Priest, the intermediary between God and Man. The High Priest did not abolish the priesthood. On the contrary, he endowed it by his authority with a unique role, a role that it has played for two thousand years.

[3] See Dale Ahlquist, *G. K. Chesterton: The Apostle of Common Sense* (San Francisco: Ignatius, 2003), 35.

[4] *The Common Man* (New York: Sheed and Ward, 1950), 22.

The priesthood is connected to the idea of sacrifice.
Almost all of Protestantism—along with the rest of the modern world—has quite forgotten the significance of sacrifice.
Not only do we want something for nothing, but we want
it any time and all the time. The result has been a growing
lack of appreciation and respect, a degradation and cheapen-
ing of good things, and it is all related to a loss of holiness.
Holiness means something set apart. Sacrifice sets something apart. To sacrifice something literally means to make
it sacred. Ancient pre-Christian religions understood the
role of sacrifice. The principal religious act was to make a
sacrifice to the gods. The sacrifice not only honored the
god and humbled the sacrificer; it made that place and that
event holy. Chesterton explains that where a religion was
strong, it was only natural that the rites associated with it
grew more elaborate and even complex. But where a religion decayed, people forgot the origins and the inmost nature
of what they were doing, and they ended up turning it
into something else, sometimes into the very opposite of
what it originally meant.

> The sacrificer builds an altar and pours wine or blood or
> something on it and holds up his hands to the sky and talks
> to somebody he can't see. A sensible fellow. Then, as time
> goes on, he turns his remarks into an ordered chant, and
> then, perhaps, into a written book; and he has a roof to
> cover the people who come to see him sacrifice, and a lectern
> to read the book from, and a sort of forum or pulpit to
> stand in and explain what he has been doing, and so on.
> And then, when civilisation has grown for some centuries,
> there comes an Ethical Society—the advance guard of barbar-
> ism. You may know it by this extraordinary fact: that it
> doesn't take away the additions and accretions round the
> old human thing; it takes away the old human thing itself.

It leaves the reading-desk and the talking-box and the people sitting still on hard seats. But it takes away the altar. It takes away the god.[5]

Only the Catholic Church has kept the God, and the sacrifice, which is the Lamb of God, and the altar. Only the Catholic Church understands the unique role of the priest as the one who has been given authority to offer the sacrifice at the altar.

There are many points on which Protestants and the rest of the world have attacked the Catholic Church, but on which they have eventually come around to agree with the Catholic Church. Most everyone admits a need for rituals, a respect for the dead, for places and times of holiness. Most everyone believes good works are good, even for our own souls. But most Protestants and most of the world still attack the Church on one issue. They want no priest to come between a man and his maker. They say they believe in direct communion with God, and that there is no need for interference from a priest.

It sounds like a great objection, as long as you don't think about it very carefully. First of all, devout Catholics know that the priest does not come between them and God. Nor does anything else. And secondly, the real irony of the objection, says Chesterton, is that most modern people do not feel they have any free access to God for anybody to interfere with. They are not conscious of any communion with Christ that anyone can interrupt.[6] They are conscious, rather, of something that *has* come between them and God. And it is not a priest. It is sin.

[5] *ILN*, March 9, 1912.
[6] See *America*, September 25, 1926.

This of course brings us to the other thing a priest is needed for: confession.

Chesterton says that a religion that has confession as one of its sacraments is a religion that deals in truth. To the critics who say it is "morbid" to confess your sins, he responds:

> The morbid thing is *not* to confess them. The morbid thing is to conceal your sins and let them eat away at your soul, which is exactly the state of most people in today's highly civilised communities.[7]

When the Protestant world did away with confession, it eventually replaced it with something far worse: psychotherapy, which is merely confession without absolution and without any of the safeguards of the confessional.[8] The sinner is now told that his sins are not sins. But knowing that doesn't seem to help him. The only thing that does help him is knowing that his sins are forgiven.

So, in defending the Catholic Faith, the primary point is that the main attacks are against the Incarnation and the priesthood. Everything else is secondary, and a mere detail. But they are details a Catholic still should be prepared to address.

And Chesterton does this very well. In doing so, he shows that the very attacks on the Church point to its truth and its centrality.

Even before his conversion, Chesterton noticed that all the attacks on the Church come for opposite reasons. The Church is accused of restraining sexuality too much at the same time it is accused of restraining it too little. It insists

[7] *Daily News*, January 8, 1908.
[8] See *The Thing*, CW 3:187.

on celibacy for those who have chosen it, but is relentless in forcing family and marriage upon men and women who have chosen that. The Church is accused of showing contempt for women's intellect. But at the same time the great sneer at the Church in most countries is that "only women" go there. The Church is attacked for its asceticism, its "sackcloth and dried peas". And the next minute it is being reproached for its pomp and its ritualism and its robes of gold. It is abused for being too plain and for being too colored. It is accused in the same breath of being prim and dull and of being garish and extravagant. It is rebuked for its disunion and dissent, and rebuked also for its union and uniformity. It is criticized for being too political and too worldly, but also for not being involved enough in politics and being too unworldly. It is blamed for despising Jews, and also despised for being too Jewish.[9]

From the way the rest of the world attacked the Church, Chesterton says it was not a question of whether or not the Church were bad enough to include any vices, but rather of whether or not any stick were good enough to beat the Church with. And that was exactly what attracted him to this "astonishing thing" that people were so anxious to contradict that in doing so they didn't mind contradicting themselves.[10]

After he became Catholic he still noticed the inconsistent criticisms from what he called a "nebulous type of Protestantism".

> They complain of our thinking too much of theology, just as they complained a few centuries before of our thinking too little of theology. But theology is only the element of

[9] See *Orthodoxy*, *CW* 1:293–94.
[10] Ibid.

reason in religion; the reason that prevents it from being a mere emotion. People will tell you that theology became too elaborate because it was dead. Believe me, if it had been dead it would never have become elaborate; it is only the live tree that grows too many branches. They accuse Catholics of false sentiment, but they are the ones who are prepared to pay Divine honors to a certain person while doubting whether he is Divine, who take off their hats in his churches while denying that he is present on the altar, who hint that he was only an ethical teacher and then hint again that he must be served as if he were not only an ethical teacher, who are always ready to treat him as a fallible individual in relation to his rivals, and then invoke him as an infallible authority against his followers; who dismiss every text they choose to think dogmatic and then gush over every text they choose to think amiable; who heckle him with Higher Criticism about most of what he said and then grovel before a mawkish and unmanly ideal made by misunderstanding the little that is left.[11]

The textual critics make amazing claims, amazingly bland, that is, after they have thrown out the texts that are not to their liking. After they prove that Christ was not divine, they prove that apostles started a Church that Christ would have hated.[12] And then that the early Fathers changed it into a Church that the apostles would have hated. Chesterton points out that the historical critics claim to prove that the Church was something suited to the conditions of the third or fourth century. But what they do not explain to us is why, if the Church is so suited to the third century, it is flourishing in our century. "While the truth of the

[11] *America*, November 27, 1926.
[12] See *The Everlasting Man*, CW 2:351.

Church is outside time, the heresies are always tied up with the times." [13]

> The Catholic Church is the only thing that saves a man from the degrading slavery of being a child of his age. [14]

In addition to the higher critics and the textual critics and the historical critics, there are simply the brick-throwing critics who think they have scored anytime they can point out one of the Church's scandals or abuses. But where these critics are most wrong is in imagining that any of their criticisms are new to us. We know our problems much better than any outsider does. We accuse ourselves more fervently and accurately than any outsider does: "The Church is not justified when her children do not sin, but when they do." [15]

We are in constant need of repentance and renewal— and of close constant scrutiny. But Chesterton says it is good to be in hot water: it keeps you clean. [16] And the greatest scandals in the Church, he says, have been pointed out not by outsiders, but by the indignant insiders, the greatest Churchmen, who, more often than not, were founders of religious orders that helped bring about renewal and reform. [17] As Chesterton says, the highest form of criticism is self-criticism. [18]

And when the critics get all offended about the Church's abuses, usually the best they can come up with is the Spanish Inquisition and St. Bartholomew's Massacre, as if these things are everyday occurrences in the Catholic Church,

---

[13] *America*, September 25, 1926.
[14] *The Catholic Church and Conversion*, *CW* 3:110.
[15] *The Everlasting Man*, *CW* 2:144.
[16] See *ILN*, March 10, 1906.
[17] See *America*, October 20, 1926.
[18] See *Nash's Pall Mall Magazine*, April 1935.

when in fact they are isolated events and are several hundred years old. The critics ignore the fact that we do not have to go back three hundred years to find cases of Catholics being killed for being Catholic. That is happening today. Right now. But as Chesterton says, "The modernist will not show the faintest interest in modern persecution." [19]

"The essential of being a good Protestant", he says, "is having a bad memory." [20] Protestants have "carefully protected [themselves] from any knowledge of Christian History".[21] They have managed to ignore the heroic work of the Catholic Church from century to century, which also means ignoring the Catholic heroes. They have performed the trick of making over a thousand years just disappear. They know who Abraham is, but they have forgotten who St. Giles is.

> The Church has been accused of hiding the Bible, which of course is not true, but even if that had been true, it would have been a less astonishing achievement than that of the Reformation, which succeeded in hiding everything else about the Faith.[22]

This bad memory of the Protestants extends to their own history as well. Chesterton points out that each Protestant sect was founded on the principle that theological truth is all that matters; but now with thousands of different denominations, theological truth does not matter so much as personal tastes in worship. Each Protestant sect was first established on the ground that no man must remain where he is if the Church is in error. Now that there are

[19] *America*, November 3, 1928.
[20] *America*, August 28, 1926.
[21] *America*, July 24, 1926.
[22] Ibid.

thousands of churches, every man is told that he may as well remain where he is, because probably nobody has it completely right and everybody has some amount of truth and probably the same amount.[23]

> Protestantism has not been merely the abandonment of Catholic doctrines. Protestantism has been the abandonment of Protestant doctrines.[24]

Chesterton also shows how those who attack the Catholic Faith steal from it at the same time. This is true not only of Protestantism, but of the rest of the world. Almost all of the important institutions and the basic assumptions in our society were borrowed from the Catholic Church. The world, he says, is living on its Catholic capital.[25] The world has taken all the good things it can from the Church, has separated them from the Church, and has tried to make those separate things in and of themselves sufficient apart from the Church. Think about it. Scientists have taken the wonder of creation and left out the Creator, philosophers have taken the analytical thinking, psychiatrists have taken the confessional (without the absolution), humanitarians have taken the social justice, fundamentalists have taken the Bible, artists have taken the art, pagans have taken the feasts, and puritans have taken the fasting. They've each taken a part of the truth and mistaken that bit of the truth for the whole truth and have rejected all the rest of it.

But Chesterton says that we must not assume that our opponents are stupid or wicked, or at least not any more stupid and wicked than we are. They are only ignorant of

---

[23] Ibid.
[24] *America*, June 28, 1930.
[25] See *The Thing*, *CW* 3:147.

things they cannot reasonably be expected to know unless we tell them. We only know them ourselves because someone told us. Chesterton suggests that the art of defending faith should be more positive and less negative. We should not be on the defensive just because this or that detail has been attacked. We still have to answer the hecklers with responsibility and charity, but we can't let the hecklers choose all the subjects. We have to start presenting the wholeness of the Catholic Faith, the richness of Catholic history, the completeness of Catholic thought.

> It will always be possible for even the wisest to miss the truth; sometimes by their own fault and sometimes by their invincible ignorance. [They want to have] Christianity without Catholicism, or . . . religion without Christianity, or . . . religious sentiment without religion. . . . I do not say that anybody exercising mental activity must come to the Catholic Faith. But I do say that many men will have to exercise great mental activity *in order* to come to the Catholic Faith. . . . Put shortly and roughly, the problem of this great educated modern world is whether people are still bright enough to be converted.[26]

Too many people who are ignorant about the Catholic Church actively maintain their ignorance. Chesterton says that in a strange way they treat the Church as a thing at once invisible and solid. They can't seem to see it, yet they are careful to avoid it.[27] But for those who are willing to look at it honestly, they discover that it is something very real and solid. The Catholic Faith not only appeals to common sense; it appeals to the senses. It is sights and sounds and smells. It is something you can taste and feel.

[26] *America*, June 9, 1928.
[27] See *America*, October 16, 1926.

Chesterton—and nobody other than Chesterton—could say that its very soul is a body.

> A gift of God that can be seen and touched is the whole point of the epigram of the creed. Christ Himself was a Christmas present. The note of material Christmas presents is struck even before he is born. The Three Kings came to Bethlehem bringing gold and frankincense and myrrh. If they had only brought Truth and Purity and Love there would have been no Christian art and no Christian civilisation.[28]

Chesterton says quite plainly that there is only the Church and its enemies. This provocative statement does not seem to leave any middle ground, and yet it does not diminish his importance as an ecumenical writer. The essence of ecumenism is found in the Gospel paradox where Jesus says, in Mark 9:40, that those who are not against us are for us, but in Matthew 12:30, he says that those who are not with us are against us. Chesterton understands the subtle distinction. He appeals to Protestants with the truths that both they and Catholics have in common; but in not compromising the truths that separate them, he offers a compelling invitation to explore the rest of the Church. At the same time he warns Catholics that there are people who may seem to be our enemies who are really our allies. This is actually a theme of his great novel *The Man Who Was Thursday*. The people we are so sure are against us, turn out in the end to be fighting for the same thing we are.

But in the end, there are only two choices. Chesterton makes the astounding statement that "if every human being lived a thousand years, every human being would end up

---

[28] "The Theology of Christmas Presents" in the *Chesterton Review*, vol. 7, no. 4, November 1981.

either in utter pessimistic scepticism or in the Catholic creed." [29] Even more astounding is that he said it long before he himself became Catholic. But long after his conversion he confirms, "Those who know the Catholic practice find it not only right, but always right when everything else is wrong." [30] If that sounds arrogant and hard-nosed, I would like to assure you that it is not. When G.K. Chesterton claims to be right, it is never a boast; it is always an act of humility. When he points out error, as he does in practically everything he writes, it is never to score points; it is always an act of love. Defending the Faith must always be an act of love. Not only do we love what we are defending, but we love who is attacking it. Our goal is not to crush our enemies but to convert them.

When G.K. Chesterton died in 1936, Pope Pius XI called him "a gifted defender of the faith". Condolences were sent to Mrs. Chesterton from the Vatican Secretary of State, Cardinal Eugenio Pacelli, who would himself become pope less than three years later. The Church knew it had lost a great soldier. But in the years since his death, it has become quite apparent that Chesterton is still fighting the battle. His abundant writings are still here for us, speaking to us directly, as timely and as timeless as when he first poured them onto page after page. And there is still much to be learned from this unwavering warrior about the art of defending the Faith.

---

[29] *William Blake* (London: House of Stratus, 2000), 57. Chesterton wrote this astonishing comment twelve years before he himself became Catholic.
[30] *The Thing,* *CW* 3:190.

16

Ten Thousand Reasons

G. K. Chesterton began his writing career by defending religion against the atheism and agnosticism of his age. He argued that doubt gets us nowhere, that religion makes us joyful about things that matter, while the new philosophies make us sad about things that don't matter. Soon he was defending not just religion in general, but Christianity as opposed to all other religions—and irreligions. He argued that the Apostles' Creed was the source of the greatest sanity in the world. Other religions not only do not offer the strength and comfort and meaning of Christianity; they do not offer the fierce joy of Christ. "Christianity", he said, "even when watered down is hot enough to boil all modern society to rags." [1]

But Chesterton noticed that much of modern society was derived from a liberalized and Protestantized Christianity that had fallen far from its origins. Ultimately Chesterton returned to those origins. He became a Roman Catholic and ended up defending the Catholic Church against the whole world. He called his conversion "the chief event" of

[1] *Orthodoxy, CW* 1:323.

his life.[2] And, yet, when he defended the Church he did not like to talk about his personal experience, because he felt that made the Faith look too small. He claimed it was the universal truth, and therefore he wished to defend it as such, by speaking in universals, by showing how it was true for everybody and not just himself.

But explaining why the truth is true is a huge task, because it means talking about everything. But that's the way it should be. As Chesterton says, "A man is not really convinced of a philosophic theory when he finds that something proves it. He is only really convinced when he finds that everything proves it."[3] Still, that does not make it any easier to explain or defend.

> The difficulty of explaining why I am a Catholic is that there are ten thousand reasons all amounting to one reason: that Catholicism is true. I could write ten thousand separate sentences each beginning with the words, "The Catholic Church is the only thing that ..."[4]

Ten thousand reasons? Well, let's go through them:

1. *The Catholic Church "is the only thing in which the superior cannot be superior; in the sense of supercilious".*[5]

This may seem like an odd one to start with, but we're sort of using Chesterton's order. When there are thousands of reasons, I guess it doesn't matter where we start. What this one means is this: the Church is of a higher

[2] *The Everlasting Man, CW* 2:141.
[3] *Orthodoxy, CW* 1:287.
[4] "Why I Am a Catholic", in *The Thing, CW* 3:127.
[5] Ibid.

nature than the world. It is, in fact, better than anything in the world. It is heavenly. It informs every other kind of knowledge. It gives an eternal perspective to every other discipline. It holds the keys. It bestows blessings over everything and everyone, over babies when they are baptized, over men and women when they are married, over the dead when they are buried. Only a superior thing can bestow a blessing. But the Church can never *act* superior. That's what supercilious means: acting superior, acting with arrogance. The Church cannot do this. It can never puff itself up and look disdainfully on the rest of the world. On the contrary, the Church, like Christ, lays itself down for the rest of the world. The Church serves the poor, elevating them like kings. The Church seeks the outcasts who have been chased away by everyone else. The Church looks after the small things, the weak things. It brings knowledge and education the way light is brought into the darkness, but at the same time it brings charity and humility and sacrifice to a world that is hateful and selfish and prideful and ... supercilious. Though the Church is the highest thing in the world; it must act like the lowest. And this is what Jesus meant when he said that the first shall be last; the last shall be first, and the greatest among you must be your servant.[6]

2. *The Catholic Church "is the only thing that really prevents a sin from being a secret".*[7]

Well, I might not have picked it as the second reason, but we'd have to get around to this unpleasant subject

[6] See Mark 9:35.
[7] "Why I Am a Catholic", *CW* 3:127.

eventually. The Church is the only thing in the world that calls sin what it is: sin. It does not explain away sin or dismiss sin or deny sin. It faces sin. It requires us to admit our sin, to confess our sin. And if we do not confess it, it destroys us. If we keep sin a secret it keeps doing its deadly deeds in the dark. If we do not confess our personal sins, we fall farther and farther away from God until we deny him altogether. When we rationalize our behavior, when we justify our misdeeds, we in effect replace God with ourselves. We have thrown out God's rules and replaced them with our own. But by turning around and facing God again, by confessing our sins and acknowledging our faults, by telling our secrets to our confessor, we enter back into communion with our Creator. And what is true for the individual is true for the whole society. When a whole society denies sin, when it tries, for instance, to claim that homosexual behavior or the slaughter of unborn babies or the neglect of the poor is perfectly acceptable, then the whole society destroys itself. It sinks into the dark and eventually disappears. Chesterton says that a whole people has a soul just as an individual does, and a whole people can repent just as an individual can.[8] As Catholics, we have to be the conscience of a society that has turned away from God. We have to be that voice that keeps telling the world to turn back and confess its sins and, as the prophet Isaiah says, "Seek the Lord, while he may be found."[9]

That's two reasons; we still have several thousand to go . . .

---

[8] See *Alarms and Discursions* (New York: Dodd, Mead, 1911), 191.
[9] Isaiah 55:6.

3. *The Catholic Church "is the only thing that frees a man from the degrading slavery of being a child of his age".* [10]

Now, this is more like it. I'm surprised we didn't start with this one. It's worth repeating: "The Catholic Church 'is the only thing that frees a man from the degrading slavery of being a child of his age'." The way of Christ and the way of the world are diametrically opposed. When we follow Christ, we are going against the way of the world. For Chesterton, this is liberating. To be caught up in the way of the world is to be a slave to fads and fashions, to trendy ideas that always fail and always flee. The Church is not burdened by fashion. And fashion *is* a burden. It is a beast that is insatiable and never satisfied. It is always changing. But "Jesus Christ is the same yesterday and today and for ever." [11] To be a child of the age is, as Chesterton says, degrading. But to transcend the age is exhilarating. It is an act of dignity to defy the fads. As Chesterton says, "A dead thing can go with the stream; only a living thing can go against it." [12]

4. *The Catholic Church "is the only thing that talks as if it were the truth; as if it were a real messenger refusing to tamper with a real message".* [13]

This is very important. One of the many things that the world does not understand about the Church—no, *two* of the many things that the world does not understand about the Church is that it speaks its message with authority and

[10] "Why I Am a Catholic", *CW* 3:127.
[11] Hebrews 13:8.
[12] *The Everlasting Man, CW* 2:388.
[13] "Why I Am a Catholic", *CW* 3:127.

that it cannot *tamper* with its message. It cannot change the truth; it can only try to convey the truth. That is why Pope Paul VI could not issue an encyclical approving contraception. He could only uphold the truth that had been passed along to him by the authority of the Church, authorized by the Author of Life, God himself. That is why a pope cannot suddenly ordain women as priests. He has no authority to do so. There is a sacred order to things. Priesthood has a specific meaning, and no one in the Church can simply change that meaning to his own liking. The pope risks being unpopular with the whole world, including even many Catholics, every time he makes a pronouncement—because people often do not want to hear the truth. But when the pope makes a pronouncement he does not say anything new; he only tries to make truths clear, truths that are very old. There are no new truths, only the Truth that makes all things new.[14]

5. *The Catholic Church "is the only type of Christianity that really contains every type of man; even the respectable man".*[15]

A typical Chesterton paradox. Something the opposite of what we expect. But think about it. Most religions appeal to the poor and the humble, to the common man. That is because religion is something natural to normal human beings. Our souls long for God as much as our bodies thirst for water. But there is a minority of people—the sophisticated, the educated, the wealthy—who, interestingly enough, are "respectable" in the world, who reject religion, and who have convinced themselves that religion is something merely

[14] See Revelation 21:5.
[15] "Why I Am a Catholic", *CW* 3:127.

for the ignorant and the unwashed. But the Catholic Church
has a way of bringing even these proud folks to their knees.
The Church satisfies the needs of the intellect. It satisfies
the needs of the senses, including the artistic sense. And it
even satisfies the needs of people who think they have everything. The Catholic Church is the only place in this world
where money has no power, where wealth is exactly the
opposite of important. The Church appeals to an amazingly wide variety of people, even to people to whom religion does not normally appeal. It reaches across class, across
borders, and even across time. It is as universal as its name
suggests.

6. *The Catholic Church "is the only large attempt to change
   the world from the inside; working through wills and not
   laws".*[16]

Attempting "to change the world from the inside" means
trying to change people only by changing their minds. Every
other large institution tries to change the world from the
outside. They rely on power, on forcing different mechanisms and environments and behaviors on people. There is
a difference between power and authority. The Church does
not act with power; it acts with authority. In fact, about
the only times it has really failed in its mission have been
when it has tried to use power. And in those cases the
Church's weakness was that it gave in to the world and
tried to use the world's devices. It undermined its own
authority by imitating the world's methods of using power.
Authority is something connected to the Author, the One
Who Authorizes. It was Christ himself who gave authority

[16] Ibid.

to his apostles, and to Peter, the Rock upon whom he built his Church. Authority is something we choose to recognize, to honor, and to obey. Power is something that is merely coercive or restrictive, something that leaves us with no choice. For Chesterton, one of the greatest doctrines of the Catholic faith is free will, what he calls the "dizzy vision of liberty".[17] It does not force anyone into the truth. We have to make the choice ourselves. And we have to make the choice every day.

7. *The Catholic Church "is the only institution that ever attempted to create a machinery of pardon. The Church is the only thing that ever attempted by a system to pursue and discover crimes, not in order to avenge, but in order to forgive them."*[18]

I was waiting for one like this. Chesterton, the lover and writer of detective stories, here likens the Church to a detective, a sleuth who pursues and discovers crimes, not in order to avenge them, but to forgive them. That is exactly what his great character, Father Brown, does so charmingly and so well in story after story. Chesterton says that the Church has a "merciless mercy".[19] The Church is an unrelenting sleuth, tirelessly and doggedly hunting down souls, in order to save them instead of slay them. And he says that what gives the adventure even more dramatic tension is that the modern world curses the Church for not saving the world, which does not wish to be saved.[20]

[17] *The Catholic Church and Conversion*, *CW* 3:120.
[18] *A Miscellany of Men* (Norfolk, Va.: IHS Press, 2004), 146.
[19] Ibid., 147.
[20] See *ILN*, March 2, 1929.

8. *The Catholic Church is the only thing that ever founded a civilization on first love, on "the single and romantic view of sex; we have the only scheme that believes in chivalry; we alone serve St. George and St. Valentine. We alone among the great religions of the world have a creed that interprets mystically these physical things; we alone believe in the resurrection of the body."*[21]

We just talked about the Church trying to change the world from the inside. But we also have to admit the fact that the Church already has changed the world. We have forgotten that our civilization is based on the Church's teachings. Not only its laws, but its everyday life. The high view of marriage and the family, the proper respect of the body, the role of chivalry, are all based on the sacraments. And our whole society declines as we move away from these basic and beautiful things.

9. *The Catholic Church "is the only continuous intelligent institution that has been thinking about thinking for two thousand years. Its experience covers nearly all experiences; and especially nearly all errors. The Church makes itself responsible for warning her people against all the blind alleys and dead ends and roads that lead to destruction. She dogmatically defends humanity from its worst foes, from those devouring monsters of the old mistakes. There is no other corporate mind in the world that is on the watch to prevent minds from going wrong. The policeman comes too late, when he tries to prevent men from going wrong. The doctor comes too late, for he only comes to lock up a madman, not to advise a sane man on how not to go mad. And all other sects and*

---

[21] *Daily News*, May 23, 1903.

schools are inadequate for the purpose. This is not because each of them may not contain a truth, but precisely because each of them does contain a truth; and is content to contain a truth. None of the others really pretends to contain the truth. None of the others, that is, really pretends to be looking out in all directions at once. The Church is not merely armed against the heresies of the past or even of the present, but equally against those of the future, that may be the exact opposite of those of the present."[22]

I am happy to say that I can't add anything to that.

10. *The Catholic Church is the only philosophy operating from first principles and not from fashionable prejudices.*[23]

First principles. Why didn't we use this one for starters? Could there be a better place to start than with first principles? Chesterton is a great defender of the faith, and one of the reasons is that he is so reasonable. He knows how to use the tool of reason. But the tool has its limits—especially in today's intellectual confusion, where people are unable to grasp the abstract concept of first principles. A first principle means "the thing with which thought has to start, since it must start with something".[24] A first principle is a thing that cannot be proved or need not be proved, either because it is self-evident, or it is accepted by most everyone. In other words, it's something like common sense.

Chesterton claims that the Catholic Church is the only philosophy operating from first principles. For instance, we

[22] "Why I Am a Catholic", *CW* 3:129.
[23] See *America*, June 6, 1929.
[24] Ibid.

could use first principles to establish the basis for one of the fundamental doctrines of the faith, which is the Fall of man. We could start by saying that it is a first principle that men desire happiness. Most everyone agrees with that idea, without us having to prove it. In fact, anybody who denies that men desire happiness is, well, cracked.

If we grant as a first principle that men desire happiness, we can go on from there to "examine the curious manner" in which they fail to get happiness. And, then, by referring to experience and reason we can show the soundness of the doctrine of the Fall. And from there we can continue to the "subsequent ideas of redemption and revelation". And then we could "consider the record of that revelation, and what it said, and in what sense it should be taken".[25] Very systematically, we could make the whole case for the truth of the Catholic Faith.

11. *The Catholic Church is the only Church that can claim to be the Church.*[26]

The most unacceptable and most unpalatable claim of the Catholic Church in today's world is the Church's claim to be the true Church.

G. K. Chesterton is one of the great ecumenical writers. He is admired by Catholics, Protestants, and even non-Christians because of his goodness and truthfulness and unconquerable joy. He is very fair to other faiths. He acknowledges that many Protestant sects have had their own saints and prophets and provided a living and inspiring faith for their adherents. But each of these sects came about

[25] Ibid.
[26] See *The Catholic Church and Conversion, CW* 3:99.

because they believed they were right and everybody else was wrong. In the end, their ultimate claim has to be weighed against the claim of the Catholic Church, from whom they broke away. And it requires far more faith or fanaticism, says Chesterton, to believe that a small chapel can sustain its own claim over the great international Church. And, as a matter of fact, most of the Protestant sects, which arose out of the claim that they were right and everybody else was wrong, gradually retreated into the stance that nobody is completely right, and everybody is probably a little wrong. And this led to the position taken by modern philosophy: that everybody is equally wrong. The rise of Protestantism led directly to the fall of Protestantism.

12. *The Catholic Church is the only institution that is "not only right but always right where everything else is wrong".*[27]

Right where everything else is wrong. This is a grand claim indeed. But the Catholic Church brings us the honesty of the confessional when the rest of the world soothes itself with the lies of psychology. The Church upholds humility when the rest of the world preaches pride. The Church brings sacrificial charity to relieve human suffering, when the rest of the world wants brutal utilitarianism. The Church teaches free will and responsibility when the rest of the world trips into determinism and irresponsibility. The Church keeps a well-defined doctrine, when the rest of the world wants broad and meaningless sentimentalism. The Church values the past, when the rest of the world wants to forget it. But the Church is also realistic about the future, as in the four last things (death, judgment, heaven, hell), when the rest of

[27] *The Thing, CW* 3:190.

the world talks only about progress and utopia. The Church embraces life in the midst of a culture of death.

Hm. It looks like we're not going to have enough room to go through all ten thousand reasons. But we did pretty well. We got through ... twelve. All good ones, too. And all amounting to the same reason: that Catholicism is true. But before we end, we should add one other reason. After his conversion, Chesterton never missed a day of obligation. One Sunday morning as he was struggling to get ready to go to Mass, he said that only a religion that was true could possibly get him out of bed so early in the morning.

17

A Sacramental Understanding

For certain skeptics[1] in the modern age, there is only one reality: the physical world. There is no spiritual reality at all, and religion is a bunch of bunk. On the other end of the spectrum, there are some modern religious cults, from Christian Science to Westernized versions of Eastern mysticism, that have not merely rejected materialism, but have rejected the very physicality of the world itself. G. K. Chesterton says this is the biggest blunder of these new religions. Being "purely spiritual", he says, is opposed to the very essence of religion. Throughout history, all religions, high and low, true and false, have had one thing in common: the idea of visible, tangible holiness. It is obvious enough that a philosophy which is purely materialist is opposed to religion. It is perhaps surprising that a philosophy that is purely spiritual is also opposed to religion. Those who reject holiness and the sacred have made their decision. They need not detain us any longer. But those who deny the visible and the tangible, those who break away from organized religion into something they call "pure spirituality", not only go against religion; they go against

[1] Sounds like an oxymoron. If they were certain, they wouldn't be skeptics.

common sense. They deny the *significance* of the material world, and in extreme cases even deny the *reality* of the physical world. But you cannot have faith-healing without having a body to heal. Neither can you do faith-healing without doing some physical act. Savages may invoke their demons over the dying, but to do them justice, says Chesterton, they dance round the dying or yell or *do something*.[2] So, whether your religion has bread and wine, or eye of newt and toe of frog, in either case there is a material aspect to it. You can't have holy water without water. You can't have holy oils without the oils.

A sacrament is soul and substance together. It is real, but it is also a riddle. That is why a mystery is a mystery. There is something about it that is begging to be figured out. It takes a plain thing like water or bread or wine, a plain act like eating or kneeling or kissing or dying, and it reveals something eternal.

The sacraments are very hard to understand, and even harder to explain. In fact, when Christ himself first explained the Sacrament of the Eucharist to his disciples, they shook their heads and murmured, "This is a hard saying. Who can accept it?"[3]

Chesterton says that the sacraments are "certain and incredible".[4] Certain and incredible: a typical Chesterton paradox. Two ideas that seem to contradict each other, and yet both are true. Certain and incredible. The sacraments have a solid physical aspect and at the same time a fantastical spiritual aspect. Or, you could even say the sacraments have a *solid* spiritual reality. The sacraments are a

---

[2] See *ILN*, November 5, 1910. Emphasis mine.
[3] John 6:60.
[4] *The Ball and the Cross*, *CW* 7:132. "Certain and incredible" is not an oxymoron. It is a paradox.

way of touching what cannot be touched and seeing what is invisible. The paradox of the sacraments reflects the great paradox of God himself. A spirit who became flesh. An eternal being who died. The cross is very real and very mystical. It is certain and it is incredible.

Now, you could argue that all of Chesterton's books are religious—and you would win the argument—but what makes that comment so interesting—that the sacraments are "certain and incredible"—is that it comes not in one of Chesterton's books that is overtly about theology or philosophy or apologetics; it comes in one of his novels. In Chesterton's fiction, we see his ideas come to life as characters and events. And it is in his fiction that we see perhaps his most creative approach to explaining the sacraments.

In his novel *The Ball and the Cross* Chesterton stages a long debate between an atheist named Turnbull and a Catholic named MacIan. Turnbull, who considers himself a freethinker, regularly publishes blasphemy in his newspaper called *The Atheist*, but cannot manage to get a rise out of anyone. But one day the devout MacIan reads one of Turnbull's grossly anti-Catholic statements, something to the effect that the story of the Virgin Mary is merely borrowed from some pagan cult where the God-figure seduced a young maiden. MacIan knows when his mother has been insulted, and he goes and confronts Turnbull and challenges him to an affair of honor, that is, a duel. Turnbull is pleased that he has finally been taken seriously and accepts the challenge. The problem, however, is that dueling is illegal, and the two gentlemen can never find a place to fight one another safely without being interrupted by the local law enforcement. And so, they scramble across the country trying to carry out their physical duel, all the while carrying on a philosophical duel.

In one of their verbal clashes, Turnbull makes the bold assertion that heretics and skeptics have actually helped the world move forward and "handed on a lamp of progress!" MacIan replies:

"Nothing is plainer from real history than that each of your heretics invented a complete cosmos of his own which the next heretic smashed entirely to pieces. Who knows now exactly what Nestorius taught? Who cares? There are only two things that we know for certain about it. The first is that Nestorius, as a heretic, taught something quite opposite to the teaching of Arius, the heretic who came before him, and something quite useless to James Turnbull, the heretic who comes after. I defy you to go back to the Free-thinkers of the past and find any habitation for yourself at all. I defy you to read Godwin or Shelley or the deists of the eighteenth century or the nature-worshipping humanists of the Renaissance, without discovering that you differ from them twice as much as you differ from the Pope. You are a nineteenth-century sceptic, and you are always telling me that I ignore the cruelty of nature. If you had been an eighteenth-century sceptic you would have told me that I ignore the kindness and benevolence of nature. You are an atheist, and you praise the deists of the eighteenth century. Read them instead of praising them, and you will find that their whole universe stands or falls with the deity. You are a materialist, and you think Bruno a scientific hero. See what he said and you will think him an insane mystic. No, the great Free-thinker, with his genuine ability and honesty, does not in practice destroy Christianity. What he does destroy is the Free-thinker who went before. Free-thought may be suggestive, it may be inspiriting, it may have as much as you please of the merits that come from vivacity and variety. But there is one thing Free-thought can never be by any possibility—Free-thought can never be progressive.

It can never be progressive because it will accept nothing from the past; it begins every time again from the beginning; and it goes every time in a different direction. All the rational philosophers have gone along different roads, so it is impossible to say which has gone farthest. Who can discuss whether Emerson was a better optimist than Schopenhauer was a pessimist? It is like asking if this corn is as yellow as that hill is steep. No; there are only two things that really progress; and they both accept accumulations of authority. They may be progressing uphill or down; they may be growing steadily better or steadily worse; but they have steadily increased in certain definable matters; they have steadily advanced in a certain definable direction; they are the only two things, it seems, that ever *can* progress. The first is strictly physical science. The second is the Catholic Church."

"Physical science and the Catholic Church!" said Turnbull sarcastically; "and no doubt the first owes a great deal to the second."

"If you pressed that point I might reply that it was very probable", answered MacIan calmly. "I often fancy that your historical generalizations rest frequently on random instances; I should not be surprised if your vague notions of the Church as the persecutor of science was a generalization from Galileo. I should not be at all surprised if, when you counted the scientific investigations and discoveries since the fall of Rome, you found that a great mass of them had been made by monks. But the matter is irrelevant to my meaning. I say that if you want an example of anything which has progressed in the moral world by the same method as science in the material world, by continually adding to without unsettling what was there before, then I say that there *is* only one example of it. And that is Us."

"With this enormous difference," said Turnbull, "that however elaborate be the calculations of physical science, their net result can be tested. Granted that it took millions of books I never read and millions of men I never heard of to discover the electric light. Still I can see the electric light. But I cannot see the supreme virtue which is the result of all your theologies and sacraments."

"Catholic virtue is often invisible because it is the normal", answered MacIan.[5]

The normal sometimes *is* invisible. Only because we don't notice the normal things. We don't notice normal things because we are used to them. Water. Bread. Wine. Oil. Marriage. These are normal things. We have to stop occasionally and realize their enormous significance. We have to make special note of them in very special acts to see their sacramental qualities—because what is holy is what is normal. What is holy is the divine order. Whatever goes against that order, whatever departs from that order, is abnormal. Virtue is normal. Vice is abnormal.

Chesterton is always trying to get us to better appreciate the normal. Perhaps his most creative work in this regard is his novel *Manalive*, where we meet one of the most fascinating characters in all of literature, a man with the wonderful name of Innocent Smith. Innocent Smith is on trial for attempted murder, for burglary, and for polygamy. He has indeed fired a gun at a man. He has indeed broken into a house and taken things. And he has indeed eloped many times. But he is, as his name suggests, innocent of all the charges. For the man he shot at was grateful because he was suddenly jolted into appreciating life. The house he broke into was his own home. And all the women he ran away with were actually the same woman: his wife. Love is one of those things that is certain and incredible, which is

[5] Ibid. 118–19.

why marriage is a sacrament. Innocent Smith is always trying to see his own life from the outside so that he can see it
better. And see it better he does. He is always trying to see
his house from a fresh angle and a completely different perspective, even if he has to walk around the world to do it. He
is always seeing his wife as if seeing her for the first time. Innocent Smith sees that life is a marvel, an undeserved gift, and
he tries to give that vision to others. It is a sacramental vision.
He says that he knows there should be priests to remind men
that they will one day die. But there should also be another
kind of priest to remind men that they are not dead yet.[6]

There is great joy in that sacramental vision of life. Innocent Smith is a happy man. And he is innocent. He is good.
But he is not good because he is happy. He is happy because
he is good.

What about the rest of us? Those who have failed to be
good? The Catholic Church has a sacrament to restore our
innocence. We need forgiveness in order to have another
chance to be good. The Sacrament of Reconciliation, confession, does that. Confessing our sins to a priest is a physical act. Penance is a physical act. Again, it is a difficult
thing to explain to non-Catholics. But Chesterton explains
it very well in one of his Father Brown stories. In it a mysterious character who committed a crime long ago has lived
as a recluse in his mansion ever since, supposedly "under
the influence of monks". A group of sympathetic people,
some of whom once knew him a long time ago, now want
to see him, to deliver him, as it were, from his deep funk
of remorse. They represent the enlightened modern types.
Father Brown urges them not to disturb the mysterious man.

---

[6] See *Manalive*, *CW* 7:378.

"You'd much better leave him alone. He knows what he's doing and it'll only make everybody unhappy."

Lady Outram ... looked at the little priest with cold contempt.

"Really, sir," she said, "this is a very private occasion, and I don't understand what you have to do with it."

"Trust a priest to have to do with a private occasion", snarled Sir John Cockspur. "Don't you know they live behind the scenes like rats behind the wainscot burrowing their way into everybody's private rooms?"...

"Oh, that's all right", said Father Brown, with the impatience of anxiety.... "His clerical tastes have been much exaggerated. I tell you he knows what he's about, and I do implore you all to leave him alone."

"You mean to leave him to this living death of moping and going mad in a ruin!" cried Lady Outram, in a voice that shook a little. "And all because he had the bad luck to shoot a man in a duel more than a quarter of a century ago. Is that what you call Christian charity?"

"Yes," answered the priest stolidly, "that is what I call Christian charity."

"It's about all the Christian charity you'll ever get out of these priests", cried Cockspur bitterly. "That's their only idea of pardoning a poor fellow for a piece of folly; to wall him up alive and starve him to death with fasts and penances and pictures of hell-fire. And all because a bullet went wrong."

"Really, Father Brown," said General Outram, "do you honestly think he deserves this? Is that your Christianity?"

"Surely the true Christianity", pleaded his wife more gently, "is that which knows all and pardons all; the love that can remember—and forget."

"Father Brown," said young Mallow, very earnestly, "I generally agree with what you say; but I'm hanged if I can follow you here. A shot in a duel, followed instantly by remorse, is not such an awful offense."

"I admit", said Father Brown dully, "that I take a more serious view of his offense."

"God soften your hard heart", said the strange lady, speaking for the first time.[7]

So, how is our hero going to get out of this one? Well, he does. But we aren't going to tell you how he does it, because the worst sin in the world is to give away the solution to a mystery story. The people who do that, says Chesterton, have a spot reserved for them at the lowest level of hell, next to Judas and the other traitors. But we are going to show you what happens *after* what happens next, after the solution is revealed. All we can tell you is that the people who were scolding Father Brown about being uncharitable find out what the criminal had *really* done. And their attitude suddenly changes. They stare at him with pale faces:

"Are you sure of this?" asked Sir John at last, in a thick voice.

"I am sure of it," said Father Brown, "and now I leave [him] to your Christian charity. You have told me something today about Christian charity. You seemed to me to give it almost too large a place; but how fortunate it is for poor sinners like this man that you err so much on the side of mercy, and are ready to be reconciled to all mankind."

"Hang it all," exploded the general, "if you think I'm going to be reconciled to a filthy viper like that, I tell you I wouldn't say a word to save him from hell. I said I could pardon a regular decent duel, but of all the treacherous assassins—"

[7] Since we're not going to tell the ending of the story, neither are we going to tell you which story it is.

"He ought to be lynched", cried Cockspur excitedly. "He ought to burn alive. . . . And if there is such a thing as burning for ever, he jolly well—"

"I wouldn't touch him with a barge pole myself", said Mallow.

"There is a limit to human charity", said Lady Outram, trembling all over.

"There is," said Father Brown dryly, "and that is the real difference between human charity and Christian charity. You must forgive me if I was not altogether crushed by your contempt for my uncharitableness today; or by the lectures you read me about pardon for every sinner. For it seems to me that you only pardon the sins that you don't really think sinful. You only forgive criminals when they commit what you don't regard as crimes, but rather as conventions. So you tolerate a conventional duel, just as you tolerate a conventional divorce. You forgive because there isn't anything to be forgiven."

"But hang it all," cried Mallow, "you don't expect us to be able to pardon a vile thing like this?"

"No," said the priest, "but *we* have to be able to pardon it."

He stood up abruptly and looked round at them.

"We have to touch such men, not with a barge pole, but with a benediction", he said. "We have to say the word that will save them from hell. We alone are left to deliver them from despair when your human charity deserts them. Go on your own primrose path pardoning all your favourite vices and being generous to your fashionable crimes; and leave us in the darkness, vampires of the night, to console those who really need consolation; who do things really indefensible, things that neither the world nor they themselves can defend; and none but a priest will pardon. Leave us with the men who commit the mean and revolting and real crimes; mean as St. Peter when the cock crew, and yet the dawn came."

"The dawn", repeated Mallow doubtfully. "You mean hope—for *him*?"

"Yes", replied the other. "Let me ask you one question. You are great ladies and men of honour and secure of yourselves; you would never, you can tell yourselves, stoop to such squalid treason as that. But tell me this. If any of you had so stooped, which of you, years afterwards, when you were old and rich and safe, would have been driven by conscience or confessor to tell such a story of yourself? You say you could not commit so base a crime. Could you confess so base a crime?" [8]

The real difficulty with the sacrament of confession, as Chesterton points out, is not forgiving the horrible sins that *others* commit. It is confessing the sins that *we* commit. Confession means coming face to face with God, but also face to face with yourself. Chesterton, after he became Catholic, realized that the Catholic Church was the only thing that was willing to go with him into the depths of himself. [9]

The sacraments always reveal more of God, but they also take away our masks. The Sacrament of Confirmation is about standing up before God and a congregation of witnesses and declaring, "This is what I believe." It is a sacrament that is then put to the test for the rest of our lives. Time after time, as doubt or sorrow or tragedy befalls us, it is as if God were asking, "Do you *really* believe it? Do you believe it even *now*?" That is the meaning of the Book of Job. And that is the meaning of Chesterton's greatest novel, *The Man Who Was Thursday*. Go read it.

---

[8] In case you have not already read footnote number 7, now is a good time.
[9] See *Autobiography*, *CW* 16:329.

And what about the Eucharist? Chesterton deals with this sacrament in *The Ball and the Cross*. Remember poor old Turnbull, the atheist? His debate and delayed duel with MacIan gets further complicated when he starts falling in love with a young Catholic woman named Madeleine. He disguises himself and starts following her to Mass every morning. She finally talks to him not only about his duel, but about the sacraments:

> "You may be right or wrong to risk dying", said the girl, simply; "the poor women in our village risk it whenever they have a baby. You men are the other half of the world. I know nothing about when you ought to die. But surely if you are daring to try and find God beyond the grave and appeal to Him—you ought to let Him find you when He comes and stands there every morning in our little church."
>
> "O God! I can't stand this! . . ."
>
> "You always go to Mass," answered the girl, opening her wide blue eyes, "and the Mass is very long and tiresome unless one loves God."
>
> . . . He advanced upon Madeleine with flaming eyes, and almost took her by the two shoulders. "I do not love God", he cried, . . . "I do not want to find Him; I do not think He is there to be found. I must burst up the show; I must and will say everything. You are the happiest and honestest thing I ever saw in this godless universe. And I am the dirtiest and most dishonest."
>
> Madeleine looked at him doubtfully for an instant, and then said with a sudden simplicity and cheerfulness: "Oh, but if you are really sorry it is all right. If you are horribly sorry it is all the better. You have only to go and tell the priest so and he will give you God out of his own hands."
>
> "I hate your priest and I deny your God!" cried the man; "and I tell you God is a lie and a fable and a mask. . . . I am sure there is no God."

"But there is", said Madeleine, quite quietly, and rather with the air of one telling children about an elephant. "Why, I touched His body only this morning."

"You touched a bit of bread", said Turnbull, biting his knuckles. "Oh, I will say anything that can madden you!"

"You think it is only a bit of bread", said the girl, and her lips tightened ever so little.

"I know it is only a bit of bread", said Turnbull, with violence.

She flung back her open face and smiled. "Then why did you refuse to eat it?" she said.[10]

In his own personal experience, Chesterton referred to the Eucharist as "that tremendous Reality".[11] It was so real, he was so in awe of it, that he only approached it in true fear and trembling. It is fitting that in his fiction, he respects it even through the character of an atheist and blasphemer.

---

[10] *The Ball and the Cross*, *CW* 7:163–65.

[11] Maisie Ward, *Return to Chesterton* (New York: Sheed and Ward, 1952), 299.

18

Saints and Sinners

One of the main points about the saints is not how saintly they are, but how human they are. Of course, one of the other main points about the saints is how saintly they are. On the one hand, they are just like us, with all the human variety and frailty and fascination and personality and pain and talent and lack of talent that you expect to find in any human being. On the other hand, they are nothing like us because of their holiness, their intimacy with God, their giant faith, and their giant humility. They are not like us, but we could be like them. If we wanted to. Sainthood is open to everybody. As Chesterton says, "When we rebuke a man for being a sinner, we imply that he has the powers of a saint." [1]

How do we become saints? By giving ourselves totally to Christ, by living the Christian life in its completeness, inside and out. Simple, right? Well, sadly for us ... it *is* simple! We make our lives complicated by *not* being saints. Sin has complicated things from the beginning. But if we let Christ deal with us, he will even deal with our sin.

The Bible tells us the good news of salvation, and it is of course very important to study Sacred Scripture. Besides

[1] *Fancies* vs. *Fads* (London: Methuen, 1929), 89.

the Gospels and the Epistles, there is a great deal to be learned from contemplating the Old Testament prophets and the psalmists, who were very intimate with God. But that kind of intimacy with God did not end with Bible times. There have been heroes of the faith throughout the history of the Church, and we really need to study them as well. The saints are the model Christians. They have successfully lived the Christian life. The saints' lives are "applied Christianity", or we could even say, "practical Christianity". Because it is Christianity put into practice.

There may be notable people in history who come along and practice some noble behavior or live out some ideal and may even get a few others to do it for a while, but then they disappear. But when a saint comes along, he puts a virtue into practice and it becomes a permanent thing, just as the Franciscans still carry on the virtue of St. Francis of Assisi. The Greeks and the Romans may have set up an ideal of virginity. But Catholicism *achieved* an ideal of virginity. Chesterton says that the Church has "a special power of virtue", because "[t]he Church is the only thing on earth that can perpetuate a type of virtue and make it something more than a fashion." [2]

> Empires break; industrial conditions change; the suburbs will not last for ever. What will remain? I will tell you. The Catholic Saint will remain. [3]

The saints are good; they are happy; they are humble; they are mystical. These qualities are all bound together and are so closely connected that it is difficult to talk about them one at a time. But we'll try. Let's talk about that last one

[2] *The Ball and the Cross, CW* 7:120.
[3] Ibid., 121.

first. Mysticism. Chesterton says that mysticism is only a transcendent form of common sense.[4] Common sense is the truths that we all know to be true. It is the common mind.

> With this mere phrase, the common mind, we collide with a current error. Commonness and the common mind are now generally spoken of as meaning ... inferiority and the inferior mind; the mind of the mere mob. But the common mind means the mind of all the artists and heroes; or else it would not be common. Plato had the common mind; Dante had the common mind. ... Commonness means the quality common to the saint and the sinner, to the philosopher and the fool. ... In everybody there is a certain thing that loves babies, that fears death, that likes sunlight. ... And everybody does not mean uneducated crowds; everybody means everybody.[5]

The truth that God has revealed is universal. We know it is true even when we deny it and run away from it. The saint runs toward it. He pursues the truth to its fullest extent. The mysticism of the saints is simply a profound appreciation of the truth that is achieved through contemplation and action. Mystics do not have their heads in the clouds. They usually have their hands in the dirt. They are at work building the Kingdom of God. Saints are often dirty. Chesterton says they can afford to be dirty, while, seducers, on the other hand, have to be clean.[6]

Next, let's talk about goodness. While we might be convinced of a saint's goodness, the saint himself is never convinced. Chesterton says that a saint is a man who really

---

[4] See *Twelve Types* (Norfolk, Va.: IHS Press, 2003), 58.

[5] *Charles Dickens*, *CW* 15:100.

[6] See *What's Wrong with the World*, *CW* 4:189.

knows he is a sinner.[7] So the first step to goodness is confession. The first step to confession is humility. I told you these things were connected.

> The great strength of Christian sanctity has always been simply this—that the worst enemies of the saints could not say of the saints anything worse than [the saints] said of themselves. It is disheartening to go on abusing a man while he is quite unconscious of your presence, but is in a low and furious undertone abusing himself. This has always been the strong point of even the most commonplace Christianity. Suppose the village Atheist had a sudden and splendid impulse to rush into the village church and denounce everybody there as miserable offenders. He might break in at the exact moment when they were saying the same thing themselves. You can say anything against a man who praises himself, but a man who blames himself is invulnerable.[8]

While the saint is certainly superior to us, he is never conscious of his superiority. Chesterton says the saint is only more conscious of his inferiority than we are of ours.[9]

We're still trying to talk about goodness here, but we keep talking about humility. The idea of being honored and rewarded for plain goodness is something that the world just doesn't get. Chesterton points out that we almost have to be reminded that a saint means a very good person. He gives an illustration to make the point.[10] Suppose we entered a foreign town and found a great pillar with a statue on top and found out that that hero was famous for his politeness and hilarity during a chronic toothache. Or suppose we

[7] See *Alarms and Discursions* (New York: Dodd, Mead, 1911), 281.

[8] *ILN*, October 26, 1907.

[9] See *Short History of England, CW* 20:432.

[10] Ibid., 473.

saw a procession come down the street with a brass band and a hero on a white horse, and we learned that he was being celebrated because he had been very patient with his half-witted maiden aunt. We would be a little surprised. That kind of honor is usually given to war heroes. But it is the inspiration of the Catholic Church to give high glory to simple goodness. That is the essence of the popular and recognized saint. The humble shall be exalted.

I think we have to give up at this point and admit that humility and goodness are connected and we cannot talk about them separately.

The other half of Christ's precept about the humble being exalted is that the exalted will be humbled. One of the things the saints do is humble the exalted. They do not do it out of envy or spite, but out of charity. They warn kings and politicians who are unjust or who are leading their people astray. They tell sinners to repent. They try to remind us about what is really important, of what is eternal, of where our treasure should be. Chesterton says, "There is one thing that Christ and all the Christian saints have said with a sort of savage monotony. They have said simply that to be rich is to be in peculiar danger of moral wreck." [11] The exalted shall be humbled.

> We are always ready to make a saint or prophet of the educated man who goes into cottages to give a little kindly advice to the uneducated. But the mediaeval idea of a saint or prophet was something quite different. The mediaeval saint or prophet was an uneducated man who walked into grand houses to give a little kindly advice to the educated. [12]

[11] *Orthodoxy, CW* 1:323.
[12] *Heretics, CW* 1:190.

As we might expect, Chesterton points out all the unexpected things about the saints. The master of paradox understands very well the paradoxical nature of the saints.

He points out that although saints are the most universal of human figures, they are also the most local. He says that the men whom we most easily connect with heaven we also most easily connect with earth.[13] That is because the local things *are* the universal things: the home, the field, food, family, fellowship. The paradox is that the very ones who had given up those things were most appreciated by those who had those things. The saints would always give spiritual help, but they would also give practical and physical help. It was because they were locally appreciated that they became universally appreciated. If we help the people around us, we can do the whole world good. Perhaps that is why Jesus simply tells us to love our neighbor as ourselves. We can worry about everybody else once we have made sure our neighbor is taken care of.

One of the other unexpected things about the saints is their humor and joy. For some reason, we expect them to be gloomy, since they have to be good and humble all the time.

If you have a good heart you will always have some lightness of heart; you will always have the power of enjoying special human feasts, and positive human good news. But the heart which is there to be lightened will also be there to be hurt; and really if you only want to be happy, to be steadily and stupidly happy like the animals, it may be well worth your while not to have a heart at all. Fortunately, however, being happy is not so important as having a jolly time. Philosophers are happy; saints have a jolly time. The

[13] See *ILN*, November 17, 1906.

important thing in life is not to keep a steady system of pleasure and composure (which can be done quite well by hardening one's heart or thickening one's head), but to keep alive in oneself the immortal power of astonishment and laughter and a kind of young reverence.[14]

Modern investigators of miraculous history have solemnly admitted that a characteristic of the great saints is their power of "levitation." They might go further; a characteristic of the great saints is their power of levity. Angels can fly because they can take themselves lightly.[15]

"Angels fly because they take themselves lightly." One of Chesterton's most famous lines. One of his other most famous lines is, "If a thing is worth doing, it is worth doing badly."[16] But we should hasten to point out that he was talking about amateurs. This line does not apply to professionals. And he says that while every professional calling has its drudgery and details to attend to, there is an ideal connected to the calling, an ideal that one strives for or aspires to. That is why the classic professions, such as soldiers or doctors, have patron saints who represent that ideal. However, in our modern world, says Chesterton, it is a serious calamity that no such ideal exists for the vast number of honorable trades and crafts on which the existence of a modern city depends. There should be, for instance, a patron saint of plumbers. "This", says Chesterton, "would alone be a revolution, for it would force the individual craftsman to believe that there was once a perfect being who did actually plumb."[17]

[14] *ILN*, January 11, 1908.
[15] *Orthodoxy*, *CW* 1:325.
[16] *What's Wrong with the World*, *CW* 4:199.
[17] *The Defendant* (London: J. M. Dent, 1907), 64.

The modern world not only has been slow to pick up on patron saints; it also does not grasp the idea of martyrdom. As Chesterton says, "Most modern martyrdom ... generally consists of a man chaining himself up and then complaining that he is not free. . . . The assumption is that if you show your ordinary sincerity (or even your political ambition) by being a nuisance to yourself as well as to other people, you will have the strength of the great saints who passed through the fire." [18]

Martyrdom is not a thing to be taken lightly, even if we take ourselves lightly. Martyrdom is the ultimate form of turning the other cheek. Although the saints love justice, they denounce vengeance. They know that vengeance is something too great for man. "Vengeance is *Mine*", says the Lord; "*I* will repay." [19] The saints take God at his word.

Being willing to die for our faith is the supreme sacrifice. But being willing to live for our faith is sometimes even more difficult. The Apostle Paul urges us to present our bodies as *living* sacrifices. [20] But, as we know, there have been many saints who were martyrs. In fact, there are many saints about whom we know nothing except that they were martyrs. The martyr knows he cannot live without the faith; he knows that if he recants the faith, he damages the faith, and he knows that if he dies proclaiming the faith, the faith lives on, stronger than ever. He knows that his death may be just the thing that is needed for a revival.

The Saint is a medicine because he is an antidote. Indeed that is why the saint is often a martyr; he is mistaken for a poison because he is an antidote. He will generally be found

---

[18] *ILN*, February 8, 1908.
[19] Hebrews 10:30.
[20] See Romans 12:1.

restoring the world to sanity by exaggerating whatever the world neglects, which is by no means always the same element in every age. Yet each generation seeks its saint by instinct; and he is not what the people want, but rather what the people need. . . . It is the paradox of history that each generation is converted by the saint who contradicts it most.[21]

The saints help hold the faith together, but they are not the whole faith. The faith is something greater than even the saints.

As long as you have a creed, which every one in a certain group believes or is supposed to believe, then that group will consist of the old recurring figures of religious history, who can be appealed to by the creed and judged by it; the saint, the hypocrite, the brawler, the weak brother. These people do each other good; or they all join together to do the hypocrite good, with heavy and repeated blows. But once break the bond of doctrine which alone holds these people together and each will gravitate to his own kind outside the group. The hypocrites will all get together and call each other saints; the saints will get lost in a desert and call themselves weak brethren; the weak brethren will get weaker and weaker in a general atmosphere of imbecility; and the brawler will go off looking for somebody else with whom to brawl.[22]

So, when the doctrine is under attack, yes, we need the saints to defend it. But we also need the rest of us to join them in the battle. We hypocrites and brawlers and weak brethren have to join together with the saints to help defend

[21] *St. Thomas Aquinas*, *CW* 2:424.
[22] *A Miscellany of Men* (Norfolk, Va.: IHS Press, 2004), 83.

the faith. In the process, maybe even we can become saints as well.

We are all inhibited. It is usually good taste that restrains us, and in most cases this restraint is fortunate for the rest of the world. If we were to let loose what is inside of us, it might not be very pretty. But there might also be some goodness in us after all, part of the common sense that does bind us together with the rest of mankind. The saints were not inhibited. They were not restrained by good taste. They let loose what was inside of them. And it was goodness. They were provocatively and uncomfortably virtuous—embracing the poor and the prisoner, sacrificing themselves to martyrdom, declaring the truth at all costs, pouring themselves out so that they could be filled with divine light.

Chesterton is always pointing to the truth, and it is interesting how often he holds up the divine light of the saints like a torch for us. There are references to well over one hundred different saints in his writings; from the very obscure, like St. Giles and St. Hugh and St. Paraskeva, to the very well known.

He talks about St. Thomas More, whom he says is even more important in our time than he was in his own, defending the Church against the State, and also defending the home against the State.[23]

He talks about St. George, who besides being patron saint of England, is the main character in every romance, because every romance is about slaying a dragon and rescuing a princess.[24]

---

[23] See "St. Thomas More", in *The Well and the Shallows*, *CW* 3:505–509.
[24] See *Appreciations*, *CW* 15:255–56. For another excellent Chesterton reference to St. George, see *ILN*, May 12, 1906.

He talks about the huge impact of St. Patrick, in whose wake there are crowds of saints who were Irishmen, even though St. Patrick was not an Irishman.[25]

He talks about St. Joan of Arc, "a diamond among pebbles", how she represents chastity and purity not as something lacking or something negative, but as a positive and powerful virtue, something flaming, a star and a thunderbolt.[26]

In the same way he talks about St. Catherine of Siena, showing that there is a difference between virtue and respectability, and we should not confuse the two. Saints have virtue; they don't always have respectability.

> Virtue can be and has been a violent thing. There was the lawlessness of felons, but there was also the greater lawlessness of saints. St. Catherine of Siena went hand-in-hand with a low criminal to the scaffold, and when his head had been cut off she lifted his head before all the people and kissed it.[27]

He talks about St. Clare, that emancipated woman who chose to live her own life, running away from home, taking a vow of poverty and chastity and starting a religious order that still profoundly affects the world.[28]

He talks of St. Peter and St. Paul and points out that while both Catholics and Protestants venerate both saints, Catholics think first of St. Peter, and Protestants think first of St. Paul.[29]

---

[25] See *A Short History of England*, *CW* 20:464.

[26] See "A Piece of Chalk", in *Tremendous Trifles* (New York: Sheed and Ward, 1955). See also *ILN*, April 12, 1924.

[27] *ILN*, April 13, 1907.

[28] See *St. Francis of Assisi*, *CW* 2:99.

[29] See *ILN*, December 29, 1928.

He talks about Santa Claus—he believes in Santa Claus—because he knows that it is really St. Nicholas, the patron saint of children.[30]

And of course he talks about St. Francis of Assisi and St. Thomas Aquinas, devoting entire books to each of them.

There is one other saint about whom Chesterton wrote, one who was very special not only to him, but to millions of others. What does he have to say about Mary, the Blessed Virgin Mother, the Queen of all the Saints?

Though Chesterton is a master of prose and can explain incredibly complex ideas with equally incredible clarity, on the subject of Mary there is remarkably little in his books and essays. But if we turn to his poetry, we find that it is filled with imagery of the Mother of God. There are dozens of poems specifically about her, and many addressed to her, some which he wrote even before he became Catholic. Mary plays a huge role in his epic poem *The Ballad of the White Horse*. And he also wrote an entire book of poems about her, entitled *The Queen of Seven Swords*.[31]

> These wells that shine and seem as shallow as pools,
> These tales that, being too plain for the fool's eyes,
> Incredibly clear are clearly incredible.
> Truths by their depth deceiving more than lies.[32]

Now there is a paradox for you. The story of the Virgin Mother of God is a deep well that looks like a shallow pool. A simple story hugely profound. A truth more deceiving than a lie.

[30] See *ILN*, June 26, 1926.
[31] See *The Queen of Seven Swords* (London: Sheed and Ward, 1926).
[32] "The Paradox", ibid., 20.

A poem is a picture painted with words. If a picture is worth a thousand words, so is a poem, even if the poem has very few words. A poem uses language as a shortcut to an idea or a feeling that would take much longer to describe in prose. A short poem can sometimes say much more than an entire book can. And, so, for these mysteries that surround Mary, Chesterton uses poetry, for the same reason that hundreds of painters have used paint, and hundreds of sculptors have used wood and marble, and hundreds of composers have used music; for the same reason that Mary has been the subject of Christian art for centuries. The fact that Mary appeals to the greatest artists is by itself evidence of her enduring greatness. That she also appeals to the lowliest and most anonymous folk artists and simple people also speaks of her universal appeal. Chesterton says that the Hottentots did not try to paint Mumbo Jumbo as Raphael painted Madonnas.[33] There is nothing in any other religion to compare with it. Artists have indeed been obsessed with her because they are trying to express some inexpressible truth about the woman who gave birth to God.

> Our Lady, reminding us especially of God Incarnate, does in some degree gather up and embody all those elements of the heart and the higher instincts, which are the legitimate short cuts to the love of God.[34]

Just as a poem or a painting is a shortcut to an idea, Mary is a kind of shortcut to the greatest of all ideas: the love of God. Ultimately, that is what creativity is all about. Ultimately, that is what all artists are always trying to

---

[33] See *The New Jerusalem*, *CW* 20:270.
[34] *The Well and the Shallows*, *CW* 3:461.

accomplish for us: the legitimate shortcuts to the love of God. And that explains why artists are drawn to the Mother of God as a subject.

In one of his poems, called "A Little Litany", Chesterton paints a word picture of a Madonna and child, with the baby Jesus crawling up from his mother's lap and looking her in the eye ...

> [he] found his mirror there; the only glass
> That would not break with that unbearable light
> Till in a corner of the high dark house
> God looked on God, as ghosts meet in the night.[35]

Can we find in all of literature a more profound and provocative image than God looking at God in the reflection of his mother's eye? The marvelous images go on forever. That is why Chesterton said, "I know that I shall never exhaust the profundity of that unfathomable paradox which is defined so defiantly in the very title of the Mother of God." [36]

That is why there are thousands of different Madonnas throughout the history of art, and why Chesterton says in another of his poems, "In all thy thousand images we salute thee",[37] and why in another poem he muses that if all the statues of Mary were smashed, we would still carve her image with a song.[38] It is an inexhaustible profundity.

When Chesterton's home parish in Beaconsfield, England, built a new church, Chesterton wanted to present it with a statue of the Madonna and Child. But he wanted to find

[35] *The Queen of Seven Swords*, 14.
[36] *The Thing, CW* 3:303.
[37] "The Black Virgin", in *The Queen of Seven Swords*, 32.
[38] See "Images", ibid., 37.

just the right one. It gave him another occasion to reflect on the many faces of the Mother of God.

I heard a story in Ireland years ago about how someone had met in the rocky wastes a beautiful peasant woman carrying a child. And on being asked for her name she answered simply: "I am the Mother of God, and this is Himself, and He is the boy you will all be wanting at the last." I have never forgotten this phrase, and I remembered it suddenly long afterwards.

I was looking about for an image of Our Lady which I wished to give to the new church in our neighbourhood, and I was shown a variety of very beautiful and often costly examples in one of the most famous and fashionable Catholic shops in London. . . . But somehow I felt fastidious, for the first time in my life; and felt that the one kind was too conventional to be sincere and the other too primitive to be popular . . . and I ended prosaically by following the proprietor to an upper floor, where there was a sort of lumber room, full of packages and things partially unpacked, and it seemed suddenly that she was standing there, amid planks and shavings and sawdust, as she stood in the carpenter's shop in Nazareth. I said something, and the proprietor answered rather casually: "Oh, that's only just been unpacked; I've hardly looked at it. It's from Ireland!"

She was a peasant and she was a queen. She was barefoot like any colleen on the hills; yet there was nothing merely local about her simplicity. I have never known who was the artist and I doubt if anybody knows; I only know that it is Irish, and I almost think that I should have known without being told. I know a man who walks miles out of his way at regular intervals to revisit our church where the image stands. She looks across the little church with an intense earnestness in which there is something of endless youth; and I have sometimes started, as if I had actually heard the words spoken across that emptiness: "I am the Mother of God and this is Himself, and He is the boy you will all be wanting at the last." [39]

One of the reasons for the Protestant dislike of Catholic art, besides the completely false charge of idolatry, was simply the puritanical dislike for anything beautiful. But Chesterton suggests that the attack on Mary is even more sinister. In his poem called "A Party Question", Chesterton actually treats the original Protestant revolt against the Catholic Church very sympathetically, acknowledging full well that the Church was indeed corrupt with "Bad men who had no right to their right reason" who were opposed by "Good men who had good reason to be wrong". But as that "tangled war" continued, it became more devious. The goal was no longer the reform of the Church. It became the destruction of the Church. The revolt had lost its innocent anger. It simply started to attack everything about the Catholic Church. When it attacked the Mother of God, the sound was recognizable. It was, says the poet, "a hiss out of hell".[40]

But just as G. K. Chesterton came to discover and embrace Christianity as a result of reading the attacks against it, the Catholic Church seems to have gained a greater appreciation of Mary as a result of the attacks against her. The widespread devotion to the Rosary arose right alongside the rise of Protestantism. The doctrine of the Immaculate Conception was declared during the height of nineteenth century anticlericalism. The doctrine of the Assumption was declared right in the middle of the bloodiest anti-Catholic century

---

[39] *Christendom in Dublin, CW* 20:80–82.
[40] "A Party Question", in *The Queen of Seven Swords*, 12–13.

in history, the twentieth century. The world may defy the Church, but the Church also has a way of defying the world.

As for the Protestant accusation that Mary is something like the pagan goddesses Isis or Cybele, Chesterton laughs. The comparison, he says, only flatters the pagan goddesses.[41] It explains nothing about the devotion to Mary, which is really a devotion to her Son. She is always pointing at her son: "This is Himself and He is the One you will be wanting at the last."

As for the accusation that this devotion to the Virgin Mary first arose during the Dark Ages, Chesterton responds that it was perfectly natural that it first arose during that time.[42] The Church was the only light in the Dark Ages, the only order amidst the chaos. And the devotion to Mary introduced the element of chivalry in those barbaric times, the importance of protecting and honoring women.

We are seeing another resurgence in the devotion to the Virgin Mary in our day, because we are in a new dark age.

> Where shall they go that have delight in honour
> When all men honour nothing but delight?[43]

Are there some Catholics who are "excessive" in their devotion to Mary? Maybe. Do they turn off Protestants? Certainly. Are they bad people? Are they pagans? Are they delusional? Are they lost in sin? Take a look at their lives. The most troubling thing to non-Catholics about those old ladies who seem to be "excessive" about Mary is that they are pious and devout and holy. We claim to be irritated by their simplistic-sounding words and their rattling trinkets,

---

[41] See "Laughter", ibid., 31.
[42] See *A Short History of England*, *CW* 20:469.
[43] "In October", in *The Queen of Seven Swords*, 29.

but what is most irritating is how their lives put our lives to shame. They know that the Madonna is always pointing to the Child. They know she is saying, "Do whatever he tells you."

But they also know something else about Mary's importance in our day and age. That is what makes them the bane of feminists and abortionists everywhere. The attack on the cult of the Virgin Mary is an attack on purity and chastity and obedience and submission to the will of God, and an attack on life itself.

In one of his poems, Chesterton says that it is our "sterile appetites" that scorn the "creative purity" of Mary:

> So: in her house Life without Lust was born,
> So in your house Lust without Life shall die.[44]

Chesterton seems to be on very intimate terms with the saints. Is it possible that this three-hundred-pound, cigar-smoking London journalist, Gilbert Keith Chesterton, is himself a saint? Maybe. There is in fact a growing popular interest in his cause. As one observer said, "We need more fat saints." But of course, it is up to the Catholic Church to make the determination. The priest that gets assigned to investigate Chesterton's cause will have *a lot* of reading to do. But what fun: he gets to read Chesterton.

---

[44] "An Agreement", ibid., 28.

19

Moments Filled with Eternity

Most of the popular songs from the last hundred years or so are love songs. But in spite of being love songs, most of them are not so much about love as about the loss of love. Or longing for a love that isn't. Very few of them are actually about actual love.

Love is basic, even if it seems to be basically missing from the world.

So why are all those songs we have to listen to so miserable? What is the problem with modern love? We seem to be aware of the great joy that love brings, which is why we want it, but why can't we hang on to it?

Well, it has something to do with the place that love naturally takes us. Love wants to take us to the altar. But the altar is a place of sacrifice. The altar is the place where the temporary and the physical touch the eternal and the spiritual. The Catholic Church has a word for it when that happens. It is called a sacrament. G. K. Chesterton describes the nature of a sacrament when he says that great joy has in it the sense of immortality. All lovers think of their love as something that cannot end. He describes this experience as "moments filled with eternity". He says,

"These moments are joyful because they do not seem momentary." [1]

But the modern world has avoided the sacrament. The modern world has tried an impossible experiment it calls "free love". But as Chesterton says, there is no such thing as "free love". It is the very nature of love that it wants to bind itself. It binds itself with a vow. It glories in being put to the test. The result is either the triumph of true love or the tragedy of false love.

"The man who makes a vow", says Chesterton, "makes an appointment with himself at some distant time or place. The danger of it is that he should not keep the appointment." [2] For the greater part of human history, the institution of marriage, he says, "merely paid the average man the compliment of taking him at his word." [3] But in the modern world, we are apparently in terror of ourselves, of our weaknesses and our changeability, so that we have tried to win love without giving the vow. We want this back door, this way of escape always available to us. And this, says Chesterton, is "the sterilizing spirit in modern pleasure. Everywhere there is the persistent and insane attempt to obtain pleasure without paying for it." [4]

> The free-lovers say: "Let us have the splendour of offering ourselves without the peril of committing ourselves; let us see whether one cannot commit suicide an unlimited number of times." Emphatically it will not work. [5]

[1] *Heretics, CW* 1:95.
[2] *The Defendant* (London: J. M. Dent, 1907), 20.
[3] Ibid., 23.
[4] Ibid., 25.
[5] Ibid., 25–46.

Chesterton makes it very clear that love involves commitment. Just as the institution of religion helps us survive our moods about divine love, so the institution of marriage is there to get us through our moods about earthly love. And, of course, there is a connection between divine love and earthly love, seen in those "moments filled with eternity". That connection, as we said, is what is known as a sacrament. True romance has something to do with Rome, as in the Church of Rome. There is nothing more romantic, and nothing more Roman, than the vow. The pledge to be faithful ... forever.

> In everything on this earth that is worth doing, there is a stage when no one would do it, except for necessity or honor. It is then that the Institution upholds a man and helps him on to the firmer ground ahead. This [is a] solid fact of human nature.... It is amply sufficient to justify the general human feeling of marriage as a fixed thing.... The essential element is not so much duration as security. Two people must be tied together in order to do themselves justice; for twenty minutes at a dance, or for twenty years in a marriage. In both cases the point is, that if a man is bored in the first five minutes he must go on and force himself to be happy. Coercion is a kind of encouragement; and anarchy (or what some call liberty) is essentially oppressive, because it is essentially discouraging. If we all floated in the air like bubbles, free to drift anywhere at any instant, the practical result would be that no one would have the courage to begin a conversation. It would be so embarrassing to start a sentence in a friendly whisper, and then have to shout the last half of it because the other party was floating away into the free and formless ether. The two must hold each other to do justice to each other. If Americans can be divorced for "incompatibility of temper" I cannot conceive why they are not all divorced. I have known many happy

marriages, but never a compatible one. The whole aim of marriage is to fight through and survive the instant when incompatibility becomes unquestionable. For a man and a woman, as such, are incompatible.[6]

The fact that marriage brings together these two incompatible beings—man and woman—is another reason it is a sacramental mystery, just as it brings together the physical and the spiritual. Chesterton says that the greatest feat of engineering in human history is the bridge that has been built between man and woman.[7]

So, that's all there is to it. Chesterton has properly diagnosed what ails modern love and he has prescribed the cure. He is one of the greatest modern defenders of the ancient institution of marriage and the ancient institution of the Catholic Church, two things that the modern world tries so hard to avoid—and even tries to destroy—but, in doing so, destroys itself.

But what about Chesterton's own love life? What about his own marriage? Did he live out the ideal that he explained so well in his writings?

Let's take a look at Chesterton's married life, and meet the woman who was Mrs. G. K. Chesterton.

Chesterton's description of himself when he first fell in love should sound somewhat familiar to anyone who has ever fallen in love. He said he awoke in the morning, washed his boots in hot water, put shoe polish on his face, put his coat on backwards, went to breakfast and poured hot coffee on the sardines, and put his hat on the fire to boil. And when he left the house by way of the

[6] *What's Wrong with the World*, CW 4:69.
[7] See *The Superstition of Divorce*, CW 4:238.

chimney, his family figured out that something was on his mind.[8]

The woman who had reduced him to this state was a very sweet and kind and witty girl with the unlikely name of Blogg. Frances Blogg. She would later become his wife. But she also played another important role in his life. Chesterton described her as the first Christian he had ever met who was happy.

Years later when he published what some consider to be his greatest masterpiece *The Ballad of the White Horse*, he dedicated the epic poem to Frances, with the words

> I bring these rhymes to you
> Who brought the cross to me.[9]

When he knew that Frances was going to be his wife, Chesterton sat down and wrote a letter to the other important woman in his life—his mother, telling her about the girl he was going to marry. It was, like everything else Chesterton ever wrote, full of paradox and profundity and joy, but perhaps the most unusual thing about the letter is that Chesterton wrote it while his mother was in the room with him, in fact, sitting across the table. In the letter, he tries to tell her that she will like his bride, even though he knows she might not be assured by such a claim, since "all young men say that to their mothers, quite naturally, and their mothers never believe them, also, quite naturally." But he is confident she will like Frances because Frances is the kind of woman his mother would like, "a Woman's Woman", very humorous and sympathetic and so on. Chesterton ends

---

[8] See Maisie Ward, *Gilbert Keith Chesterton* (New York: Sheed and Ward, 1943), 92.

[9] *BWH*, Dedication, 53–54.

the letter by thanking his mother for the cup of cocoa she
has just handed him.[10]

After Gilbert proposed to Frances and she accepted, he
wrote *her* a letter. But she was not in the room with him,
as his mother had been. She was quite far away. He was on
the English coast, looking at the sea, and looking into the
future.

He wrote down all the things he had to offer his bride,
which were all the things he had in the world: a straw hat,
a walking stick, a pocket knife, a little money from his job
in a publisher's office, a tennis racket (believe it or not), a
copy of Walt Whitman's poems, the half-written volume of
his own poetry that would eventually be his first published
book, the letters that Frances had written to him—and his
soul, his body, and his heart.

He suggested that when they get married, Frances should
do the shopping. He said he was not good at shopping. He
was able to spend the money, but not very good at bringing home the things that he had paid for or even remembering what they were. So Frances was duly warned about
what she was getting into. And then he proceeded to describe
his vision of their life together. He wanted to have a simple
house, a sofa for her, and no chairs, for he preferred sitting
on the floor. There would be a box of chocolates, and the
rest would be bread and water. They would have bad things
in their house and make them good things. They would
invite an occasional dragon to dinner, and he pictured her
teaching Sunday school to a group of little devils who would
look up at her in "savage wonder" and "see the most glorious and noble lady that ever lived ... with a halo of hair
and great heavenly eyes" and their tails would drop off, and

---

[10] See Ward, *Chesterton*, 89–91.

wings would sprout: and they would become angels in six lessons.[11]

Then he returned to a more pressing matter at hand: the fact that Frances' mother seemed quite reluctant to let her daughter marry him.

I cannot profess to offer an ... explanation of your mother's disquiet but I admit it does not wholly surprise me. You see I happen to know one factor in the case, and one only, of which you are wholly ignorant. I know you. ... I know one thing which has made me feel strange before your mother—I know the value of what I take away. I feel (in a weird moment) like the Angel of Death.

My views about death are bright, brisk and entertaining. When Azrael takes a soul it may be to other and brighter worlds: like those whither you and I go together. The transformation called Death may be something as beautiful and dazzling as the transformation called Love. It may make the dead man "happy," just as your mother knows that you are happy. But none the less it is a transformation, and sad sometimes for those left behind. A mother whose child is dying can hardly believe that in the inscrutable Unknown there is anyone who can look to it as well as she. And if a mother cannot trust her child easily to God Almighty, shall I be so mean as to be angry because she cannot trust it easily to me? I tell you I have stood before your mother and felt like a thief. I know you are not going to part: neither physically, mentally, morally nor spiritually. But she sees a new element in your life, wholly from outside—is it not natural ... that you should find her perturbed? ... Your mother would certainly have worried if you had been engaged to the Archangel Michael (who, indeed, is bearing his disappointment very well): how much more when you are engaged

[11] Ibid., 94–99.

to an aimless, tactless, reckless, unbrushed, strange-hatted, opinionated scarecrow who has suddenly walked into the vacant place. I could have prophesied her unrest: wait and she will calm down all right, dear. God comfort her: I dare not.[12]

And then he went on to recount the story of how he came to meet Frances, and how he fell in love with her the first time he laid eyes on her. And now after a two-year court-ship, she has agreed to spend the rest of her life with him. And here he is, sitting overlooking the sea, thinking of how undeserving he is:

> Gilbert Keith Chesterton ... sees how far he has gone wrong and how idle and wasteful and wicked he has often been: how miserably unfitted he is for what he is called upon to be. Let him now declare it and hereafter for ever hold his peace. But there are four lamps of thanksgiving always before him. The first is for his creation out of the same earth with such a woman as you. The second is that he has not, with all his faults, "gone after strange women." You cannot think how a man's self restraint is rewarded in this. The third is that he has tried to love everything alive: a dim preparation for loving you. And the fourth is—but no words can express that. Here ends my previous existence. Take it: it led me to you.[13]

And so they were married in 1901. On his wedding day, he wrote a poem to Frances entitled "Creation Day", for the world began utterly new when they began their life together. The poem ends with the lines

---

[12] Ibid., 100–101.
[13] Ibid., 101, 105.

> The world is many and is mad,
> But we are sane and we are one.[14]

The life they began together was truly remarkable. It is safe to say that Gilbert Keith Chesterton could not have been the man and the writer he was if Frances Blogg Chesterton had not been the woman and helpmate she was. She knew he was a great man of great ideas, and she made it possible for him to devote his life to writing so that he could share his fabulous mind with the rest of the world. She freed him from the distractions of diurnal details. She looked after her husband, who proved to be utterly incapable of looking after himself. Without her, he was lost. There is, of course, the famous story of his sending a telegram to her saying, "Am at Market Harborough. Where ought I to be?" There are also wonderful accounts of his turning up at lectures wearing his bedroom slippers because Frances had not been around to make sure he had put his shoes on. When they were together in public, he literally never took his eyes off her. It can be said, that he also looked after her. He adored her as his "bride", his "queen", and his "friend". He became a world-renowned writer, and she was always at his side. They started with nothing, and while they never became rich, his writing eventually provided a relatively comfortable middle-class life that enabled them to give away money with true charity. It was a relationship of mutual devotion and great happiness. But it was never easy.

The fairy tales said that the prince and princess lived happily ever afterwards: and so they did. They lived happily, although it is very likely that from time to time they threw

[14] *Collected Poetry, CW* 10, Part 1:345.

the furniture at each other. Most marriages, I think, are happy marriages; but there is no such thing as a contented marriage. The whole pleasure of marriage is that it is a perpetual crisis.[15]

In their happily ever after life, there was one tragedy that certainly affected them deeply. They both loved children, but Frances was unable to have a baby. Neither of them were ever in very good health, but neither of them complained of their various ailments. They consulted several doctors about Frances' fertility problems, but to no avail. They made up for it, however, by always having their house full of other people's children: neighbors and relatives and guests. Their secretary, Dorothy Collins, became like a daughter to them. In addition to that, they had two dogs named Winkle and Quoodle, a cat named Perky, and a donkey named Trotsky: "Trotsky because he wouldn't walksky."

Their house was never empty and was always known as a place of great joy and great jokes. Just as they depended on each other's strengths, they were able to laugh at each other's weaknesses.

A man and a woman cannot live together without having against each other a kind of everlasting joke. Each has discovered that the other is not only a fool, but a great fool.[16]

There was one other major difficulty in their happy marriage. Though Frances brought Chesterton to Christianity, she remained a devout Anglican, while he continued to be drawn toward the Catholic Church. For over twenty years Chesterton defended the Catholic Faith without being a

[15] *Appreciations*, *CW* 15:333.
[16] *Charles Dickens*, *CW* 15:188.

Catholic himself. Finally, in what was surely an excruciating decision, G. K. Chesterton, for the first and only time in his married life, acted alone. He did something without his wife joining him. He became a Catholic. He entered the Church in 1922, at the age of forty-eight. It was a bittersweet day for both of them. She knew he was happy, as indeed he was, but they both were aware of something huge that they suddenly did not share. But this part of the story also has a happy ending. Four years later, Frances was also received into the Catholic Church, as one of the many, many converts who found their way to Rome because of G. K. Chesterton.

It is interesting, and poignant, that Frances, who could not have children, had a mystical devotion to the Nativity of Christ. She even wrote several poems about it. The most famous is "How Far Is It to Bethlehem?"

How far is it to Bethlehem? Not very far.
Shall we find the stable room lit by a star?
Can we see the little child, is he within?
If we lift the wooden latch may we go in?
May we stroke the creatures there, ox, ass, or sheep?
May we peep like them and see Jesus asleep?
Great kings have precious gifts, and we have naught,
Little smiles and tears are all we brought.
For all weary children Mary must weep,
Then here, on his bed of straw, sleep, children, sleep.
God in his mother's arms, babes in the byre,
They sleep as they sleep who find their heart's desire.

Our heart's desire is ultimately found only in Christ.

When G. K. Chesterton wrote his autobiography, which he completed just before his untimely death at the age of sixty-two, there is one character from his life oddly missing from the book: his wife. Because of her modesty and humility, she asked him not to talk about her. It must have been a difficult task for him to write about his own life without mentioning the greater half of it. But she probably knew, as he did, that if she had not made that prohibition, Chesterton's autobiography would not have been about himself; it would have been about her.

Chesterton's last words on this earth were a greeting to his wife. "Hello, My Darling." He died of congestive heart failure on June 14, 1936. Frances died only two years after her husband. George Bernard Shaw, who knew and loved them both, said the cause of her death was widowhood. They were indeed inseparable. Two shall become one. Gilbert and Frances are buried in the same grave in Beaconsfield, England.

G. K. Chesterton understood the breadth and depth of romantic love, and he lived it. His great book on St. Francis of Assisi was written during those few years when he was Catholic and his wife was not. He describes the romance, the love affair that St. Francis had with God. It is a love that only a lover can understand. It reveals both oneness and separation at the same time, both fulfillment and longing, the mystical connection between joy and suffering. In this book about the saint who has the same name as his wife, Chesterton says plainly: "Now there are those who do not believe that a heavenly love can be as real as an earthly love. But I do." [17]

---

[17] *St. Francis of Assisi*, CW 2:99.

20

Recovering the Lost Art of Common Sense

The most famous thing Chesterton said is something he didn't say. He is always quoted as saying that when a man stops believing in God he doesn't believe in nothing, he believes in anything. It is a great line, and it is well worth quoting, and I have no doubt that Chesterton would agree with it and would be pleased to hear it quoted. But it's just not what he said. What he said was, "The first effect of not believing in God, is that you lose your common sense." [1]

Since the line never gets quoted correctly, let's quote it correctly again: "The first effect of not believing in God, is that you lose your common sense." That means that in order for us to recover our common sense, we have to recover our faith. In order for us to recover our faith, we need religious renewal and reform. History shows that reform is a thing that is indeed needed from time to time. And usually it is botched up every time it is needed.

> In the matter of reforming things, as distinct from deforming them, there is one plain and simple principle; a principle which will probably be called a paradox. Let us say, for the

---

[1] And he gave the line to Father Brown, who said it in a story called "The Oracle of the Dog".

sake of simplicity, that there is a fence or gate erected across a road. The more modern type of reformer goes gaily up to it and says, "I don't see the use of this; let us clear it away." To which the more intelligent type of reformer will do well to answer: "If you don't see the use of it, I certainly won't let you clear it away. Go away and think. Then, when you can come back and tell me that you *do* see the use of it, I may allow you to destroy it." This paradox rests on the most elementary common sense. The gate or fence did not grow there. It was not set up by somnambulists who built it in their sleep. It is highly improbable that it was put there by escaped lunatics who were for some reason loose in the street. Some person had some reason for thinking it would be a good thing for somebody. And until we know what the reason was, we really cannot judge whether the reason was reasonable. It is extremely probable that we have overlooked some whole aspect of the question if something set up by human beings like ourselves seems to be entirely meaningless and mysterious. There are reformers who get over this difficulty by assuming that all their fathers were fools; but if that be so, we can only say that folly appears to be a hereditary disease. But the truth is that nobody has any business to destroy a social institution until he has really seen it as an historical institution. If he knows how it arose, and what purposes it was supposed to serve, he may really be able to say that they were bad purposes, or that they have since become bad purposes, or that they are purposes which are no longer served. But if he simply stares at the thing as a senseless monstrosity that has somehow sprung up in his path, it is he and not the traditionalist who is suffering from an illusion.[2]

So, the problem with reformers is that they so often want to do away with things they don't understand. They apparently regard their lack of understanding as proof that the

[2] *The Thing, CW* 3:157.

thing is not needed. It does not occur to them that the tradition they are trying to destroy may have been put into place for a very good reason. Chesterton says, "A tradition is generally a truth",[3] and, "Common sense often comes to us in the form of a tradition."[4] The successful reforms in history have occurred when people reconnected with their roots and where they recovered their lost traditions. It is not the tradition that has gone wrong; it is we who have gone wrong.

In order to have reform, says Chesterton, to return to the form, we must have repentance. We must admit that we have gone wrong. The point of repentance is starting over, beginning fresh. The only fresh beginning is that which starts from first principles, which will always be fresh when all novelties are stale.[5]

Chesterton, as we know by now, favors the common sense of the common man as the basis for democracy. And when it comes to the idea of reform, he reminds us famously of the democracy of the dead. True democracy means respecting tradition: "It means giving a vote to the obscurest of all classes, our ancestors." It means not submitting to the "oligarchy of those who merely happen to be walking about".[6] To get at what we have in common, we have to go backward. It is ancient history that will unite us, while modern history has only divided us.

To say that new things like [rapid transportation and communication] have united nations is simply false. . . . It is not new but old things that unify mankind; it is at the back of

---

[3] *The Everlasting Man*, *CW* 2:204.
[4] Ibid., 163.
[5] See *ILN*, September 4, 1920.
[6] *Orthodoxy*, *CW* 1:251.

history that we rediscover humanity; it is quite strictly, in Genesis or the beginnings that we find the brotherhood of men; even if some controversy continues about ... Abel and Cain.[7]

It is true that the first family had its problems and didn't exactly set a good precedent for the rest of us. But the fact remains that the basic unit of society is still the family. Strong families make for a strong society. If the family is weakened, the society is fundamentally weakened. But even if we try to break the basic unit of society into smaller pieces, those pieces still have to be held together by a very strong cement in order for the larger structure of society to hold up, and the smaller the pieces the stronger the glue must be. Chesterton says the only glue strong enough to bind people together is religion.[8] If people abandon religion, they abandon each other. Art and culture, sports and games, political causes and commercial ventures all have their place in a society but a very secondary place. None of them are broad enough or deep enough to be a substitute for religion. And when we try to make them a substitute for religion, our society is in decline.

Most people are aware that something is quite wrong with our society. But most of us are in a daze about it. We feel quite lost. Man has always lost his way, says Chesterton, but our problem is that we have not only lost our way; we've lost our address.[9]

We have all read in scientific books, and in romances, the story of the man who has forgotten his name. This man walks about the streets and can see and appreciate everything; only he cannot remember who he is. Well, every

---

[7] *The Well and the Shallows, CW* 3:460.
[8] See *ILN*, January 13, 1912.
[9] See *What's Wrong with the World, CW* 4:77.

man is that man in the story. Every man has forgotten who
he is. . . . The self is more distant than any star. We are all
under the same mental calamity; we have all forgotten our
names. We have all forgotten what we really are.[10]

The reason we have forgotten who we are is that we have
been cut off from our traditions. We have not only lost the
common sense that connects us to others; we have lost our
own sense of identity. And, again, the thing that defines us,
as individuals and as a community, is religion. That is the
only thing that can give us an ultimate meaning and sense
of purpose. When the majority of people lose their religion and their common philosophy, they are easy prey for
what Chesterton calls the "thin and theoretic minorities".[11] By simply *having* a philosophy, even if it is a fallacy
or a perversion, a small group can conquer the vast majority who have lost their philosophy. The abnormal gains an
advantage over the normal. And this is exactly what we
have seen happen in our society. A few small minorities
with some strong but wrong philosophies, such as those
that favor abortion and homosexuality, have managed to
spread their poisonous ideas to the rest of society, because
the rest of society has no cohesive ideas but only "a sort of
broad bewilderment produced by the reading of newspapers".[12] (And Chesterton would certainly have added "by
the watching of television".) Those thin and theoretic minorities do not represent the masses, yet because of the media,
they seem to be everywhere, and they have contrived to
destroy the role of religion in our society. The result, says
Chesterton, is that now "there is no mental machinery for

[10] *Orthodoxy, CW* 1:257.
[11] *ILN*, December 20, 1919.
[12] Ibid.

common sense."[13] In order to have common sense, a society must have what Chesterton calls "spontaneous mental discipline".[14] We have lost ours.

How do we get it back?

First of all, we cannot deal with these problems superficially. Chesterton says we have to get down to fundamentals. We have to recognize that there is a battle between good and evil. And we have to recognize evil, which is always very recognizable and very obvious. But we choose to ignore it.

> Men do not differ much about what things they will call evils; they differ enormously about what evils they will call excusable.[15]

One of the most insidious philosophies of the modern world is the bland tolerance of every other philosophy, the idea that it doesn't matter what you do or what you believe. Evil rushes in through the door of indifference.

> Right is right, even if nobody does it. Wrong is wrong, even if everybody is wrong about it.[16]

In a confusing world we have to speak clearly. People will sneer at our words, calling them catchwords. But Chesterton says, "The words used by ordinary hardworking people have to be ordinary and rather hard-worked words."[17] We do not have to apologize for using the common words of common sense. Chesterton says, the great men of history had the common mind and they are great not because they

---

[13] Ibid.
[14] Ibid.
[15] *ILN*, October 23, 1909.
[16] *ILN*, May 11, 1907.
[17] *ILN*, July 3, 1920.

make every man feel small, but because they make every man feel great.[18] They help us to regain our vision of what's important, and to rise up and defend it or reclaim it.

There is something that is not plain about the plain truth. There is something uncommon about common sense. It is has to be repeated over and over again because a million small distractions draw us away from the great truths. Chesterton is sometimes accused of repeating himself, but that is only because we need to be reminded of the simple, vital, basic things. Things like this: we must have a code of morals in a society; we have to teach this code of morals to our children; we have to believe our own beliefs enough to act on them in order to expect our children to believe us.

Everything has its place and proportion and proper use, and it is rational to trust its use and to distrust its abuse. The idea of "everything in its place" is the idea of the ordinary. G. K. Chesterton was an extraordinary man who defended ordinary things:

> I am ordinary in the correct sense of the term, which means the acceptance of an order; a Creator and the Creation, the common sense of gratitude for Creation, life and love as gifts permanently good, marriage and chivalry as laws rightly controlling them, and the rest of the normal traditions of our ... religion.[19]

According to Chesterton, Christianity is the religion that is most at one with common sense. It proclaims basic truths that can be relied on: that the world is real; that our actions have consequences; that truth itself is something solid and absolute; that we didn't just make it up. He says that all

[18] See *Charles Dickens*, *CW* 15:43.
[19] *The Thing*, *CW* 3:169.

religious history shows that this common sense perishes except where there is Christianity to preserve it. Other religions and philosophies and heresies have tried to reduce Christianity to something less than itself, but they always make it too simple to be sane. The temptation of the philosophers is simplicity rather than subtlety.

The commands of Christ, says Chesterton, may sound impossible, but they are not insane. They are, rather, "sanity preached to a planet of lunatics".[20] When someone strikes you on one cheek, offer the other. When someone steals your shirt, give him your cloak as well.[21] Why is that sanity? Because it really does make more sense to turn the other cheek in order to stop the insane cycle of revenge. It really does make more sense to give the thief more than he has stolen because he may need it, and what he needs most of all is grace and charity. That will serve to save his soul. His soul is more important than our clothes. And the main point of Christ's commands is that we should not take ourselves so seriously. Being able to laugh at ourselves is the key to humility and obedience. "If the whole world was suddenly stricken with a sense of humour it would find itself automatically fulfilling the Sermon on the Mount."[22]

The reason that Christianity is at one with common sense is that both are all about what is good for everybody. Only a religion of charity can be the glue to hold a society together. Christianity teaches us to feed the hungry and clothe the naked and give shelter to the homeless. And Chesterton points out that this applies to spiritual poverty as well as physical poverty.

---

[20] *Twelve Types*, 66.
[21] See Matthew 5:39–40.
[22] *Twelve Types* (Norfolk, Va.: IHS Press, 2003), 66.

As we should be genuinely sorry for tramps and paupers who are materially homeless, so we should be sorry for those who are morally homeless, and who suffer a philosophical starvation as deadly as physical starvation.[23]

The Christian saints were famous for their great charity, and their charity was exactly what the world needed. They were mystics, but they were also very practical. The two go together. And that is why Chesterton says we will never recover common sense until we recover the mysticism of the saints. The saints are "wild and perfect".[24] They put their idealism in the right place and their realism in the right place. We have both things displaced. The saints put their dreams and sentiments into their aims, where they ought to be, and their practicality into their practice, where it ought to be. We have it backwards. Our dreams, we insist, are quite practical. But our practice is quite impractical. Our aims fall far short of heaven. Our practice falls short even of earth. And one of the main problems with our practice is that we don't do anything ourselves. We don't take responsibility. We leave it to the expert or to the public servant or to the private servant. We don't grow our own food; we don't build our own homes. We don't teach our own children; we don't even raise our own children. We leave everything up to someone else. We don't even think for ourselves. We even let others tell us what our tastes are. And, we don't even practice our own religion. It has become more convenient to leave that to others, too.

Once men sang together round a table in chorus; now one man sings alone, for the absurd reason that he can sing

[23] *ILN*, November 24, 1934.
[24] *ILN*, March 28, 1908.

better. If our civilization goes on like this, only one man will laugh, because he can laugh better than the rest.[25]

Whenever we have some crisis in society, rather than solving the crisis ourselves, we immediately make demands of the government for a solution. But a solution from the government always means a new set of laws and regulations. Chesterton says, "Modern man is in favor of introducing order into everything except his own ideas."[26] Excessive regulation and organization rests on a fallacy. It basically means turning men into machinery, and it is a mistake to think that machinery made out of men will be very efficient. The other problem with such schemes is that they must be enforced, which usually just means forced.

The point is, it is up to us to solve the crisis. It cannot be done for us. That is the disadvantage as well as the advantage of having free will. Common sense works only if we use it. Chesterton offers common sense both as a challenge and a comfort:

> If men cannot save themselves by common sense, they cannot save each other by coercion.[27]

> But what more can we have on our side than the common sense of everybody?[28]

In this book, we have covered some of the main ideas in Chesterton's writing. These are not mere literary themes; they are fundamental truths, and if we would take the trouble to understand them, they would rejuvenate our lives.

[25] *Heretics, CW* 1:164.
[26] *ILN*, April 1, 1922.
[27] *ILN*, September 29, 1923.
[28] *The Napoleon of Notting Hill, CW* 6:308.

And they would help us recover the lost art of common sense. Let's review them very briefly:

First: our whole approach to life should be filled with wonder and gratitude. Thanks are the highest form of thought.

Second: truth is paradoxical. That explains why it is dignified and tragic when a man suffers, and why it is undignified and funny when a man sits on his hat.

Third: we are created in the image of God, which means we also are creators. Art is the signature of man. But art must connect. It has to connect to people, and it must also be connected to the eternal.

Fourth: we have a responsibility to pass truth on to our children. Therefore, education must be controlled by parents.

Fifth: temporary trends must never take precedence over permanent things. Fads and fashionable ideas always undermine the authority of the family and the Faith.

Sixth: democracy operates on the principle of common sense, the idea that people really can rule themselves if they truly have the freedom and independence to do so. Democracy means that self-government is better than big government, and that self-employment is better than wage slavery.

Seventh, eighth, and ninth: the world constantly tries to attack the Catholic Church or replace the Catholic Church or reduce and redo the Catholic Church, and in every case the result is something less satisfying, less balanced, and less complete than the Catholic Church.

And tenth: poems should rhyme.

Of course, there is one more thing we can do to help recover the lost art of common sense: read G. K. Chesterton.

21

The Battle Goes On

This book ends where another one begins. And since we are ending with a beginning, we will have the decency and good sense to be brief.

In the early pages of Chesterton's masterpiece *The Man Who Was Thursday*, the poet Gabriel Syme is recruited by a policeman to become an undercover detective, to help fight a war. Against whom? The policeman explains that the educated class is the "class that contains most of our enemies". It is the intellectuals who are at war against the common man and the normal way of life. They defy common sense. He says:

> We believe that a purely intellectual conspiracy will soon threaten the very existence of civilization, that the scientific and artistic worlds are silently bound in a crusade against the Family and the State. We have formed a special corps of policemen, policemen who are also philosophers. It is our business to watch the beginnings of this conspiracy.[1]

Syme is surprised and intrigued. He asks, "Do you mean that there is really as much connection between crime and the modern intellect as all that?"

[1] *The Man Who Was Thursday*, CW 6:508.

The policeman responds by assuring him that he is not talking about the "poor criminal ... the ignorant and the desperate".

> We say that the dangerous criminal is the educated criminal. We say that the most dangerous criminal now is the entirely lawless modern philosopher. Compared to him, burglars and bigamists are essentially moral men; my heart goes out to them. They accept the essential ideal of man; they merely seek it wrongly. Thieves respect property. They merely wish the property to become their property that they may more perfectly respect it. But philosophers dislike property as property; they wish to destroy the very idea of personal possession. Bigamists respect marriage, or they would not go through the highly ceremonial formality of bigamy. But philosophers despise marriage as marriage. Murderers respect human life; they merely wish to attain a greater fullness of human life in themselves by the sacrifice of what seems to them to be lesser lives. But philosophers hate life itself, their own as much as other people's.[2]

Thus G. K. Chesterton identified the culture of death long before Pope John Paul II gave it its proper name. He understood that we are fighting a battle. Chesterton says that we all wake up on a battlefield.[3] We know there is a fight going on. We see the effects of it everywhere. But it often takes us a long time to realize what the fight is about or even who is fighting whom. For a battle is a complicated thing. And in the midst of the battle, in the modern intellectual world we see flags of many colors. The one thing we cannot see is the map. We cannot see in one simple statement, the thing that tells us what is the origin of all the trouble.

[2] Ibid., 509.
[3] See *William Blake* (London: House of Stratus, 2000), 54.

All of our modern problems go back to the original trouble. It is Original Sin. The thing that first brought death into the world is still bringing it.

But instead of being discouraged by what looks like a hopeless mess, Chesterton says that this world "can be made beautiful again by beholding it as a battlefield. When we have defined and isolated the evil thing, the colours come back into everything else. When evil things have become evil, good things, in a blazing apocalypse, become good. There are some men who are dreary because they do not believe in God; but there are many others who are dreary because they do not believe in the devil."[4]

When we identify evil, we can do battle with it. We can join the battle with enthusiasm when we know which side we are fighting for.

G.K. Chesterton was a warrior. But it was a battle of love. He did not want to crush his enemies. He wanted to convert them. He was dedicated to helping his fellow man, to bringing justice to the poor, to bringing hope to the hopeless. He was a loving, charitable man who was always ready to fight. A paradox? What else? Only G.K. Chesterton could point out the mystical connection between soldiers ... and nuns.

In a lovely little play called *The Surprise* (a play you should see, by the way, if someone would bother staging it), there is a princess who says to another character named Maria:

> You puzzle me very much, my dear, sometimes. I always thought you were a sort of nun; and you talk like a musketeer. I don't understand your oddly assorted enthusiasms. What is the common idea, that makes you like nuns and like soldiers?

[4] *Charles Dickens, CW* 15:202.

And Maria responds:

> Obedience. The most thrilling word in the world; a very
> thunderclap of a word. Why do all these fools fancy that
> the soul is only free when it disagrees with the common
> command? Why should mere disagreement make us feel
> free? I know you are fond of dancing; do you want to dance
> to a different tune from your partner's? You are a fine horse-
> woman; do you want to think of walking northward all by
> yourself, when you and your horse are going southward
> together? You have called me a nun; I am not a nun, I am
> not good enough to be a nun. I do not . . . I have not set
> . . . (She breaks off the sentence.) But do you suppose that
> nuns are unhappy? I never see them pass, silent and hooded,
> through their quiet cloisters but I have a vision: a vast vision
> of Amazons, wilder than any heathen Valkyries, riders rush-
> ing into battle; a charge of chivalry going all one way, and
> every rider as free as Joan of Arc; galloping, galloping to
> God. That is the real vision of Obedience.[5]

Chesterton calls obedience "the most thrilling word in the
world". The world, of course, has it backwards. The world
thinks that obedience is demeaning, that it goes against freedom. But the highest expression, the greatest achievement
of free will, is obedience. There is no virtue in disobedience. Disobedience is the first sin. And the glory of obedience is that it is the result of free will. There is no virtue
in obedience if it is not from free will. That is slavery.

But why are we talking about obeying here? We are talking about obeying God, as the Virgin Mary did. Her act of
obedience stands in direct contrast to Eve's act of disobedience. The first act brought sin into the world; the second
brought redemption.

[5] *The Surprise*, *CW* 11:313–14.

If we are to win the war against the culture of death, we must start by being completely obedient to the Giver of Life.

> Obedience is and has been often the most passionate form of personal choice. . . . If we believe in the sanctity of human life, it must be really a sanctity; we must make sacrifices for it, as the old creeds made for their sanctities. There must be no murdering of men wholesale because they stand in the path of progress. There must be no committing suicide because the landlady is unsympathetic and the books of Schopenhauer impressive. If human life is mystical and of infinite value, murder must be really a crime. Suicide must be a greater crime than murder, since it is the murder of the only man whose happiness we can appreciate. The faithful of the ancient creeds gave up for the sake of their sanctities the ultimate and imperious cravings of human nature, the desire of love and liberty and home. We profess to believe in the divinity of life, and we cannot give up for it a few grimy political advantages and a few sullen psychological moods. They gave up their joys, and we cannot even surrender lamentations. They denied themselves even the virtues of common men, and we cling openly, in art and literature, to the vices which are not even common. In this mood, we are not likely to open a new era.[6]

Chesterton knew what was under attack. In his lifetime, he saw that the family had already faded into the background. He was worried that it would fade even from the background as well.[7]

He knew that the enemy included "snobs who seem to think they can atone for being hard-hearted by being soft-headed".[8] He knew that reason was under attack, and

---

[6] *Daily News*, December 13, 1901.

[7] See *Irish Impressions*, *CW* 20:105.

[8] *G.K.C. as M.C.* (London: Methuen, 1929), 115.

that "when men are accustomed to being mentally wrong, they will become accustomed to being morally wrong."[9]

He knew that there was only one force that could stand against the decay and degeneration and destruction of the culture of death: the Catholic Church. It is only the saints who can lead us into battle against the modern world.

> If the world grows too worldly, it can be rebuked by the Church; but if the Church grows too worldly, it cannot be adequately rebuked for worldliness by the world.[10]

Chesterton said that we do not need a Church that moves with the world; we need a Church that will move the world.[11] He knew that it was a fallacy that people would ever flock to a church where nothing of substance is preached, where doctrine is avoided, where beliefs are kept quiet, where everything that happens inside the church apes what is happening outside.[12] As he said, "A dead thing can go with the stream, but only a living thing can go against it."[13] And G. K. Chesterton was a living thing who went against the stream.

Instead of questioning the traditional truths of the Catholic Church, Chesterton questioned the modern ideas that have tried and failed to replace the Church. Instead of being skeptical about the ancient ideas, he was skeptical about the modern ideas. Instead of swallowing all the claims of modern science, he put them to the test, just as he put the claims of psychology and sociology and economics and political theory to the test. He revolted against the crass

[9] *ILN*, March 7, 1908.
[10] *St. Thomas Aquinas*, *CW* 2:424.
[11] See Maisie Ward, *Gilbert Keith Chesterton*, 468.
[12] See *America*, August 17, 1929.
[13] *The Everlasting Man*, *CW* 2:388.

commercialism of the age instead of being swept away by
it. He recognized that marriage and the family were under
attack and he defended them valiantly at every point. He
defended the rights and dignity of the independent family
against the collective forces of Big Government and Big
Business that are always trying to undermine them. He knew
that what the modern world calls emancipation is actually
slavery. What it calls fulfillment is emptiness. He used the
newspaper to do what newspapers almost never do: tell the
truth. He revolted against catchwords that were used as a
substitute for thinking. He revolted against art that merely
tried to shock, and instead he shocked people with the claim
that the Catholic Church is not only right, but right where
everything else is wrong. He knew that compromise is not
the answer. Only the Truth is the answer, and the Truth
does not change. He knew that in a fallen world we must
preach forgiveness, but we cannot preach forgiveness without first preaching repentance. That is what the greatest of
prophets, St. John the Baptist, did before Jesus came into
the world. He preached repentance. G. K. Chesterton, a
modern prophet, was also a voice crying in the wilderness,
trying to turn the world around, completely contradicting
the age—and converting it. And Chesterton is still making
converts. I know. I am one.

Reading Chesterton is fun. But it is also serious. We are
fighting a battle. I would like to invite you to join the battle.
Help make Chesterton's voice heard. Help get Chesterton's
books back into the classroom. Help get Chesterton's ideas
back into the public arena. Join the argument about what's
wrong with the world, about who the heretics are, about what
orthodoxy is, and about Who the Everlasting Man is. Be a
living thing that goes against the stream. Help bring sanity
back to a world gone mad.

AN ALMOST BRIEF, SLIGHTLY ANNOTATED, MOSTLY CHRONOLOGICAL CHESTERTON BIBLIOGRAPHY

Chronological List

1900

Greybeards at Play. Available in *G. K. Chesterton's Early Poetry.* Seattle: Inkling Books, 2004.

> Chesterton's first book; a slim volume of light verse with his own illustrations.

The Wild Knight and Other Poems. Available in *G. K. Chesterton's Early Poetry.* Seattle: Inkling Books, 2004.

> Includes such favorites as "The Donkey" and "By the Babe Unborn".

1901

The Defendant. London: J.M. Dent, 1907. Out of print.

> Essays reprinted from Chesterton's literary reviews in *The Speaker*; includes "A Defence of Ugly Things", "A Defence of Nonsense", "A Defence of Patriotism", "A Defence of Detective Fiction", "A Defence of Baby Worship", and even "A Defence of Skeletons". The second edition includes "A Defence of a Second Edition".

1902

Twelve Types. Norfolk, Va.: IHS Press, 2003

>   Essays from the *Daily News* and *The Speaker*, on fig-
>   ures such as Charlotte Brontë, Leo Tolstoy, Robert Louis
>   Stevenson, and St. Francis.

1903

Robert Browning. New York: Macmillan, 1903. Also, London: House of Stratus, 2000.

>   Chesterton's first real book, which established his
>   unique approach to both literary criticism and biog-
>   raphy. He uses his subject merely as a device to expound
>   on his own philosophy.

1904

The Blatchford Controversies. In Vol. 1 of *The Collected Works
of G. K. Chesterton.* San Francisco: Ignatius Press, 1986.

>   Four essays in defense of Christianity, written in
>   response to publisher and atheist Robert Blatchford.
>   These essays established Chesterton as a controversial-
>   ist to be reckoned with.

G. F. Watts. London: Duckworth, 1974. Out of print.

>   Art criticism of the portrait painter and allegorist
>   George Frederick Watts. A wonderful discourse on lan-
>   guage, art, and allegory. Includes thirty-seven sepia tone
>   reproductions of his paintings.

The Napoleon of Notting Hill. In Vol. 6 of *The Collected Works of G. K. Chesterton*. San Francisco: Ignatius Press, 1991. Also, Mineola, N.Y.: Dover Publications, 1991.

> Chesterton's first novel; a story about the residents of a London suburb who take up arms and declare their independence from England.

Time's Abstract and Brief Chronicle. In Vol. 11 of *The Collected Works of G. K. Chesterton*. San Francisco: Ignatius Press, 1989.

> A dialogue in four acts that really never was intended for the stage. Sections were first published in *The Fortnightly Review*. With no holds barred, the characters debate politics and religion with surprising conclusions, and we are left wanting more.

1905

The Club of Queer Trades. In Vol. 6 of *The Collected Works of G. K. Chesterton*. San Francisco: Ignatius Press, 1991. Also, Mineola, N.Y.: Dover Publications, 1988.

> Six adventures of Basil and Rupert Grant, who encounter what seem to be strange, unexplainable crimes, all of which turn out to have even stranger explanations. With illustrations by Chesterton.

Heretics. In Vol. 1 of *The Collected Works of G. K. Chesterton*. San Francisco: Ignatius Press, 1986. Also (annotated) Reformation Press.

> An often overlooked book that contains some of Chesterton's strongest writing, as he takes on the

"heresies" of modern thought, such as negativism, relativism, neo-paganism, puritanism, aestheticism, and individualism. Includes one of his best essays, "On Certain Modern Writers and the Institution of the Family".

1906

Charles Dickens. In Vol. 15 of *The Collected Works of G. K. Chesterton*. San Francisco: Ignatius Press, 1990.

Considered by T. S. Eliot, Peter Ackroyd, and others, to be the best book on Dickens ever written, this literary biography was largely responsible for creating both a popular revival for Dickens' works and serious reconsideration of Dickens by scholars.

1907

The Man Who Was Thursday. In Vol. 6 of *The Collected Works of G. K. Chesterton*. San Francisco: Ignatius Press, 1991. Also, Mineola, N.Y.: Dover Publications.

Chesterton's most famous novel; utterly unique, it is a detective fantasy about a policeman who infiltrates a secret organization of anarchists.

1908

All Things Considered. New York: Sheed and Ward, 1956. Out of print. Last reprinted in 1969 by Dufour Editions, but all of the original essays from this book are available in Vols. 27 and 28 of *The Collected Works of G. K. Chesterton*. San Francisco: Ignatius Press, 1986 and 1987.

A book of essays reprinted from Chesterton's weekly column in the *Illustrated London News*. Includes "On

Running after One's Hat", "Cockneys and their Jokes", and "Wine When It Is Red".

Orthodoxy. In Vol. 1 of *The Collected Works of G. K. Chesterton*. San Francisco: Ignatius Press, 1986. Also, published separately. San Francisco: Ignatius Press, 1995.

> Considered by many to be Chesterton's best book, it is certainly his most indispensable book, and a unique and refreshing spiritual autobiography and defense of the Christian faith. Everyone should read this book. Everyone should read it every year.

Varied Types. New York: Dodd, Mead, 1905 and 1909.

> *Twelve Types* plus a few more, including essays on Bret Harte, Queen Victoria, and Tennyson.

1909

George Bernard Shaw. In Vol. 11 of *The Collected Works of G. K. Chesterton*. San Francisco, Ignatius Press, 1989.

> Chesterton and Shaw were friends but disagreed on most everything. This critique of Shaw's philosophy, politics, and plays is, in effect, a critique of the prevailing ideas of the twentieth century. (Volume 11 also includes additional Chesterton essays on Shaw, collected for the first time.)

Tremendous Trifles. New York: Sheed and Ward, 1955.

> Essays reprinted from Chesterton's weekly column in the *Daily News*. Includes "A Piece of Chalk", "On Lying in Bed", "The Twelve Men", and "What I Found in My Pocket". A great introduction to Chesterton.

The Ball and the Cross. In Vol. 7 of *The Collected Works of G. K. Chesterton*. San Francisco: Ignatius Press, 2004. Also, Mineola, N.Y.: Dover Publications, 1995.

> A novel that acts out the debate between Christianity and atheism, as embodied by two characters who propose to fight a duel but can never manage to carry it out. Filled with humor, rich dialogue, and striking allegorical imagery.

1910
William Blake. London: House of Stratus, 2000.

> Chesterton discusses the art, poetry, and mysticism of Blake. Includes several plates of Blake's art and poems.

Alarms and Discursions. New York: Dodd, Mead, 1911. Out of print.

> Essays reprinted from the *Daily News*. Includes "On Gargoyles", "The Futurists", "How I Found the Superman", and "Cheese" (a subject about which poets are mysteriously silent).

What's Wrong with the World. In Vol. 4 of *The Collected Works of G. K. Chesterton*. San Francisco: Ignatius Press, 1987. Also, published separately. San Francisco: Ignatius Press, 1994.

> Chesterton systematically takes on big government, big business, compulsory education, and feminism. More timely today than when he wrote it.

1911
The Ballad of the White Horse. With notes by Sister Bernadette Sheridan. San Francisco: Ignatius Press, 2001.

Chesterton's epic poem about King Alfred's defeat of the Danes in 878. An unjustly neglected masterpiece about an unjustly neglected historical event. One of the most outstanding narrative poems of twentieth century English Literature.

Appreciations and Criticisms of the Works of Charles Dickens. In Vol. 15 of *The Collected Works of G. K. Chesterton.* San Francisco: Ignatius Press, 1990.

Also known as *Chesterton on Dickens.* A collection of introductions to each of Dickens' works. Reveals the breadth and depth of Chesterton's acquaintance with Dickens but also an insiders' view of the creative process and the art of the written word.

The Innocence of Father Brown. In Vol. 12 of *The Collected Works of G. K. Chesterton.* San Francisco: Ignatius Press, 2005. Also, Mineola, N.Y.: Dover Publications, 1998. And in *The Penguin Complete Father Brown.* New York: Penguin Books, 1981.

The first collection of Father Brown mysteries. Twelve yarns that helped introduce the world to the humble little priest who was also a clever sleuth. Includes "The Blue Cross" and "The Invisible Man".

1912
A Miscellany of Men. Norfolk, Va: IHS Press, 2004.

A collection of essays reprinted from the *Daily News.* Includes "The Miser", "The Mystagogue", and "The Romantic in the Rain".

Manalive. In Vol. 7 of *The Collected Works of G. K. Chester-ton*. San Francisco: Ignatius Press, 2004. Also, Mineola, N.Y.: Dover Publications, 2000.

> A novel about Innocent Smith, a man who picnics on rooftops, breaks into his own house, and has an affair with his own wife. There are any number of Chesterton books that offer us a window to his thoughts, but this book grabs us and pulls us in the front door. This is the book on how to *live* Chesterton.

A Chesterton Calendar. London: Kegan Paul, Trench, Trib-ner and Co., 1911. The second edition, New York: Dodd, Mead & Co., 1912, was reprinted as *Chesterton Day by Day*. Seattle: Inkling Books, 2002.

> Chesterton's witticisms and epigrams were already being collected and published in his own day. This was a Chesterton "quote of the day" compilation.

1913

The Victorian Age in Literature. In Vol. 15 of *The Collected Works of G. K. Chesterton*. San Francisco: Ignatius Press, 1990.

> A sweeping yet succinct volume of literary criticism; packed with Chestertonian surprises, such as the point that one of the principal literary influences on the Victorian poets and novelists was a writer named Darwin.

Magic. In Vol. 11 of *The Collected Works of G. K. Chesterton*. San Francisco: Ignatius Press, 1989.

> Chesterton's most successful play, which served as the basis for Ingmar Bergman's film *The Magician* (though the two shouldn't be compared too closely). The question: Is the magic real or not?

1914

The Flying Inn. In Vol. 7 of *The Collected Works of G. K. Chesterton.* San Francisco: Ignatius Press, 2004. Also, Mineola, N.Y.: Dover Publications, 2001.

> A novel that Chesterton said was one of the books he most enjoyed writing. Imagining what England would be like under Prohibition, Chesterton follows the adventures of two men who travel through the country with a barrel of rum and a temporary inn sign that they hang up at every occasion. It is a romp, filled with amusing characters and wonderful drinking songs, such as "The Song of the Vegetarian", "The Song of Right and Wrong", and "The Song of Quoodle".

The Wisdom of Father Brown. In Vol. 12 of *The Collected Works of G. K. Chesterton.* San Francisco: Ignatius Press, 2005. Also, in *The Penguin Complete Father Brown.* New York: Penguin Books, 1981.

> The second collection of mysteries featuring the beloved priest-detective. The twelve stories include "The Absence of Mr. Glass" and "The Head of Caesar".

1915

Poems. Out of print, but the annotated "Lepanto" is available in *Lepanto.* San Francisco: Ignatius Press, 2004.

> A collection of Chesterton's poems, including "Lepanto", "The Wise Men", "The House of Christmas", and the hymn "O God of Earth and Altar".

Wine, Water, and Song. Out of print.

> All of the songs and poems from *The Flying Inn* (see above).

The Appetite of Tyranny. In Vol. 15 of *The Collected Works of G. K. Chesterton*. San Francisco: Ignatius Press, 1990.

> Reprinted articles from the London *Daily Mail*, written at the outset of World War I. This book attacks German philosophy and politics, and is surprisingly prophetic about World War II and the reasons for defending against German aggression. Includes the previously published *The Barbarism of Berlin* and "Letters to an Old Garibaldian".

The Crimes of England. In Vol. 5 of *The Collected Works of G. K. Chesterton*. San Francisco: Ignatius Press, 1987.

> Another wartime book, in which Chesterton responds to the typical German attacks on England by explaining what the real weaknesses, the real "crimes", of England have been in its history.

1916

Divorce vs. Democracy. In Vol. 4 of *The Collected Works of G. K. Chesterton*. San Francisco: Ignatius Press, 1987.

> Essay reprinted from *Nash Magazine*, along with an introduction. An argument that divorce is not democratic, that the vast majority of people are against it.

1917

Utopia of Usurers. In Vol. 5 of *The Collected Works of G. K. Chesterton*. San Francisco: Ignatius Press, 1987.

> A collection of essays reprinted from the *Daily Herald*. A critique of the "strange poetry of plutocracy" and

other modern developments that still afflict the common man, robbing him of his dignity, his autonomy, and his simple pleasures.

A Short History of England. In Vol. 20 of *The Collected Works of G. K. Chesterton*. San Francisco: Ignatius Press, 2002.

Known as the history book with no dates in it (but see if you can find some), Chesterton at once paints the big picture but also includes the most overlooked details of English history: the landscape, the buildings, the ruins, the little things, and "The Meaning of Merry England".

1919

Irish Impressions. In Vol. 20 of *The Collected Works of G. K. Chesterton*. San Francisco: Ignatius Press, 2002.

Chesterton's portrait of Ireland's distinct culture is sympathetic and perceptive. Written in the midst of the events surrounding Ireland's fight for Home Rule.

1920

The Superstition of Divorce. In Vol. 4 of *The Collected Works of G. K. Chesterton*. San Francisco: Ignatius Press, 1987.

Arguing that divorce is, at best, a failure, Chesterton is more interested in finding the cure than allowing the disease to complete its deadly effects. This book is a marvelous defense of the sanctity of the family.

The Uses of Diversity. Out of print, but all the *Illustrated London News* essays from this collection are available in

Vols. 28, 29, and 30 of *The Collected Works of G. K. Chesterton*. San Francisco: Ignatius Press, 1987 and 1988.

> A collection of essays reprinted from *The Illustrated London News* and *New Witness* on subjects ranging from the Japanese, the Mormons, the Christian Scientists, and the Futurists to Shakespeare, Shaw, and Jane Austen.

The New Jerusalem. In Vol. 20 of *The Collected Works of G. K. Chesterton*. San Francisco: Ignatius Press, 2002.

> Written during a trip to the Holy Land, Chesterton's observations combine history, literature, religion, social criticism, and whatever else comes to his mind. Includes a controversial chapter on Zionism.

1922
The Ballad of St. Barbara and Other Poems. Out of print.

> Includes "Elegy in Country Churchyard" and "The Convert".

Eugenics and other Evils. In Vol. 4 of *The Collected Works of G. K. Chesterton*. San Francisco: Ignatius Press, 1987. Also, Seattle: Inkling Books, 2000.

> A powerful and prophetic book that gets at the root of the evils which would give rise to Nazi Germany and which still plague modern society. Chesterton shows how evil wins through ambiguity and "through the strength of its splendid dupes".

What I Saw in America. In Vol. 21 of *The Collected Works of G. K. Chesterton*. San Francisco, 1990.

A thick book of essays written during Chesterton's trip to America in 1921, with his unique and incisive observations of "the only nation ever founded on a creed".

The Man Who Knew Too Much. In Vol. 8 of *The Collected Works of G. K. Chesterton.* San Francisco: Ignatius Press, 1999. Also, Mineola, N.Y.: Dover Publications, 2003.

A collection of mysteries featuring another amateur detective, the rather languid Horne Fisher. No connection to the Alfred Hitchcock film(s) of the same name.

1923

St. Francis of Assisi. In Vol. 2 of *The Collected Works of G. K. Chesterton.* San Francisco: Ignatius Press, 1986.

A marvelous book about St. Francis, putting him into his context, taking him through the phases of his spiritual development, showing us that "he was a poet whose whole life was a poem", and finally, explaining that he reflects the divine light as the moon reflects the light of the sun.

Fancies Versus Fads. London: Methuen, 1923. Out of print. Some of the essays are available in Vol. 32 of *The Collected Works of G. K. Chesterton.* San Francisco: Ignatius Press, 1989.

A collection of essays reprinted from *London Mercury, New Witness,* and *Illustrated London News.* Includes an introduction by Chesterton. He takes on modern poetry, modern history, modern laws, and even another modern thing called "film".

1924

The End of the Roman Road. In Vol. 14 of *The Collected Works of G. K. Chesterton.* San Francisco: Ignatius Press, 1993.

> Subtitled "A Pageant of Wayfarers", this short piece is neither an essay nor a short story, but something of both, about the Roman influence on English culture.

1925

The Superstitions of the Sceptic. Cambridge: W. Hefner and Sons, 1925. Out of print.

> The text of a speech Chesterton delivered to the I.D.K. Club, followed by correspondence between Chesterton and the Medieval scholar (and skeptic) G. G. Coulton. Chesterton criticizes the philosophy that is founded on doubt. Coulton criticizes Chesterton's interpretation of history. I.D.K., by the way, stands for "I Don't Know".

William Cobbett. London: House of Stratus, 2000.

> Cobbett (1763–1835) was a popular journalist, a defender of rural England and the rights of small property owners, and a critic of the rise of industrialism. In other words, he was an early version of Chesterton, and certainly one of Chesterton's heroes (and of distributists everywhere).

Tales of the Long Bow. In Vol. 8 of *The Collected Works of G. K. Chesterton.* San Francisco: Ignatius Press, 1999.

> "These tales concern the doing of things recognised as impossible to do; impossible to believe; and, as the weary reader may well cry aloud, impossible to read

about." So begins a series of what seem to be unconnected stories, which end up being connected, in which
pigs fly, sows' ears are sown into silk purses, and a
gentleman eats his hat.

The Everlasting Man. In Vol. 2 of *The Collected Works of G. K.
Chesterton.* San Francisco: Ignatius Press, 1986. Also, published separately. San Francisco: Ignatius Press, 1993.

> One of Chesterton's greatest and most important
> books. A compact presentation of the history of the
> world, in two parts: "On the Creature Called Man"
> and "On the Man Called Christ". Chesterton argues
> that the central character in history is Christ, and
> that no explanation other than the Christian one makes
> as much sense. When the book was first published,
> *The Times Literary Supplement* wrote: "Mr. Chesterton
> has a quite unusual power of seeing the obvious, and
> it is quite true that many learned men seem to have
> lost that power. There are many modern theories
> whose origins we can understand only on the hypoth-
> esis that their authors have spent their whole lives in
> one room."

1926

The Outline of Sanity. In Vol. 5 of *The Collected Works of
G. K. Chesterton.* San Francisco: Ignatius Press, 1987.

> Chesterton's most systematic treatment of distribut-
> ism, a scathing critique of communism, capitalism, and
> commercialism, leaving the only logical alternative: the
> wide distribution of capital, private ownership, and pro-
> ductive property.

The Incredulity of Father Brown. In Vol. 13 of *The Collected Works of G. K. Chesterton.* San Francisco: Ignatius Press, 2005. Also in the *Penguin Complete Father Brown.* New York: Penguin Books, 1981.

> The third collection of Father Brown mysteries. Eight stories, including "The Oracle of the Dog", "The Miracle of Moon Crescent", and "The Resurrection of Father Brown".

The Queen of Seven Swords. London: Sheed and Ward, 1926. Out of print.

> A book of 24 religious poems. The title poem refers to the seven swords of sorrow that pierced Mary's heart as she witnessed the sufferings of her son.

1927

The Catholic Church and Conversion. In Vol. 3 of *The Collected Works of G. K. Chesterton.* San Francisco: Ignatius Press, 1990. Also published separately. San Francisco: Ignatius Press, 2006.

> Written five years after his conversion, Chesterton describes the feeling of discovering that the Catholic Church is "larger on the inside than on the outside". He addresses both the common objections and the real obstacles to conversion.

The Collected Poems of G. K. Chesterton. New York: Dodd, Mead, 1949. Out of print, but all of Chesterton's poetry is being made available in Vol. 10 (in three parts) of *The Collected Works of G. K. Chesterton.* San Francisco: Ignatius Press, 1994–.

Several new poems, along with most of the previous collections, except *Greybeards at Play* and *The Queen of Seven Swords*.

The Judgment of Dr. Johnson. In Vol. 11 of *The Collected Works of G. K. Chesterton.* San Francisco: Ignatius Press, 1989.

Chesterton's play about Samuel Johnson, the great eighteenth century man of letters. Chesterton was often compared with Dr. Johnson, and for good reason. Both were poets, critics, journalists, essayists, and conversationalists of great wit. The dialogue Chesterton gives Dr. Johnson in this play blends Johnson's aphorisms seamlessly with his own.

Robert Louis Stevenson. In Vol. 18 of *The Collected Works of G. K. Chesterton.* San Francisco: Ignatius Press, 1991.

The author of popular works from *A Child's Garden of Verses* to *Treasure Island* and *Kidnapped*, Stevenson was treated harshly by the "higher" critics, and Chesterton's criticism of the critics is as extensive—and as enjoyable—as his defense of Stevenson and his lively, romantic, and adventurous view of life. Chesterton's description of childhood is exquisite.

The Secret of Father Brown. In Vol. 13 of *The Collected Works of G. K. Chesterton.* San Francisco: Ignatius Press, 2005. Also in the *Penguin Complete Father Brown.* New York: Penguin Books, 1981.

The fourth collection of Father Brown mysteries. In addition to a prologue and epilogue, the eight stories include "The Man with Two Beards", "The Red Moon of Meru", and what some fans think is the best Father Brown mystery, "The Chief Mourner of Marne".

The Return of Don Quixote. In Vol. 8 of *The Collected Works of G. K. Chesterton.* San Francisco: Ignatius Press, 1999.

> Chesterton's last novel, which, in one sense, is the sequel to *Tales of the Long Bow*; in another sense, it is the sequel to all his novels: softly whimsical and sharply pointed. Some consider it Chesterton's most finely crafted novel. Michael Herne, a mild librarian, playing the role of a medieval king in a play, decides at the end of the performance to keep wearing his costume and head off into the real world as the champion of trade unions to do battle against the modern industrial state.

Social Reform vs. Birth Control. In Vol. 4 of *The Collected Works of G. K. Chesterton.* San Francisco: Ignatius Press, 1987.

> A short work in which Chesterton argues that the advocates of birth control are merely dupes of industrial capitalism.

Culture and the Coming Peril. Out of print. Last reprinted in the *Chesterton Review,* Vol. 18, no. 2, August, 1992.

> The text of a speech delivered at the University of London, warning about "standardization by a low standard".

1928

Do We Agree? In Vol. 11 of *The Collected Works of G. K. Chesterton.* San Francisco: Ignatius Press, 1989.

> The text of a debate between Chesterton and George Bernard Shaw, mostly about socialism vs. distributism. Hillaire Belloc serves as moderator, and, truth be told, wins the day.

Generally Speaking. Out of print, but all of the essays from this collection are available in Vols. 32, 33, and 34 of *The Collected Works of G. K. Chesterton.* San Francisco: Ignatius Press, 1989, 1990, and 1991.

> A collection of essays reprinted from Chesterton's weekly column in the *Illustrated London News* from 1923 to 1927. The usual variety of subjects are covered, from leisure to funeral customs to Buddhism.

1929

The Poet and the Lunatics. London: House of Stratus, 2000. Also, in New York: Sheed and Ward, 1955.

> Eight mysteries featuring the poet-detective, Gabriel Gale, who solves (or prevents) crimes committed by madmen. The lunatics all represent the modern breakdown of reason.

Father Brown Omnibus. Also Vols. 12 and 13 of *The Collected Works of G. K. Chesterton.* San Francisco: Ignatius Press, 2005. Also, in the *Penguin Complete Father Brown.* New York: Penguin Books, 1981. (This book is not "complete", by the way; it's missing two Father Brown stories.)

> The four previously published collections all under one roof. (Reissued in 1947 to include *The Scandal of Father Brown* and in 1953 to include the story, "The Vampire of the Village".)

The Thing: Why I Am a Catholic. In Vol. 3 of *The Collected Works of G. K. Chesterton.* San Francisco: Ignatius Press, 1990.

> The word "Catholic" means "universal" and in this book Chesterton not only defends his Catholic Faith

from attacks on all sides, but shows how it is the right answer to all questions. He applies "The Thing" (i.e. the Faith) to all other things: worldly philosophies, economic theory and practice, nationalism, Protestantism, agnosticism, art, history, education, and sports. Universal.

G. K. C. as M C. London: Methuen, 1929. Out of print.

A collection of 37 introductions by Chesterton to books by others, with the subjects ranging from Gilbert and Sullivan, Jane Austen, and Oliver Wendell Holmes, to Boswell, Belloc, and George MacDonald. Includes one of Chesterton's most transcendent essays, "Introduction to the Book of Job".

1930

Come to Think of It. Out of print, but all of the essays from this collection are available in Vols. 34 and 35 of *The Collected Works of G. K. Chesterton.* San Francisco: Ignatius Press, 1991 and 1992.

A collection of essays reprinted from Chesterton's weekly column in the *Illustrated London News* from 1928 and 1929. The usual variety of subjects includes Abraham Lincoln, encyclopedias, mythology, and scientists.

The Resurrection of Rome. In Vol. 21 of *The Collected Works of G. K. Chesterton.* San Francisco: Ignatius Press, 1990.

Chesterton's "travel book" about his trip to Rome in 1929, drawing together history and art and current events (and his meetings with Pope Pius XI and Mussolini!).

Four Faultless Felons. Mineola, N.Y.: Dover Publications, 1989.

> Four mysteries about men who are, respectively, a murderer, a fraud, a thief, and a traitor. All quite guilty ... except for the fact that they're completely innocent, proving that "through the worst one could imagine comes the best one could not imagine".

1931

All is Grist. In Vol. 35 of *The Collected Works of G. K. Chesterton*. San Francisco: Ignatius Press, 1992.

> A collection of essays reprinted from Chesterton's weekly column in the *Illustrated London News* from 1930 and 1931. The usual variety of subjects include Swinburne, the Renaissance, lotteries, heredity, and "The Thrills of Boredom".

1932

Christendom in Dublin. In Vol. 20 of *The Collected Works of G. K. Chesterton*. San Francisco: Ignatius Press, 2002.

> Written while attending the World Eucharistic Congress, this short book manages to create a perspective that is at once both inside and outside of the Catholic Church.

Sidelights on New London and Newer York. Vol. 21 of *The Collected Works of G. K. Chesterton*. San Francisco: Ignatius Press, 1990.

> (Also known simply as *Sidelights*.) A collection of essays reprinted from *G. K.'s Weekly* and several other periodicals, divided into three sections: observations on

England, on America, and some essays of literary criticism.

Chaucer. In Vol. 18 of *The Collected Works of G. K. Chesterton.* San Francisco: Ignatius Press, 1991.

Chesterton shines in this work on Chaucer and his Age, both of which Chesterton praises as being more sane, more cheerful, and more normal than the writers and ages that came after them. Includes an important discussion about Shakespeare.

1933

All I Survey. Out of print.

A collection of essays reprinted from Chesterton's weekly column in the *Illustrated London News* from 1931 and 1932. The usual variety of subjects includes taxes, the solar system, literary cliques, and eating and sleeping.

St. Thomas Aquinas. In Vol. 2 of *The Collected Works of G. K. Chesterton.* San Francisco: Ignatius Press, 1986.

(Subtitled *The Dumb Ox* in some subsequent editions.) "I consider it as being without possible comparison the best book ever written on St. Thomas", so wrote the renowned international scholar Étienne Gilson. But besides being merely the best book ever written about St. Thomas, Chesterton's book has the virtue of being the most readable.

1934

Avowals and Denials. Out of print.

A collection of essays reprinted from Chesterton's weekly column in the *Illustrated London News* from 1932 and 1933. The usual variety of subjects include jazz, monsters, free verse, dogs and apes.

G. K.'s Weekly: A Miscellany. London: Rich and Cowan, 1934.

> A collection of essays reprinted from *G. K.'s Weekly*.

1935

The Scandal of Father Brown. Stories available in Vol. 13 of *The Collected Works of G. K. Chesterton*. San Francisco: Ignatius Press, 2005. Also, in *The Penguin Complete Father Brown*. New York: Penguin Books, 1981.

> The fifth and final set in the series of Father Brown mysteries. Eight stories, including "The Blast of the Book" and "The Insoluble Problem".

The Well and the Shallows. In Vol. 3 of *The Collected Works of G. K. Chesterton*. San Francisco: Ignatius Press, 1990. Also published separately. San Francisco: Ignatius Press, 2006.

> This book could be called *More of The Thing*. It is the natural sequel to that book, a collection of essays reprinted from a number of different periodicals, which apply "The Thing" to everything else, including sex, materialism, nihilism, Puritanism, capitalism, free thought, Luther, and the rest. Includes the essay "Babies and Distributism", which is cast down like a gauntlet against modern thought.

The Way of the Cross. In Vol. 3 of *The Collected Works of G. K. Chesterton*. San Francisco: Ignatius Press, 1990.

> A commentary on The Stations of the Cross, which is a commentary both on art and on the vividness of

the events surrounding the Crucifixion, and seems to anticipate the critics of Mel Gibson's movie *The Passion of the Christ* seventy-five years ahead of time.

1936

As I Was Saying. Out of print. (The essays will be available in Vols. 36 and 37 of *The Collected Works of G. K. Chesterton*. San Francisco: Ignatius Press, in preparation.)

> A collection of essays reprinted from Chesterton's weekly column in the *Illustrated London News* from 1934 and 1935. The usual variety of subjects includes traffic, blondes, shirts, the telephone, and mad metaphors.

Autobiography. Vol. 16 of *The Collected Works of G. K. Chesterton.* San Francisco: Ignatius Press, 1988. Also published separately. San Francisco: Ignatius Press, 2006.

> It is hard for a humble man to talk about himself, so Chesterton talks about several other things instead, giving us glimpses along the way of what is ostensibly the subject of this book, which was completed just before his death and published just after it.

Posthumous books

1937

The Paradoxes of Mr. Pond. Mineola, N.Y.: Dover Publications, 1990.

> A collection of eight mysteries, featuring Mr. Pond (whose first name we never learn), an obscure bureaucrat who, wouldn't you know it, has a surprising way

of solving crimes. Includes the remarkable story, "The Three Horsemen of the Apocalypse".

1938

The Coloured Lands. New York: Sheed and Ward, 1938. Out of print, but the short stories are in Vol. 14 of *The Collected Works of G. K. Chesterton*. San Francisco: Ignatius Press, 1993.

> A collection of stories, poems, essays, and drawings, which Maisie Ward, Chesterton's biographer, assembled with the intention of re-creating what it would be like to spend a weekend with Chesterton.

1940

The End of the Armistice. In Vol. 5 of *The Collected Works of G. K. Chesterton*. San Francisco: Ignatius Press, 1987.

> A collection of essays from *G. K.'s Weekly*, compiled by Frank Sheed, to demonstrate Chesterton's acute awareness of "future history". He predicted the coming of World War II, even that it would begin on the Polish border. Says Sheed, "Now when a man is as right as that in his forecasts, there is some reason to think he may be right in his premises."

1950

The Common Man. New York: Sheed and Ward, 1950. Out of print.

> A collection of essays from several different periodicals, compiled by Dorothy Collins, Chesterton's secretary and literary executrix. Includes "If I Had Only One Sermon to Preach", "Rabelasian Regrets",

and a wonderful essay on "A Midsummer Night's Dream".

1952

The Surprise. In Vol. 11 of *The Collected Works of G. K. Chesterton.* San Francisco: Ignatius Press, 1989.

A delightful play, written in 1932, but never produced in Chesterton's lifetime. A play within a play, in which the Author of the play gives his characters free will, and don't you suppose they make a mess of it? (The 1952 edition includes an introduction by Dorothy L. Sayers.)

1953

A Handful of Authors. New York: Sheed and Ward, 1953. Out of print.

A collection of 37 essays compiled from different sources by Dorothy Collins about literary figures and subjects, including Mark Twain, Victor Hugo, Oscar Wilde, Henrik Ibsen, Lewis Carroll, and Louisa Alcott.

1955

The Glass Walking-Stick. Out of print, but all of the essays from this collection are available in Vols. 32, 33, 34, and 35 of *The Collected Works of G. K. Chesterton.* San Francisco: Ignatius Press, 1989, 1990, 1991, and 1992.

A collection of essays compiled by Dorothy Collins from Chesterton's columns in the *Illustrated London News* from 1920 to 1928, which were not included in previous collections. The usual variety of subjects includes

Camelot, Tom Jones, Napoleon, and "A Plea for the Heroic Couplet".

1958

Lunacy and Letters. New York: Sheed and Ward, 1958. Out of print.

A collection of essays compiled by Dorothy Collins from Chesterton's columns in the *Daily News*, half a century earlier. Includes "The Meaning of Dreams", "Tommy and the Traditions", and the parable-like "The Roots of the World".

1961

Where All Roads Lead. In Vol. 3 of *The Collected Works of G. K. Chesterton.* San Francisco: Ignatius Press, 1990.

A collection of essays that originally appeared in *Blackfriars* magazine in 1922 and 1923, just after Chesterton's conversion.

1965

The Spice of Life. Beaconsfield: Darwen Finlayson, 1964. Out of print.

A collection of essays compiled from different sources by Dorothy Collins. Includes "On the Essay", "The Macbeths", "The Philosophy of Islands", and "On Losing One's Head".

1972

Chesterton on Shakespeare. Out of print.

Chesterton had been commissioned to write a book on Shakespeare, but, alas, he died before he was able to do it. Dorothy Collins compiled thirty-two of his essays on Shakespeare's plays and characters, many of which are from previous collections, but some of which are collected here for the first time, including early articles from *The Speaker* (1901–1902).

1975

The Apostle and the Wild Ducks. London: Paul Elek, 1975. Out of print.

Dorothy Collins' final compilation of essays from several different sources. Includes "On Manners", "For Persons of the Name of Smith", "Asparagus", and the incomparable "What's Right with the World" (which Chesterton was asked to write in response to his own book *What's Wrong with the World*).

1984

The Spirit of Christmas. Out of print.

Stories, poems, and essays about Christmas, compiled by Marie Smith, most of which appear in previous collections, but some of which are collected here for the first time.

1986

Daylight and Nightmare. Out of print, but most of the stories are available in Vol. 14 of *The Collected Works of G. K. Chesterton*. San Francisco: Ignatius Press, 1993.

Stories and fables by Chesterton, compiled by Marie Smith, many of which are collected for the first time.

Includes "A Picture of Tuesday", "The End of Wisdom", "The Tree of Pride", and "The Conversion of an Anarchist".

1990

Brave New Family. San Francisco: Ignatius Press, 1990.

Subtitled "G. K. Chesterton on Men & Women, Children, Sex, Divorce, Marriage & the Family". Essays, short quotations, and poems compiled by Alvaro de Silva. An excellent and well-organized collection, which includes some great material that is not available elsewhere.

1997

Platitudes Undone. San Francisco: Ignatius Press, 1997.

A facsimile of the book *Platitudes in the Making* by Holbrook Jackson, which was presented by the author to Chesterton. Chesterton's written responses, in green pencil, to each "platitude", present a microcosm of his debate with modern thinking. Not only a good introduction to Chesterton, but a welcome discovery for those who can't get enough Chesterton.

2000

On Lying in Bed and Other Essays. Edited and introduced by Alberto Manguel. Calgary: Bayeux Arts, 2000.

A wonderful new collection bringing together some of Chesterton's best essays which have long been out of print, including many of those from *Tremendous Trifles*.

2001

Basil Howe: A Story of Young Love. London: New City, 2001. Edited with an introduction by Denis Conlon.

> Chesterton's first novel, probably written in 1894, and previously unpublished (though a version of it can be found in Vol. 14 of *The Collected Works of G. K. Chesterton*). Denis Conlon pieced this early literary effort together and the result is quite pleasing. We see a lot of Jane Austen in the young GKC.

Note: *The Collected Works of G. K. Chesterton* published by Ignatius Press will eventually contain all of Chesterton's books, a definitive collection of his poetry, and thousands of essays, the bulk of which have not been collected previously.

Books by category (however, these categories are not "pure" since Chesterton has a way of bringing every discipline together in everything he writes):

Novels:
The Man Who Was Thursday
The Napoleon of Notting Hill
The Ball and the Cross
The Flying Inn
Manalive
Tales of the Long Bow
The Return of Don Quixote

Literary Criticism:
Robert Browning
Charles Dickens
Chaucer
Robert Louis Stevenson

A Handful of Authors
The Victorian Age in Literature

Philosophy/Theology:

Heretics
Orthodoxy
St. Thomas Aquinas

History:

A Short History of England
The Crimes of England
The Everlasting Man
The End of Armistice

Travel:

Irish Impressions
The New Jerusalem
What I Saw in America
The Resurrection of Rome
Sidelights

Religion:

The Thing: Why I Am a Catholic
Catholic Church and Conversion
St. Francis of Assisi

Art:

William Blake
G. F. Watts

Society and Economics:

What's Wrong with the World
The Superstition of Divorce
Eugenics and Other Evils
The Outline of Sanity

Essays:

> *All Things Considered*
> *Tremendous Trifles*
> *The Defendant*
> *Alarms and Discursions*
> *Fancies vs. Fads*
> *The Common Man*
> *Lunacy and Letters*

Plays:

> *Magic*
> *The Judgment of Dr. Johnson*
> *The Surprise*

Poetry:

> *The Ballad of The White Horse*
> *Lepanto*
> *The Queen of Seven Swords*
> *Collected Poetry*

Detective Fiction:

> *Father Brown Stories*
> *The Poet and the Lunatics*
> *The Club of Queer Trades*
> *Four Faultless Felons*
> *The Paradoxes of Mr. Pond*

A Selection of Books about Chesterton:

Ahlquist, Dale. *G. K. Chesterton: The Apostle of Common Sense.* San Francisco: Ignatius Press, 2003.

> An introduction to Chesterton's writings and an overview of several important books.

Conlon, Denis, ed. *G. K. Chesterton: The Critical Judgments*. Antwerp: Antwerp Studies in English Literature, 1976.

Contemporary views of Chesterton's books.

Conlon, Denis, ed. *G. K. Chesterton: A Half-Century of Views*. Oxford: Oxford University Press, 1987.

Assessments of Chesterton from a variety of major writers, including George Orwell, Ronald Knox, Evelyn Waugh, Garry Wills, W. H. Auden, C. S. Lewis, and Anthony Burgess.

Dale, Alzina Stone. *The Outline of Sanity: A Life of G. K. Chesterton*. Grand Rapids: Eerdmanns, 1982.

Includes a helpful account of the times in which Chesterton lived.

Kenner, Hugh. *Paradox in Chesterton*. New York: Sheed and Ward, 1948.

A penetrating treatment of Chesterton's most important theme. Introduction by Marshall McLuhan.

Pearce, Joseph. *Wisdom and Innocence: A Life of G. K. Chesterton*. San Francisco: Ignatius Press, 1996.

The best modern biography of Chesterton.

Ward, Maisie. *Gilbert Keith Chesterton*. New York: Sheed and Ward, 1943.

The definitive biography.

Ward, Maisie. *Return to Chesterton*. New York: Sheed and Ward, 1952.

> Fascinating sequel with supplemental biographical material.

Periodicals about Chesterton

The Chesterton Review. A scholarly journal published quarterly by the G. K. Chesterton Institute, Seton Hall University, South Orange, N.J.

Gilbert Magazine. A popular general interest magazine published eight times a year by The American Chesterton Society, Minneapolis, Minn.